THINKING AGAIN

A later lithograph of the painting is accompanied with
some verses to the following effect:

Charming child, absorbed in play,
we smile at your precarious efforts.
But, just between ourselves, which is more solid—
our project, or your house of cards?

THINKING AGAIN

Education After Postmodernism

Nigel Blake, Paul Smeyers,
Richard Smith, and Paul Standish

Critical Studies in Education and Culture Series
Edited by Henry A. Giroux

BERGIN & GARVEY
Westport, Connecticut • London

Library of Congress Cataloging-in-Publication Data

Thinking again : education after postmodernism / by Nigel Blake . . .
[et al.].
    p.   cm.—(Critical studies in education and culture series.
ISSN 1064–8615)
   Includes bibliographical references and index.
   ISBN 0–89789–511–8 (alk. paper).—ISBN 0–89789–512–6 (pbk. :
alk. paper)
   1. Education—Philosophy.   2. Education—Great Britain—
Philosophy.   3. Postmodernism and education.   4. Postmodernism and
education—Great Britain.   I. Blake, Nigel.   II. Series.
LB14.7.T55   1998
370′.1—dc21   97–27886

British Library Cataloguing in Publication Data is available.

Library of Congress Catalog Card Number: 97–27886
ISBN: 0–89789–511–8
       0–89789–512–6 (pbk.)
ISSN: 1064–8615

First published in 1998

Bergin & Garvey, 88 Post Road West, Westport, CT 06881
An imprint of Greenwood Publishing Group, Inc.

Printed in the United States of America

The paper used in this book complies with the
Permanent Paper Standard issued by the National
Information Standards Organization (Z39.48–1984).

10 9 8 7 6 5 4 3 2 1

Contents

Series Foreword

Educational reform has fallen upon hard times. The traditional assumption that schooling is fundamentally tied to the imperatives of citizenship designed to educate students to exercise civic leadership and public service has been eroded. The schools are now the key institution for producing professional, technically trained, credentialized workers for whom the demands of citizenship are subordinated to the vicissitudes of the marketplace and the commercial public sphere. Given the current corporate and right wing assault on public and higher education coupled with the emergence of a moral and political climate that has shifted to a new Social Darwinism, the issues which framed the democratic meaning, purpose, and use to which education might aspire have been displaced by more vocational and narrowly ideological considerations.

The war waged against the possibilities of an education wedded to the precepts of a real democracy is not merely ideological. Against the backdrop of reduced funding for public schooling, the call for privatization, vouchers, cultural uniformity, and choice, there are the often ignored larger social realities of material power and oppression. On the national level, there has been a vast resurgence of racism. This is evident in the passing of anti-immigration laws such as Proposition 187 in California, the dismantling of the welfare state, the demonization of black youth that is taking place in the popular media, and the remarkable attention provided by the media to forms of race talk that argue for the intellectual inferiority of blacks or dismiss calls for racial justice as simply a holdover from the "morally bankrupt" legacy of the 1960s.

Poverty is on the rise among children in the United States, with 20 percent of all children under the age of eighteen living below the poverty line. Unemployment is growing at an alarming rate for poor youth of color, especially in the urban centers. While black youth are policed and disciplined in and out of the nation's schools, conservative and liberal educators define education through the ethically limp discourses of privatization, national standards, and global competitiveness.

Many writers in the critical education tradition have attempted to challenge the right wing fundamentalism behind educational and social reform in both the United States and abroad while simultaneously providing ethical signposts for a public discourse about education and democracy that is both prophetic and transformative. Eschewing traditional categories, a diverse number of critical theorists and educators have successfully exposed the political and ethical implications of the cynicism and despair that has become endemic to the discourse of schooling and civic life. In its place, such educators strive to provide a language of hope that inextricably links the struggle over schooling to understanding and transforming our present social and cultural dangers.

At the risk of overgeneralizing, both cultural studies theorists and critical educators have emphasized the importance of understanding theory as the grounded basis for "intervening into contexts and power . . . in order to enable people to act more strategically in ways that may change their context for the better."[1] Moreover, theorists in both fields have argued for the primacy of the political by calling for and struggling to produce critical public spaces, regardless of how fleeting they may be, in which "popular cultural resistance is explored as a form of political resistance."[2] Such writers have analyzed the challenges that teachers will have to face in redefining a new mission for education, one that is linked to honoring the experiences, concerns, and diverse histories and languages that give expression to the multiple narratives that engage and challenge the legacy of democracy.

Equally significant is the insight of recent critical educational work that connects the politics of difference with concrete strategies for addressing the crucial relationships between schooling and the economy, and citizenship and the politics of meaning in communities of multicultural, multiracial, and multilingual schools.

Critical Studies in Education and Culture attempts to address and demonstrate how scholars working in the fields of cultural studies and critical pedagogy might join together in a radical project and practice informed by theoretically rigorous discourses that affirm the critical but refuse the cynical, and establish hope as central to a critical pedagogical and political practice but eschew a romantic utopianism. Central to such a project is the issue of how pedagogy might provide cultural studies theorists and educators with an opportunity to engage pedagogical practices that are not only transdisciplinary, transgressive, and oppositional, but also connected to a wider project designed to further racial, economic, and political democracy.[3] By taking seriously the relations between culture and power, we further the possibilities of resistance, struggle, and change.

Critical Studies in Education and Culture is committed to publishing work that opens a narrative space that affirms the contextual and the specific while simultaneously recognizing the ways in which such spaces are shot through with issues of power. The series attempts to continue an important legacy of theoretical work in cultural studies in which related debates on pedagogy are understood and addressed within the larger context of social responsibility, civic courage, and the reconstruction of democratic public life. We must keep in mind Raymond Williams's insight that the "deepest impulse (informing cultural politics) is the desire to make learning part of the process of social change itself."[4] Education as a cultural pedagogical practice takes place across multiple sites, which include not only schools and universities but also the mass media, popular culture, and other public spheres, and signals how within diverse contexts, education makes us both subjects of and subject to relations of power.

This series challenges the current return to the primacy of market values and simultaneous retreat from politics so evident in the recent work of educational theorists, legislators, and policy analysts. Professional relegitimation in a troubled time seems to be the order of the day as an increasing number of academics both refuse to recognize public and higher education as critical public spheres and offer little or no resistance to the ongoing vocationalization of schooling, the continuing evisceration of the intellectual labor force, and the current assaults on the working poor, the elderly, and women and children.[5]

Emphasizing the centrality of politics, culture, and power, *Critical Studies in Education and Culture* will deal with pedagogical issues that contribute in imaginative and transformative ways to our understanding of how critical knowledge, democratic values, and social practices can provide a basis for teachers, students, and other cultural workers to redefine their role as engaged and public intellectuals. Each volume will attempt to rethink the relationship between language and experience, pedagogy and human agency, and ethics and social responsibility as part of a larger project for engaging and deepening the prospects of democratic schooling in a multiracial and multicultural society. *Critical Studies in Education and Culture* takes on the responsibility of witnessing and addressing the most pressing problems of public schooling and civic life, and engages culture as a crucial site and strategic force for productive social change.

Henry A. Giroux

NOTES

1. L. Grossberg (1996). Toward a genealogy of the state of cultural studies. In C. Nelson & D. P. Gaonkar (Eds.), *Disciplinarity and dissent in cultural studies*. New York: Routledge, p. 143.

2. D. Bailey & S. Hall (1992). The vertigo of displacement. *Ten 8*, 2(3), p. 19.

3. My notion of transdisciplinarity comes from M. Zavarzadeh & D. Morton (1992). Theory, pedagogy, politics: The crisis of the 'subject' in the humanities. In M. Zavarzadeh & D. Morton (Eds.), *Theory pedagogy politics: Texts for change*. Urbana: University of Illinois Press, p. 10. At issue here is neither ignoring the boundaries of discipline-based knowledge nor simply fusing different disciplines, but creating theoretical paradigms, questions, and knowledge that cannot be taken up within the policed boundaries of the existing disciplines.

4. R. Williams (1989). Adult education and social change. In *What I came to say*. London: Hutchinson-Radus, p. 158.

5. The term "professional legitimation" comes from a personal correspondence with Professor Jeff Williams of East Carolina University.

Acknowledgments

This book is the product of two years' collaborative work. The idea originated with an invitation to us from Wilfred Carr to present a symposium on postmodernism and education at the annual conference of the Philosophy of Education Society held in Oxford, England, in 1995. The project developed in a way that neither he nor we would have imagined at the time. We are grateful to him for providing the original impetus.

In the course of this project we have met together on numerous occasions. We thank the Society for the grants we received in support of this work. We also thank the Katholieke Universiteit Leuven, the University of Dundee, the University of Durham, and the Open University for their support and for contributions to our expenses. The Penn Club in Bedford Place, London, provided friendly and congenial accommodation for our meetings.

Special thanks are due to Betty Vanden Bavière for the great care and unfailing patience she has shown in preparing the text for publication.

THINKING AGAIN

Retrospect

In a world that identifies success with saving time, writes Jean-François Lyotard, thinking has a fatal flaw: it wastes time (1986, p. 122). To think *again*, then, will be to waste time twice over, unless the presuppositions of the modern world are themselves faulty. This book will not save the reader time. It offers, unlike much that is published on the subject of education these days, no advice, prescriptions or ready solutions to practical problems. That approach—the quest for efficient solutions to problems—is characteristic of modernity, and of course we owe to modernity much that makes our lives safer and more comfortable. Solutions have been sought, and found, for all kinds of conditions afflicting the human race. But there comes a point where modernity begins to parody itself, pursuing answers without any sense of the original questions, proliferating devices for achieving ever greater "efficiency," in education as in other spheres. This is the point that some call "high modernism," and others the condition of postmodernity. As we look back at what has happened in education over the last quarter of a century or so, in the United Kingdom, in much of the English-speaking world, and in Europe, it seems evident that this is the point that we have reached.

A profound objection to modernity has always been that the modern technical genius for finding effective means to ends has too much diverted attention from serious consideration of our chosen or implicit ends themselves, whether ethical, economic or educational. Modernity is instrumentalist—an objection heard no less from traditionalists than from the Left or any other quarter. Under the "postmodern condition," as Lyotard (1984) has described it, the obsession with efficiency and effectiveness that he criticised, and memorably labelled as "performativity," has finally parted company altogether from controversial, political questions of what we should be trying to achieve. "In matters of social justice and of scientific truth alike, the legitimation of . . . power is based on its optimising the system's performance—efficiency" (Lyotard, 1984, p. xxiv). Under performativity, deliberation over ends is eclipsed (see further below, Ch. 9). All kinds of business and activity are measured and ranked against each other, with ever less concern for the rationale for doing so.

Thus performativity obscures differences, requiring everything to be commensurable with everything else, so that things can be ranked on the same scale and everyone can be "accountable" against the same standards. This in turn entails the disvaluing, and perhaps the eradication, of what cannot be ranked. Everything must be "operational (that is, commensurable) or disappear" (Lyotard,

1984, p. xxiv). Schools in the United Kingdom, to give one example, are now ranked in gigantic league tables on the basis of the tested achievements of their pupils. They have learned to worry about their position in the columns of near-identical results, regardless of the statistical vacuity of all but the largest distinctions. Yet while their examination scores are neurotically compared, their social and moral ethos goes by the wayside. (Recent attempts to bring spiritual education under the remit of United Kingdom government agencies highlight this neglect by their intrinsic absurdity.) University departments are graded for the quality of their research on a seven-point scale, despite the incongruity of comparing wholly different kinds of research even within the same subjects, let alone between them. Academic league tables appear, based on subject, university, and degree of improvement since the last assessment exercise (never mind that that was based on different criteria). Elsewhere, under the same conditions of performativity, privatized railway companies are ranked by the percentage of their trains that arrive punctually. They adjust their timetables accordingly: it is easier for trains to arrive on time if they are not required to reach their destinations so quickly.

Despite this drive to "optimize the system's performance" under centralized control, there has also been a countervailing tendency toward dispersal and differentiation. The United Kingdom government, for example, while instituting the first national curriculum for schools in the nation's history at the same time contrived to commit itself to educational *diversity*, at any rate to the extent of promoting the development of schools of different kinds (more grammar schools, city technology colleges, grant-maintained schools . . .). Such variety would, supposedly, empower consumers by giving them a wider range of choice in the marketplace. In itself this apparent contradiction is easily related to historic trends in modernity: to secularization and bureaucratization in the sphere of culture, and rationalization and liberalization in the sphere of society. What is new are the terms in which these processes have come to be understood and celebrated. Commenting on the White Paper, *Choice and Diversity* (1992), which set out this policy, *The Daily Telegraph*, a sympathetic Conservative newspaper, commented that "there is really no such thing as Education: there are schools" (25 July 1992). This echoed former prime minister Margaret Thatcher's famous declaration that "There is no such thing as society. There are only individuals and families."[1]

While this might constitute a healthy acknowledgment of diversity and particularity, behind it we glimpse a feature often taken to be definitional of our postmodern times: the fall into disrepute of "grand narrative," particularly the narrative of emancipation from ignorance and superstition, which has come down to us from the Enlightenment. If there is really no such thing as society then there can be no widely accepted criteria for deciding on shared values, or for agreeing on what amount and kinds of ignorance might be tolerable. If there is really no such thing as education then all the discussions of rationality, autonomy and "worthwhile activities" undertaken by mid- and late-twentieth-century philosophers of education were entirely misconceived, and were perhaps politically partial and culturally biased. If there is really no such thing as society it will not be possible to study education with any pretence of disinterestedness and of going beyond personal predilection. Finally, if there is really no such thing as education, it will not be possible to study it at all.

And things have indeed proceeded as if this were so. The authority of the "foundation disciplines" (interestingly so called, in this context) of the history, philosophy, psychology, and sociology of education has faded and their institutional standing has been eroded. Nor have they been replaced by any other *discipline* of study: instead, the personal (but largely atheoretical) reflection of the "reflective practitioner" is supposed to do whatever job here needs doing, with the help of a few *Introductions to Management* nostrums and Learning Method techniques. In a neat marrying of the themes of performativity and the rejection of grand narratives or foundational theories, governments in many parts of the world have intervened in the curriculum of what used to be called teacher education in order to replace the study of education for prospective teachers with training in "effective skills" and classroom competencies. In 1992 the United Kingdom Minister for Education, Kenneth Clarke, famously castigated "barmy theoretical" courses for teachers.

It was in terms of disciplines and disciplinarity that Michel Foucault found the dimensions of knowledge and power conjoined. ("Discipline" here means, loosely, an institutionalized practice.) In these terms, we may see here a reversion in education from the sway of academic discipline to something closer to "confessional disciplines." For Foucault, confessional discipline characterized early modernity and informed the "carceral" society of early capitalism: a carceral society that numbered schools among its agencies, alongside prisons, hospitals, and factories. Schools are now required to "speak their truth" on pain of punishment, like the penitent in the confessional, the prisoner at trial, or the psychiatric patient in assessment. This they are to do in the methodical and routine terms of examinations and tests: making their pupils "speak their truth" in turn and moreover in the format acceptable to management. (In all sorts of ways schoolchildren and college students are monitored more closely and continuously than ever before: continual assessment replaces terminal examination, and journals, learning logs and diaries proliferate as part of course requirements.) Schoolteachers and academics are now routinely reviled as past beneficiaries of a producer culture who attempted to protect their own interests and privileges, not least by appeal to arcane professional knowledge. Power has moved elsewhere, to consumers rather than producers, or at any rate to those (advertising agencies, marketing consultants and "facilitators" of all kinds) who have the expertise to manipulate consumer choice and sell the educational product just like any other. It is to the consumers that educators must now make "confession." Thus confession supplants profession, method replaces thoughtfulness, and presentation skills and image management come before scholarly authority.

But through the commodification and image management of postmodernity the very distinction between what is real and what is simulated, fictive or imaginary becomes hard to sustain, a process exacerbated by the new technologies with their capacity to create virtual reality (see Baudrillard, 1983). Education replicates such confusions. Schools and universities that must sell themselves to consumers attend to self-presentation as much as to substance. University prospectuses improve dramatically, and depict a nostalgic world of college scarves, ivy-covered walls, and students clutching teddy bears straight from *Brideshead Revisited* alongside the high-tech laboratories and computer screens; schools re-institute uniforms, designed along reassuringly 1950s lines; the curriculum emphasizes the national "heritage" and there is a constant harking back to "traditional values" (e.g., formal grammar, desks facing the front, attempts to revive corporal punishment). This creates the education heritage experience, a theme park like the ones where actors tell you what it's like working in a factory in the industrial revolution. All must attend to how they appear, not how they are, and that distinction itself comes to be problematic. For is it not, precisely, a certain kind of *image* that the consumer is shopping for?

These changes are often a source of bewilderment to those who work in education. Teachers and academics who entered their profession out of a sense that they liked children or young people, or were engrossed in their specialist subject, are confronted with new and alien imperatives. The drive for "quality," for example, may seem to have little to do with any deep engagement with the young or with the academic subject, and everything to do with getting the documentation right to appease the relevant (usually governmental) monitoring agencies. Student charters setting out entitlements and "learning contracts" in explicit terms replace initiation into the mysteries of the academic disciplines. The reasonable requirement that information be supplied and records kept turns into the demand to feed the hungry bureaucracy of information gathering, collating and comparing. New kinds of educational jargon occasion further bewilderment. Those who had been confident in the value of reading fairy stories to young children, or reading Flaubert or Emily Dickinson with young adults, struggle to articulate the outcomes of such programs in terms of the skills and competencies acquired.

The family, too, suffers bewilderment in its attempts to educate the young. Like teachers, parents find themselves the objects of suspicion and distrust. An ethos of care sits uneasily with an emphasis on children's rights and, above all, on the individual child's right to choose. The family is scrutinized for its outcomes: how are your chances of good examination results, or your earning potential, affected by being brought up by a single parent? Children in this position may be compensated by being offered, in that most revealing phrase, "quality time" by the parent who has left, as if this improves the child's opportunity of turning into a quality product (by the standards of quality control). If something here strikes us as being not quite right ethically we can always insist that schools deliver more moral education, thus taking on more of the traditional function of the home. Any remaining gaps will be filled by the relevant experts. Their courses in parenting skills will help obscure the fact that bringing up children is not really regarded as valuable in a society dominated by economic rationality.

But the demands of performativity cause more than bewilderment: as Lyotard (1984) tells us, they cause "terror." We have to "be operational or disappear":

to fit in with bureaucratic systems, to do the things that can be entered on computer databases, or pay the penalty. To one British educationist, Tim Brighouse, "terror" is the appropriate word to describe the regime of inspection currently being inflicted on the schoolteachers of England and Wales: "We have a massive OFSTED [Office for Standards in Education] caravan which is rushing round the country. We are living in a reign of terror" (*The Guardian*, 15 January 1997). Newspapers regularly report the loss to the profession of teachers and administrators on whom this regime has taken its toll of stress.

Less dramatically, one effect of postmodernity has certainly been a kind of intellectual paralysis. Who could be against the raising of academic standards, for example, or against effective teaching? Who could be opposed to more extensive choice in education, or to the transmission in schools of the nation's heritage? The key words of postmodernity seem to carry with them a self-evident desirability, an appeal to the instincts of all reasonable and civilized men and women. Even those who have the uneasy feeling that all is not straightforward beneath the reasonable surface find it difficult to sustain a critique of the shibboleths of the age.

In such a context it has become hard to think, and we need to find new resources for thinking again. The academic disciplines of education, as they have been practiced in the West for the last half-century or so, seem to get little purchase here, not least because of what many feel is their underlying commitment to values that have been rendered ambivalent. For instance, how could philosophers ever again ask "Who is the educated man?", as if there might be one answer for all times and cultures, and no issue of gender to consider? How could psychologists talk of child development without problematizing the linearity, and assumption of progress, of the idea of development? Meanwhile the media generally and even the quality press offer little to the discussion of education beyond stale and sterile polarities: phonics versus "real books," progressivism versus traditionalism, selective versus non-selective schooling.

This is the context in which we have turned to a number of writers and theorists who show us a way out of the intellectual paralysis of postmodernity. These writers—chiefly Jacques Derrida, Jacques Lacan, Jean-François Lyotard, and Michel Foucault—have mostly repudiated the title of postmodernists, yet they are clearly postmodernist thinkers in the sense that they help us think about the postmodern condition in which we find ourselves. (There are complex debates about intellectual lineage, and about poststructuralism as against postmodernism, that we have not engaged with here.) It is worth emphasizing that at least some of the hostility that attaches to postmodernists clearly should be directed not at these writers, but at postmodernity itself, or modernity and its excesses. For example, it is common to find postmodernists accused of being relativists. Yet relativism seems to spring from the condition of our age itself. If the market is the sovereign source of value, then what is valuable will change as people's choices and desires change. What it this but relativism?

These writers show us new directions, they "change the subject" in ways that are stimulating and thought-provoking. They make the familiar look strange, as it often ought to look, perhaps. They shake us out of established patterns of thinking and writing. If they are not always "clear," by certain standards of clarity, that is because they are inclined to doubt that there are any indubitable realities to be seen through to, under ideal conditions of transparency. We write "*after* postmodernism" both in the sense that we feel these writers have shown us interesting directions in which to go, and also in the sense that we ask: after the insights that they have helped us toward, where, in thinking about education, do we go from here?

NOTE

1. Interview reported in *Woman's Own*, October 1987.

Chapter 1

Poststructuralism and the Spectre of Relativism

The kinds of ideas about language explored in this book are associated with the broad continental tradition in theory which may be identified with poststructuralism and deconstructionism, or with their echoes and answers within the Anglo-Saxon tradition. As such, they excite immediate resistance in many quarters. In particular, this is a territory typically characterized as postmodernist. And supposedly we all know what that entails. Postmodernism is cultural relativism and social pluralism, revived in new and more insidious guises. It is taken to threaten both the value of culture and the cohesion of society: in fact, the whole normative foundation of our lives. It must be resisted; and resisted first and foremost in education.

Accordingly, we live in a moment of intensified conflict over relativism in education. For the educational relativism that has come down to us from the 1970s (misidentified as the 1960s) is conceived by many as the precursor of postmodernism. This relativism/postmodernism is ritually anathematised by politicians, journalists and a new cadre of state educational functionaries. And relativism has indeed some great crimes against its name. It has been alleged, not without reason, that in the past it emptied the curriculum of content; perverted the relationship between teacher and student, be it that of authority or of care; trivialized education in relation to the other functions and roles of society; and left the young ignorant and rudderless.

And it has to be admitted that where questions arose or changes have been proposed in education, relativism has in many ways exerted a bad influence. There remain good reasons for fighting such relativist notions as: that there is no objective knowledge; that truth is as you see it; that "what's true for you" is one thing and "what's true for me" is another; that individual children can and must construct their own idiosyncratic knowledges; that different groups (races, classes, nations, religions) have different knowledges; that teaching someone to see things your way is at best an empty charade and at worst an act of violence. These arguments have been grounded in philosophical scepticism and tend to present all knowledge claims, disastrously, as arbitrary. Whether or not they have ever attained a genuine hegemony, in Britain and the English-speaking world these ideas certainly have exerted an obscurantist and destructive effect on thinking about curriculum, teaching methods and, in consequence, the very social importance of education; and they have needed dealing with, somehow or other.

It is almost certainly wrong, of course, to see the general educational practice of those times and since in terms of such a holocaust of knowledge. But there are indeed still those in educational theory (and adjacent fields such as social work) who cleave to relativism, and who look to postmodernism or poststructuralism to sustain their relativist commitments. Nonetheless, in Britain relativist ideas have been neutralized in practice by political and institutional means. Relativism has been silenced virtually by edict, and the principal edict in question has been the new UK National Curriculum. By imposing the National Curriculum, the government has simply left no practical option for the relativist teacher to operate in her preferred ways, and thus no room for influence for the relativist teacher educator. This political process—which of course has far more than a fight against relativism as its aim—has been subtended by two other interlinked ideological currents, anti-theoreticism and managerialism.

The British government has sold its educational reforms as responses to the demands of common sense, which in turn it typically identifies with traditionalism. British common sense is a social (and discreetly philosophical) tradition characterized by anti-intellectualism and thus too anti-theoreticism—a suspicion of the motives of theorists, impugning their pragmatic competence, and a hostility to theoretical ideas. Thus, those academics who were authorized to construct new national curricula in various subject areas perforce steered very clear of any strong theoretical commitments. Furthermore, they were pushed culturally as far to the right as they would go, under pressure from the highest levels of government. Moreover, the legitimation of the National Curriculum appealed to "parent power" and the common sense of parents, on the assumption that parents just won't put up with any "fancy theoretical nonsense." Thus, in effect, populism was also excited against relativism.

By the same token, managerialism has been not merely useful in installing, monitoring, and enforcing the National Curriculum and its correlative reforms, but appropriate to the ideological outlook informing the Curriculum. We noted in the Retrospect the kinds of processes that constitute managerialism as an educational movement. These processes are inimical to the free creative development of theoretical ideas and practical experiment with them. Consequently, the appeal to common sense is the only credible way for managerialists to sustain their claims to knowledge. Thus managerialism and conservative anti-theoreticism work hand-in-hand. Anti-theoreticism is a view that might be summarized like this: facts are facts—they are aspects of the Real World in which we cannot but live and which we cannot but recognize on pain of stupidity. Facts are not theory-relative. It follows that educational research, if it relates at all to the Real World, can only be a limited process of the discovery of additional and hitherto unrecognized facts. What we need is opinion surveys modeled on market research and more common sense understanding of how children learn. As to education itself and the process of teaching, theory can have little or nothing to tell us here either. Necessarily, intelligent people must have some idea of how to learn and how to teach. They have all succeeded in learning. And down the centuries, some have successfully taught; for had this not been so, the culture would have died. By the same token, we have broadly agreed intentions and aims for education—and indeed cannot but have them, for otherwise, again, the culture would have died. Appeals to theory can only cloud the issue and of their very nature involve a detour from our chosen path, with no traditional record of success to justify them and no apparent short-term success to inspire confidence. Educational theory is a snare and delusion.

Fundamentally, anti-theoreticism appeals against relativism; and by that token, anti-theoreticists will view askance the approach of this book if they take it to be relativist. But there's something of a puzzle here. For these days, what most excites reaction is the spectre specifically of moral relativism: the view that there are no objective moral or ethical standards, that each must live according to her own lights and, most fundamentally, each is immune to moral critique by others. The problem with such views is that they fatally obscure the distinction between having a different morality and no morality at all. So conservatives in Britain (including those on the Left) and fundamentalists in the United States of America inveigh desperately against moral relativism in the sphere of education. Moral disintegration is the current focus of educational concern.

But the poststructuralist views about language that we investigate here do not refer primarily or most obviously to the use of language in ethics. Canonically, one explains structuralist linguistics in relation to denotative uses of language—its epistemological use to state facts or describe states of affairs. But there is virtually complete consensus that moral language is not denotative. So does it matter to educational debate if poststructuralism is a form of relativism? Conversely, won't we be sidestepping the real issue, the moral issue, even if we can convincingly defend poststructuralism—as we intend to do—from the worst charges of epistemological relativism?

We think not. If the distinction between epistemological and ethical relativism is clear, the two are nonetheless intertwined both in theory and practice. For a philosophical question confronts anyone who wants to be a moral relativist: whether that position is itself a moral position or grounded rather in more general considerations about knowledge and language. There is a moral view, arguably a coherent one, which some call relativist, that we should cherish and respect genuine moral diversity while fearing moral dogma and pressures toward moral conformity. We are hesitant, though, to use the word relativism here (preferring pluralism), because such a view clearly pulls certain non-negotiable commitments back in by the back door: commitments to, for instance, a certain moral humility and respect for the judgments of others. And these commitments look like covert moral absolutes.

Such was the fervor of radical educationists in the 1970s (and it lingers in some quarters today) that this moral approach seemed dangerous. It would have reintroduced the possibility of moral debate, which to radicals seemed the prime site of ideological manipulation. Far better, it apparently seemed, to ground one's moral relativism in pre-moral, and thus effectively epistemological, considerations. We suggest that the motives of radicals were ethical, but their arguments epistemological. And for that very reason, the political reaction against moral relativism has relied quite heavily on epistemological considerations.

In part these considerations were those of common sense anti-theoreticism; but more considered epistemological arguments have also played a role. Epistemological relativists in education commonly represent knowledge as a theory of the world, as theory-relative. They usually assume either that meaning is somehow a private matter, and thus a private theory, or refer to the different conceptual repertoires of different languages and treat these as theoretical. Anti-theoreticists commonly appeal to a fairly well-known and generally sound set of arguments against these kinds of relativism. Typically, they rely on some version of the correct insight that if relativism claims the potency and legitimacy of a genuinely philosophical position, then it must apply to all knowledge claims whatever; but if so, then it must also apply to itself, and this generates intolerable paradoxes. If relativism is true, then it is only 'relatively true'; which is to say, in effect, not true at all. Counter-relativist arguments have taken a variety of forms often much more complex than this. But, at root this is what they generally boil down to.

However, things aren't quite so simple. There are those, including good philosophers, to whom such arguments seem cheap. They will protest that the tradition of relativist argument is much richer than can be rebutted so simply and much more illuminating than such simple counter-arguments allow. Three points must be made in response.

First, our target here is not all forms of philosophical relativism, but those comparatively naïve forms that have been deployed in educational theory to impugn the validity of knowledge, and hence too of teaching and moral authority. And these naïve versions actually do bend and break in the face of quite simple objections.

Secondly, those forms of relativism that tend to be seen as less noxious are typically best at emphasizing genuine radical differences and incommensurabilities between 'knowledges', conceptual repertoires, languages or whatever; whereas the more naïve varieties hurry to the conclusion that the learner, the knowing subject, can never step from one to another, never understand one from the position of another, never choose rationally between them. These are very different emphases, though. If the former is often illuminating (for instance vis-à-vis genuine practical difficulties in multicultural education), the latter can be practically incapacitating.

If and when educators genuinely do face the prospect of communicating across barriers of radical difference or incommensurability, it makes all the difference in the world whether they view that prospect as hugely difficult or flatly impossible. Where short-term or small scale projects are concerned, we are used to making a pragmatic equation between the too difficult and the impossible. Some tasks seem so overwhelming they may as well be impossible. But increasingly, modern societies face problems of communicating across linguistic barriers and epistemic gulfs as large-scale and long-term difficulties of considerable magnitude. If we see these problems as hugely difficult, the rational response is to invest in them—to invest insight, enquiry, ingenuity and, of course, time and money. If, on the other hand, we see them as *a priori* impossible, then we give up on them completely and put our energies into other things. The practical difference between very difficult and impossible is potentially vast.

By the same token, we should recognize that the more drastic forms of relativism do nothing to help us understand and accommodate diversity; quite the contrary. They tell us *a priori* that no such understanding is possible. Yet why this should necessarily foster tolerance and democratic social forbearance is obscure. If no mutual understanding is possible, why shouldn't we persecute others? If they're really so completely different from us, how do we know they will care? Conversely, the moment we accept that they do care, that we can actually see them suffer, is the moment we concede in effect that at least some basic form of mutual understanding is possible; and that it's on such things that we should aim to build our bridges to understanding across radical differences. Recognizing incommensurability is important. Treating it as an ineffable Otherness is dangerous. Assuming there is nothing but incommensurability is disastrous.

It's for these practical and ethical reasons that we will address epistemological relativism here, and in its most narrow and reductive forms. This kind of relativism does have its own social manifestation, and important and dangerous it is too.

However, notwithstanding its epistemological inconsistencies and moral inadequacies, relativism did have at least two virtues. First, in insisting that knowledge was problematic in certain ways, it attempted, in tune with the sceptical tradition in Western philosophy, to secure the necessary intellectual space for theory and for theoretically guided research. Second, it supported attempts at a contestation of the dominant culture. What can credibly fulfill these functions in its place?

We believe that the poststructuralist and postfoundationalist movements in philosophy have the appropriate potential but that this has been overlooked because of their popular misalignment with relativism. There is indeed a powerful contemporary movement calling itself the Postmodern Position, whose widely accepted support of pluralism is supported by a similarly widely resisted appeal to relativism. This is often grounded in readings of poststructuralist writers such as Foucault or Lyotard. But these seem to us often to be significant misreadings. And if that is what one means by postmodernism, then we would sooner not lay claim to the term. This in itself is a shame, however, for we also believe that there are points to be made about the current stage of development of modernism and modernity, or even their supercession—and these points are important and equally deserve the name 'postmodernist' yet have no intrinsic connection to relativism. What's more, we associate these with the same authors that relativist postmodernists appeal to.

The potential of poststructuralism and postfoundationalism, then, is first to secure a place for theory in the study and practice of education but without opening the door to scepticism and the arbitrary. Secondly, as we hope to show, these movements conceive of intellectual, academic and theoretic contestation not as some external assault on the Western tradition, but on the contrary as being internal to it and indeed at its very heart. We read these movements not, as do some conservatives, as alien, antinomian forces for cultural Dadaism but rather as important elements of the High Tradition itself. We also see them as resources for rehumanizing and liberalizing educational practice.

One of our tasks, then, is to dissociate poststructuralism (and, in the next chapter, postfoundationalism) from those naïve forms of relativism familiar in educational theory. This leads us to a position that can take the politics of knowledge more seriously, without construing that politics either as authoritarian or as a relativistic play of arbitrariness and unscrupulous interestedness. There will be those who suspect that in embracing ideas that undermine the realism of anti-theoreticism, or which prioritize the pluralism of versions of knowledge, we simply reinvent or reinstate relativisms of different kinds. But we shall argue here and in the next chapter that the kinds of view in question just don't have the noxious consequences of familiar relativisms.

POSTSTRUCTURALISM IS NOT RELATIVISM

Educational relativism has typically come in two varieties, though rarely clearly distinguished: varieties that we may safely name subjectivism and linguistic relativism. Both kinds of relativism repudiate empiricist and rationalist conceptions of knowledge as something somehow given.

The subjectivist variety has been particularly tempting for educationists of a progressive bent. Progressivists can in fact find something congenial in empiricism. It does at least claim that the given in knowledge is given in experience, and that experience is inalienably individual and private. This appeals to romantics and progressives. Subjectivists have clung to the empiricist picture of the human subject as one immured in her own consciousness. If this subjective isolationism looks sad from the outside, it looks safe from the inside. Privacy is the realm of personal authenticity; and to insist on the primacy of the private is to protect the subject, and thus the student, from the depredations of a repressive and aggressive outside world.

The subjectivist twist, which has often been legitimated by appeal to misunderstood phenomenology, is to claim that meanings are just as private as experience. Indeed, empiricists have typically viewed meanings as constructs abstracted from experience by the subject. The subjectivist simply adds the claim that there is no self-evidently correct way of making the abstraction; and thus any subject can only do so in her own idiosyncratic way. Since knowledge is determined by the meanings available, and meanings must differ from person to person, what is "knowledge for you" and "what's knowledge for me" cannot be the same.

This is light years away from poststructuralism. One of the most fundamental (and, we hope to show, interesting) claims of poststructuralism is that subjectivity is constructed by discourse. Who we are and who we become is determined by the things both said to us and, importantly, said about us. (We will explore this idea in depth in chapter eight on Lacan's account of the self.) But more profoundly still, we do not become anyone at all *unless* we are spoken to and spoken about. According to poststructuralists, there is no transcendental ego or given subjectivity prior to an individual's immersion in the discourse of others. We just don't exist as subjects prior to the discourse of others, according to the poststructuralist.

But if this is so, then one cannot view meanings as something generated primarily by the private, solipsistic self. For there is no such original self, prior to interaction with other people and their discourses, who could generate them. And once there is such a self, it is necessarily a self attuned to the flux of meanings in discourse that occurs outside the self. For that is how the self is constituted. The only meanings available to the self are those given to it in public discourse, or reconstructed in discourse between the self and others in the public domain.

It should be clear, then, that subjectivist forms of relativism *cannot even be stated* within a poststructuralist framework. Philosophical readers will have noticed, moreover, some significant affinity between poststructuralist and Wittgensteinian views on the primacy of the public realm where meaning is concerned. Readers trained in psychology also may find the emphasis on the constructive role of others in the development of mentality very congenial. So how does poststructuralism stand in relation to linguistic relativism?

Like the subjectivist, the linguistic relativist is primarily concerned with meanings. However, like the poststructuralist, she does actually locate meanings in the public realm. Our meanings are given us, she supposes, in our language. But different languages give us different meanings. The work of the linguisticians Edward Sapir and Benjamin Lee Whorff have been influential in describing such putative differences. Innuits are said to have many words for snow where we English speakers have one. It follows, say the linguistic relativists, that they can know things about snow that we can't. Similarly, there are Amerindian languages whose grammar, apparently, makes it far easier to formulate Einstein's relativity theory than English does.

This is interesting as far as it goes; but the linguistic relativist sees us all as immured in our own language just as the subjectivist finds us immured in our subjectivity and equally finds in this as much solace as regret. (We can all agree that to protect a language is to protect an identity. The relativist seems to infer that the more hermetic a language, the sturdier the identity in the face of outside pressures.) If what we can know is delimited by our conceptual stock, and this is given in our language, then we cannot reach beyond this stock to other languages. (How the linguistic relativist deals with bi- or multilingualism is never very clear. But it's noteworthy that, according to comparative linguists, bi- or multilingualism is actually the norm across the globe. We British and American whites are unusual in our indolent monolingualism.)

The attraction of linguistic relativism for educationists is unclear. Aren't they supposed to be primarily concerned with monolingual communities? If so, where might practical problems arise? Obviously, multiculturalism has been a fertile field for linguistic relativism. Inducting students into education in a different tongue from their own is certainly not just a matter of switching lexical codes. There are indeed significant psychological if not epistemological problems involved. But further, the relevance of linguistic relativism depends in part on how narrowly one defines a language. Empirical work in linguistics tends to confirm that there are significant differences between, say, the Englishes of different regions, different classes or age groups; and, importantly, between genders. Much depends on how deep these differences go, but linguistic relativism can seem useful in cautioning us against assuming that language and hence knowledge is some unproblematic monolith.

Now, is not the term *discourse* more or less a synonym for *language*? And if so, is not the poststructuralist just a linguistic relativist in Left Bank *haute couture*? The answer is no, to both questions. There are at least two meanings of discourse. Certainly it is often used to refer quite generally to the activity of linguistic intercourse. But for poststructuralists and discourse theorists, a discourse is a unit of analysis in epistemology, rather than a language.[1] A discourse is a collection of statements (involving knowledge or validity claims) generated at a variety of times and places, in both speech and writing, and which hangs together according to certain principles as a unitary collection of statements. A great variety of discourses can be generated within any one language. And, moreover, a single discourse can include statements in a variety of different languages. (Think of scientific discourse.)

If the linguistic relativist tends to think of us as located within a single language or some polylingual hybrid, by contrast, the poststructuralist claims that we are constituted as subjects within an indefinite plurality of disparate discourses. Much of what is said to us either sits within a particular discourse or is informed by presuppositions that do so. But since the discourses that contribute to our constitution are indefinitely plural, and indeed multilinguistic, there is no *a priori* guarantee that they are conceptually consistent with each other; and contingently, indeed, they are not so. So the poststructuralist could never be a linguistic relativist. She could never see the individual as trapped within the confines of a unique set of meanings given by a particular language.

Indeed, discourses need not even be internally consistent. Within any discourse, it is possible and indeed typical to find starkly conflicting claims. For instance, within the discourse of criminology it is possible both to affirm and deny a connection between crime and mental pathology. What is shared by both those who affirm and deny this are the concepts of crime and pathology and, moreover, access to research and argument both supportive and conficting but couched in similar terms and referring to shared criteria for judgment of the evidence—and much else besides. Discourses are sites of conflict.

Being constituted by a discourse, then, is not at all like being trapped within some coherent but unpliable metaphysical framework. But that is precisely the predicament that some linguistic relativists have attributed to us. Linguistic relativism and poststructuralism pull in very different directions.

An inherent fault of linguistic relativism has been its failure to see, moreover, that meanings are indefinitely malleable. It speaks of the meanings available in a language as if, being givens, they cannot possibly be subject to change, extension or addition. By contrast, Anglo-Saxon philosophical analysis itself has been very alert to just these possibilities. And so too, but in different ways, has poststructuralism. Discourse theorists describe sets of combinatorial rules which generate the conceptual and epistemological possibilities within a given discourse. This emphasis on recombination and reiteration of rules helpfully reminds us of the ways in which concepts (and hence knowledge) can be refurbished, distorted, added to, and otherwise modified. Furthermore, deconstructionism has pointed to the intrinsic *impossibility of stabilizing* meaning, of ensuring identity of meaning from one occasion of the use of a word to another. Where the linguistic relativist claims to be trapped in the confines of the stable set of meanings given in her language, the deconstructionist is apt to see this as a covert nostalgia for a spurious stability.

WHY DISCOURSE?

One can readily argue then that the poststructuralist, as a discourse theorist, cannot be a relativist; and this should shield her from a counter-relativist attack. But this is unlikely, on the other hand, to cut much ice with the relativist. The relativist will be asking why she should side with the discourse theorist (a kind of poststructuralist) anyway. She will be tempted to say that talk about discourses, which are public entities, is all very well; but my understanding of any given discourse is still, inevitably, different from yours, surely. And the counter-relativist, who tends to traditionalism, also will want reasons for taking anything as elaborate and strange as poststructuralism seriously, especially if it is going to be turned against her. So we need to consider why poststructuralists give primacy to public discourse over private experience. It is easiest to see why if we turn to the basic ideas of structuralism, the precursor of poststructuralism.

The turn by preeminent thinkers in Paris from phenomenology and existentialism to structuralism (born in Prague and Moscow) seemed in some ways a turn away from philosophy itself. It is worth emphasizing that structuralism began to thrive in the 1960s not primarily in philosophy but across a wide range of social and cultural studies—anthropology (Levi-Strauss), mathematics (the Bourbaki group) and literary criticism (Barthes) being the best-known examples. Famously, Wittgenstein, in the analytic tradition, wanted to find a way to stop doing philosophy. The structuralists seemed to just stop without any fuss.

This turn away from philosophy was primarily a turn from any interest in private experience to an interest in public discourse, an early episode in what Habermas has identified as a turn in philosophy from a "paradigm of consciousness" to a "paradigm of communication," a turn also made in the analytic tradition. So why did structuralism not have a place for any interest in experience? And what echoes does this find in the analytic tradition?

The father of structuralism was the Swiss linguistician Ferdinand de Saussure. It's important to recognize that Saussure's project was to put his own discipline on sounder and stronger methodological foundations by asking the fundamental question: What is it that students of language study? Structuralism was not born out of revolutionary scepticism. Saussure's proposal was to consider language as composed of signs, and to seek illumination by investigating the general nature of signs. He posited that the sign has two aspects. It functions both as a signifier and as a signified. As a signifier, it typically takes the form of a written or spoken word. As a signified, a sign may be identified with a concept or a representation. But fundamentally, Saussure proposes that (with certain minor provisos) the connection between any signifier and its signified is *arbitrary*. Everything follows from this.

In one sense this is a familiar and banal idea. Clearly there is no philosophical reason why the English word for a river must be *river*. (Obviously, there is an historical explanation for this linguistic fact, but not one that makes it in any sense logically necessary.) In this simple sense, there is no intrinsic connection between a signified and its signifier. But as a linguistician, Saussure notes a deeper kind of arbitrariness. Signifiers, he insists, do not together constitute any kind of nomenclature. When attempting to translate between one language and another, we cannot simply substitute a French or Sanskrit signifier for some English signifier. Translation is much more than swapping one nomenclature for another. For it is a linguistic fact that different languages make available not just different signifiers, but different signifieds. For instance, where English has the single signified of a river, French has two—*rivière* and *fleuve*. (The distinction is that the latter flows into the sea; the former doesn't.) In translation, one is not simply switching into a different set of signifiers, but trying to match up signifieds, which may not actually be commensurable.

It's important to bear in mind that this is not a philosophical insight but a linguistic one; for it is misleading to put some kind of transcendentalist gloss on such a proposition. Nonetheless, it does have strong philosophical resonances. For it is impossible to explain the differences between the signifieds available in a language if meaning is private, a function of personal experience and of individual, asocial attempts to make sense of that experience. If that were so, if the construction of meaning were indeed a purely personal and solipsistic affair, it would be a mystery as to how any individual comes to isolate just those signifieds used by others who use the same signifiers. Why doesn't the nascent English speaker construct for herself the signifieds of *rivière/fleuve*, but home in, so conveniently, on the single signified of a river?[2] Structural linguistics requires a view of meanings as public constructs and identifies meaning with signifieds as aspects of public signs. It requires this, not as a philosophical thesis, but as a corollary of its empirical theory about language.

But can we say anything to explain why signifieds differ from language to language? We can at least explain how these differences are possible by reference to the postulate of the arbitrary connection between signifier and signified. If signifieds are public constructs, but bear no intrinsic relation to signifiers, then a repertoire of spoken or written signs does not predetermine what signifieds there may be. If experience does not do so either, then the signifieds of a given language are radically underdetermined. Different languages have different signifieds simply because there is nothing to stop them.

But how then are signifieds constructed? Meaning, says Saussure, is differential. To understand, say, the meaning of the signifier green is not a matter of treating it as a label and asking what the label is attached to (grass, for instance). Rather, to understand the word is to know how to draw practical distinctions between green and not-green. To understand a sign is always to understand it in relation to some other sign. To understand green is to understand its relations to not-green and its correlates—blue, red and so on. Meaning is relational and the primary relation for analysis is the relation of difference.

But why is this? What's wrong with seeing 'green' as simply the label for the color of grass? The suggestion begs the question of how we understand the word 'grass'; for if we don't understand that, we can't identify the color of grass and label it green. According to Saussure, the meaning of grass must be differential too. We identify grass by contrast with, for instance, other plants. In pursuing meanings, we never escape from differential structures. In structural linguistics, our categories for thinking about the world can never be taken as given.

If there are no givens, then, all we have in language is a collection of differential relations. But Saussure further claims that these differences are not disordered. They interrelate with each other. For instance, the differrential pair mother/father relates both to the pair male/female and to the pair parent/child. Differences interconnect like this to form structures, hence the term *structuralism*. These structures may be extensive and elaborate, but not necessarily unitary. A language need not be thought of as a single structure. But to learn a language is nonetheless in part to learn structures of signifieds. And it is just wildly implausible to suppose that the solipsistic subject of (vulgarized and distorted) phenomenology could ever construct such structures on her own, far less marry them to those of her fellow language speakers.

AND WHY POSTSTRUCTURALISM?

Philosophers in the analytic tradition can find much here with which to sympathize. One of the fundamentally important ideas of modern analysis is Wittgenstein's argument that hermetically private languages are logically impossible. No subject could construct a set of meanings derived wholly from her own experience without reference to the language and meanings of other people. In a nutshell, she would have no means of knowing whether she was using her own language consistently or mistakenly, and thus it would be an idle instrument for making sense of even her own world. In a real sense it would be no language at all, just pointless words lost on the air. To use a language is to use complicated sets of rules. And to know whether you are following a rule correctly requires confirmation or correction from something outside yourself. Only other people could possibly provide this.

The analytic philosopher should recognize that the structuralist must be right in thinking that language must be public rather than private. And with her interest in rules, she should at least take an interest in the idea of linguistic structures, for these are as much structures of rules as structures of signifieds: rules, for instance, for marking differences such as green/not-green or male/female. And like the structuralist, the analyst does not believe either that there are any givens of experience, because experience alone simply cannot determine what meanings we construct. And in saying that there are no givens of experience, the analyst makes explicit something that is implicit in structuralism and elaborated in poststructuralism: that there are no foundations of knowledge.

Structuralism proper has arguably had its day. One characteristic that probably alienated the interest of analytic philosophers was the formalism and reductive tendency of structuralist analysis, in particular its narrow focus on binary oppositions. As we have seen, poststructuralism, and in particular its deconstructionist version, springs from insight into the limitations of attempts at defining language in terms of determinate structures. But what survives, in particular, is a concern with the idea of difference, though of difference as something itself mutable and unstable. Later chapters will explore these developments. What remains in common between these approaches is an understanding of discourse as multiple, contingent, unstable, external to, and constitutive of the subject or the self: conceptions that remain incompatible with the familiar forms of educational relativism.

We shall return to this idea that there are no foundations of knowledge in Chapter two. As we noted at the outset, the kind of thinking loosely characterized as postmodern is typically taken to include not only poststructuralism but also the kinds of development in the Anglo-Saxon analytic tradition which we have decided to call *postfoundationalism*. These too excite fear and loathing in traditionalist and managerialist quarters. These too are seen as threats to the canon and as undermining the Western intellectual tradition. These too are taken to be forms of relativism. But these reactions rest on profound misconceptions, as we shall argue.

A more substantial question at this point might be this: if postfoundationalism is important for the kind of rethinking that we aim to further in this book, why don't we confine ourselves to the more familiar and arguably the epistemologically more rigorous analysis available in the Anglo-Saxon tradition? If analytic postfoundationalism has important things to say, for instance, about the self, identity and culture, why take the poststructuralist/deconstructionist route at all?

Our concern in this book is with questions that arise within the philosophy of education. Philosophy of education needs more than epistemology alone. It is inherently, perhaps primarily, concerned with questions about education as a social institution or a collection of institutions; about teaching and the medium of teaching, which is primarily language; and about knowledge as a social product as much as a philosophical problem. A philosophy of education which is able to engage with the quotidian realities of educational practice needs analytic tools for describing institutions, language and discourses, their interrelationships and the knowledge that is discovered, produced, and maintained within their context.

Poststructuralism offers some useful tools here, in particular its conception of difference, its grasp of the looseness of fit between language and reality, its awareness of the opacity of language (permeated by hidden and unsuspected layers of metaphor), and its insistence on the actual instability of language even, perhaps particularly, where language is intended to be most monumentally transparent and stable—for instance, in the language of managerialism. Poststructuralism has also investigated, in illuminating ways, the notion of a discourse, its principles of unity and the interplay between the generation of knowledge claims and the social practices that subtend them. This too seems important to us in the analysis and critique of educational practice.

We offer the chapters that follow as a series of explorations with critical intent. They use or examine a variety of aspects of poststructuralist, postfoundational and postmodernist analyses, without attempting to force these into a carefully elaborated synthesis. We do not believe it desirable to do this at this moment, if at all. We are more concerned with helping to keep educational theory alive and well. We are prepared to live with the uncertainties, equivocations, and live controversies which necessarily characterize any healthy discipline. We do not believe that the practice of education can be well served in the long run by the intellectual inertia of anti-theoreticism. It strikes us as too ironic for words that we should find ourselves invited by functionaries, journalists and politicians to stop thinking imaginatively and innovatively about education—to stop thinking about the very institution whose job it is to sustain and reproduce a thinking society.

NOTES

1. We are taking Foucault's conception in *The Archaeology of Knowledge* as paradigmatic here.

2. The example is borrowed from Jonathan Culler's *Saussure*.

Chapter 2

Foundations Demolished, Sovereigns Deposed: The New Politics of Knowledge

It is almost received wisdom in recent philosophy that there are no foundations of knowledge, no grounds exterior to ourselves that guarantee the truth of our factual claims, and no supra-human warrant for universal truths in the realm of ethics.

But might postfoundationalism be some kind of scandal? We noted in Chapter one that conservatives often see it that way. For instance, might its implicit repudiation of universalism in ethics lead to negligence of the moral claims that others have on us? How can a postfoundationalist such as Richard Rorty, for instance, honor these claims if postfoundationalism undercuts any appeal to moral universalism? Is he not left in the position of a moral relativist? He might answer:

Solidarity is not discovered by reflection but created. It is created by increasing our sensitivity to the particular details of the pain and humiliation of other, unfamiliar sorts of people. Such increased sensitivity makes it more difficult to marginalise people different from ourselves by thinking, "They do not feel it as *we* would," or "there must always be suffering, so why not let *them* suffer?"

This process of coming to see other people as "one of us" rather than as "them" is a matter of detailed description of what unfamiliar people are like and of redescription of what we ourselves are like. (Rorty, 1989, p. xvi)

Here, Rorty appeals to postfoundationalism precisely *not* as a form of relativism. It is rather a strategy for avoiding moral relativism (seeing our own morals as irremediably parochial), and a means to sidestep the misleading moral dichotomy between relativism and universalism. But what sense can we make of this? What does postfoundationalism come to? And why should anyone prefer to be a postfoundationalist? As in our previous chapter, let's look first to the epistemological field.

FROM PLURALISM TO SOVEREIGNTY—AND BACK AGAIN

If we think of philosophy as beginning with the thought of the pre-Socratics (Thales, Anaximander, Anaximenes, Parmenides, Pythagoras, Heraclitus), then we may see it as rooted in some quasi-religious urge to answer the deep questions of existence, the ambitions of cosmology and metaphysics. In the twentieth century, this kind of view of philosophy was preeminently Heidegger's at a certain moment. It speaks to the astonishment the lone thinker may feel in face of the transcendent fact of the very existence of anything. But modern training in philosophy typically starts not with the pre-Socratics but with Socrates and Plato; and this shows us a significantly different picture of the discipline. If Socrates' typical question was "What is X?" (what is justice? love? knowledge? piety?), his guiding motive was to become clearer as to what he (and others) really knew or really did not know. But why so? Was this an unmotivated curiosity, like that which motivated the pre-Socratics? Or was it not rather, as some have suggested, a response to puzzlement at human differences: differences of opinion, taste and practice, but primarily differences in ethics? With the emergence of the Greek city-states as strong and cherished homelands, Greeks found the confidence to travel afield and experience far more of human diversity. And Socrates' Athens was the most modern, the most cosmopolitan, in such respects.

For Socrates and Plato, as for us today, cultural plurality presented problems—moral, political and philosophical. And just as elements in our own society sidestep the problem of diversity by resort to instrumentalist practices more concerned with efficiency than truth or justice (as Lyotard argues), so in Socrates' day the sophists (so Plato tells us) taught the manipulation of language and of one's audience for opportunistic and morally shallow purposes:[1] manipulation which helped the speaker avoid addressing the difficult questions and problems for dialogue raised by cultural differences. Socrates saw sophism as pernicious, not least in its corrupting foreclosure on intellectual openness in debate. One might suggest that one of his fundamental concerns in practice, if not in theory, was with the ethics of dialogue: its proper conduct and the proper attitudes of participants to the conversation and to each other. He[2] evinces this concern in for instance his frequent pauses to consider which way the dialogue should properly turn next or his care for the character of his colleagues as they manifest it in their discussions. Such an ethics would impugn the sophist as corrupting the pursuit of knowledge.

It is arguably no mere coincidence that so many contemporary and recent philosophers have revived a concern with dialogue and its conduct.[3] In some ways it seems an important and critical response to modernity, instrumentalism and the fragmentation which characterizes pluralism at its most inflexible. And herein lies an irony. If the earliest complete works of philosophy are presented as dialogues, nonetheless the genre of dialogue soon takes a back seat in the literature. Even in some of Plato's later works, where he is less the secretary of Socrates and more his own man, the dialogue form already begins to seem vestigial, an empty formal device. And none of Aristotle's dialogues survive, perhaps by mischance, yet possibly by neglect as well. Either way, the genre of dialogue is soon marginalized.[4] Why is this?

Since Plato, one of the most central concerns of philosophy has been to establish the foundations of knowledge—both knowledge of fact and "ethical knowledge"; to discover, that is, which are the knowledge claims on which all genuine knowledge is built. If one knows this, then one can distinguish genuine from specious knowledge as that which does or does not fit in the edifice with the proper foundations. We need rehearse here only briefly the remarkable variety of candidates for foundational status: such as Plato's commitment to a transmundane realm of Forms, Descartes' search for clear and distinct ideas, Kant's account of transcendental and analytic conditions of mundane experience or Locke's and Hume's concern with the irreducible givens of sensory experience. These are the classic versions of foundations of knowledge to which most other versions relate in some way or other.

The search for foundations has been a fundamentally important strategy with regard to the politics of knowledge since Plato and in particular in that period between Descartes and A. J. Ayer which we now retrospectively characterize as the modern age. That is to say, it has had fundamental influence on conceptions of the appropriate behaviour and conventions of association of those engaged in the pursuit of knowledge. In philosophy, as in many of the humanities, attitudes to the conduct of discussion and the conventions of lecturing and publication have been of central importance in the politics of knowledge. In that connection, the search for foundations of knowledge has been central to philosophy's idea of itself and of its importance. And this, in turn, has informed educational theory's notion of its own status as a serious, even earnest pursuit. For classical educational theory, the more firmly grounded in philosophy it felt itself to be, the more confident it felt of its own status. Even Dewey, an early proponent of the idea of "the death of philosophy," felt it appropriate to ground his deepest educational thinking in ideas which began as philosophy, wherever he felt them to lead.

Tightly linked to the metaphor of foundations of knowledge has been that of the sovereign subject of knowledge; and this has been strategically important. The strategy has been to see dialogue across personal differences as irresolvable in its own terms, such that one could only bring resolution by stepping outside it. To do philosophy was to withdraw from the overtly political world of dialogue to seek truth in the supposedly apolitical realm of monologue. (For Descartes, for instance, this involved a physical retreat to his solitary stove.) And in monologue, the most fundamental and general of concerns was to examine the nature and the givens of one's own consciousness. If knowledge was an attribute of consciousness, nothing exterior to consciousness had prior authority over consciousness. Thus, the conscious individual was the sovereign subject of knowledge. The strategic, "political" value of this epistemic autonomy is in its legitimation of resistance to the "corrupting" influence of "mere opinion"—the mere opinion of others which should not easily outweigh the evidence of one's own experience or most rigorous and principled reflections.

The apparent abnegation of the politics of dialogue in this "paradigm of consciousness" has nonetheless had potent political implications for the relationship of knowledge and power. It is in abstracting itself, apparently, from the interpersonal play of power in dialogue, that philosophy in the modern period has acquired whatever authority it has ever seemed to have. It was famously Immanuel Kant's concern that the philosopher should "speak the truth to power:"[5] that the political sovereign, the king, should knock up against the recalcitrance of the disinterested philosopher who bows only to the authority of transcendental and categorical moral imperatives. Ironically, any political power accruing to the philosopher inhered in his repudiation of any politics of knowledge. As Derrida puts it,[6] writing of Kant's *The Conflict of the Faculties*, "The university is there *to tell the truth*, to judge and to criticize in the most rigorous sense of the term, namely to discern and decide between the true and the false: and when it is also entitled to decide between the just and the unjust, the moral and the immoral, this is insofar as reason and freedom of judgment are implicated there as well. Kant, in fact, presents this requirement as a condition for struggles against all 'despotisms'" (1992a, p. 17).

This, we may infer, includes despotism within the bounds of dialogue. Thus we can understand the apparent scandal of the Hegelian and Marxist traditions: the former disclaiming any pretence of disinterest, the latter denying its very possibility.

This picture of the relations of knowledge and power has been profoundly influential in our educational thinking. This is most obvious in relation to higher education and the still potent appeal of the notion of academic freedom as a fundamental value in a democratic society. Where truth cannot stand up to power, democracy and freedom wither. But until recently—in some ways still—this picture has also informed mainstream attitudes to school knowledge. Here too we have typically feared and resisted the politics of knowledge as the begetter of a politicized curriculum. On the one hand, we have supposed that any view of knowledge as having its own politics led straight to the bog of relativism, discussed in Chapter one. On the other, we have suspected that, relativist or not, the politics of knowledge would always, if not necessarily, be a proxy for politics *simpliciter*, political indoctrination and anti-democratic politics at that.

For such reasons as these, educationists and the educated public cannot be indifferent to those recent and contemporary philosophies that repudiate the very notions of foundations of knowledge and with it that of the individual as the sovereign subject of knowledge. (The latter is a particularly raw issue where, as in Britain, even the Left has acceded to the aggressive individualism of the New Right.) Once those ideas are abandoned, we are arguably thrust back into Socrates' predicament of finding some way to cope with the interminable and circuitous processes of dialogue, in a pervasively politicized ethos. If this is so, it raises problems as to the legitimacy of all and any knowledge claims: problems which in turn prompt questions about the authority and autonomy of educational institutions in general.

Moreover, it does so at a time when, ironically, the managerialist pressures mentioned in Chapter seven also come from the Right. The political conflict between cultural conservatism and the conservatism of capitalism manifests itself in difficulties over education and epistemology. Market individualism treats as mere opinion the very knowledge that cultural conservatism would suppose to be authoritative. It denies authority to ideas and invests it rather in ungrounded and non-accountable individual choices. The educational problem about foundations is in part the problem of the Right in saving itself from itself.

THE MODERNIST CRITIQUE OF FOUNDATIONS

Not surprisingly, then, postfoundationalist ideas in philosophy are regarded with the same conservative suspicion as relativism; and even within philosophy there are those who treat them as actually an aspect of relativism (e.g., Harré & Kransz, 1996). Certainly postfoundationalism can take relativist forms. But it need not do so unless, unhelpfully, one simply defines the repudiation of foundations as a form of relativism. (We will return to this.) Nonetheless, scepticism and unease may suggest that postfoundationalism is some kind of radical abrogation of intellectual responsibility, typically associated with postmodernism. (Lyotard makes an explicit connection between postmodernism and postfoundationalism [Lyotard, 1984, pp. 37-41, esp. p. 39]) though he certainly doesn't equate the two.) Indeed, this sometimes shows up in the personal animus which some express toward such thinkers as Rorty or Derrida. But this view is a mistake, and an important one—important to correct not only because one would wish to defend the reputation of some major thinkers, but because in brushing postfoundationalism aside, one fails to register something fundamentally serious about modern, no less than postmodern, culture.

First, it should be understood that truly rigorous forms of postfoundationalist argument can be found in the dryest and most punctilious of analytical writings, and amongst the most authoritative of contemporary contributions. In the Anglo-Saxon tradition, the pervasive influence of the later Wittgenstein is postfoundationalist. It informs both the analytic theory of truth, elaborated by Strawson in debate with Austin, and postanalytic philosophy of science, pursued by for instance Kuhn, Lakatos and Feyerabend. Similarly, the American tradition of philosophical pragmatism affords searching postfoundationalist insights from Dewey to Rorty by way of Quine, Davidson, Putnam and Sellars.

But secondly, we should also properly appreciate the range and variety of sources of postfoundationalism. Certainly it is also found in more speculative versions, including some in continental philosophy. In Germany, the hermeneutics of Heidegger on the one hand, Gadamer on the other fall in this tradition. So too does the later work of the Critical Theorist Jürgen Habermas, a critic of both of them. In France, poststructuralist and deconstructionist thinking are forms of postfoundationalism. Postfoundationalism is a broad and important current, and probably represents a secular shift in the Western intellectual tradition. In signing up for postfoundationalism, one does not mortgage one's position to a few specific arguments. If Derrida's postfoundationalism fails, one has still to confront Strawson's. If Habermas gets it wrong, it may yet be that Lakatos gets it right; and so on.

Sceptics should notice something about the politics of this distinguished crew. First, many of them have little or no overt professional interest in political, social or cultural theory. One does not associate Strawson or Quine, Austin or Davidson or even very much Wittgenstein with these concerns. The central, sometimes exclusive interest of such thinkers is in problems of logic and knowledge. On the other hand, those postfoundationalists who do have explicit political commitments are as likely to veer to the Right as to the Left. The Leftist Habermas is balanced by the conservative Gadamer. The radicalism of Barthes and Baudrillard is countered by the conservatism of Heidegger. And the very visible politics of Foucault and Derrida remain nonetheless enwrapped in Left/Right ambiguity. Thus postfoundationalism is not, in itself, any form of political or social radicalism. But neither does any particular political stance weigh against it.

It is hardly credible to see, in this roll call of major thinkers, an army of the intellectually challenged. Thus the only credible critical strategy for marginalizing them could be to accuse them of an oversophistication which has lead them away from fundamental, indeed foundational, common sense. But this is glib. Postfoundationalism is in fact a product of philosophical "business as usual."

If one of the central commitments of the modern Western tradition in philosophy is to the evaluation of the validity of arguments, then another is to critique. And the two are tightly intertwined. To test a view or a position for validity is in itself a form of critique. And while critique of an intellectual position involves more than this, such as evaluating the range of implications of a view or its compatibility with other strongly held commitments, critique without commitment to the evaluation of validity is canonically reckoned worthless in the modern Western tradition. But notice that a commitment to critique is actually a position in the politics of knowledge. Whilst overtly, in its monological mode, abjuring such a politics, Western philosophy has always, we suggest, retained not just a political recalcitrance vis-à-vis temporal power but also a set of covert commitments within a politics of knowledge which it overtly disavowed.

It has been tempting to conservative sceptics nonetheless to take post-foundationalism for a radical or subversive move in the politics of knowledge. They have assumed that a more traditional politics of knowledge could not but deliver their favoured product. The opposite is the truth of it. It is actually the determined but principled pursuit of foundations which finally discloses their elusiveness. Foundationalist arguments have failed as a result of the rigorous and sustained evaluation of validity; in other words, in the observance of the same, characteristically modern kind of politics of knowledge which cultural conservatives appeal to against postfoundationalism. Conservatives are not the only ones to have mistaken this dynamic. Postmodernists such as Kiziltan, Bain and Canizares in educational theory (1990) have argued that a postmodern critique of foundations forces us into a newly politicized relation to knowledge. As Paul Smeyers has written,

Kiziltan and others (1990), following Feinberg, argue that education in the twentieth century has mainly been driven by the impulse to replace the moral certainty of the last century with the scientific certainty of this one. "Consequently, in today's lexicon 'to educate' has come to be underwritten by various types of 'scientific' knowledges" (ibid., p. 353). Given that, "the postmodern critique of the foundations, the function, and the status of scientific knowledge (and of reason) is certain to have profound and unsettling effects upon the practices, rationalisation and the legitimation of education" (ibid., p. 353). (Smeyers, 1995, pp. 115-116)

They too get it the wrong way round. It is rather our modern and already critical relation to knowledge which undermines belief in foundations. Arguably both the moral and scientific modern certainties alluded to are historical illusions.

Modern culture in the humanities, social sciences and natural sciences—in contrast to modern managerialism—has a long involvement with uncertainty and doubt. Cultural modernism, in particular, was never marked by any apolitical relation to knowledge, or apolitical insistence on fundamental givens, as so often claimed by *soi-disant* postmodernists. On the contrary, fundamentals were something to discover, and the process of discovery a demanding and critical one. The critical stance in the politics of knowledge (in philosophy and any other discipline) is itself a paradigmatically modern position. If modernism grows out of the Enlightenment Project, it is surely a commonplace that the Enlightenment was concerned with the critical sifting of valid from invalid claims to knowledge.

This sifting was never done by appeal to neutral "givens" apprehended above or before discussion, debate or enquiry, even if such givens were assumed to exist. Modernists have argued that Kant gave a particular twist and a special impetus to the Enlightenment Project in providing the example of a discipline, philosophy, critically examining its own limits and its own potential.[6] The modernist cultural critic Clement Greenberg argued, in the heyday of modernism in the 1950s and 1960s, that Kant's example constituted the paradigm for processes of self-critique in other disciplines, not least the arts (Greenberg, 1961). Self-critique eventually entrenched them each as valid by testing them for their potential autonomy. (To fail this critique was to sacrifice credibility, as Greenberg thought theology had done.) To survive and thrive, each art had to show what it itself had to offer which other arts or disciplines could not. If it succeeded in doing so, then by that token it disclosed fundamental "rules of the game" for itself, which themselves entailed particular ontological and epistemological commitments—foundations.

But just as Kant's critique of philosophy was itself conducted as an exercise in philosophy, so too the critique of painting, for instance, was also a self-critique, conducted in terms of artistic experiment rather than in terms of verbal reasoning or appeal to extra-artistic philosophical argument. The radical experiments of modern painting, for instance, are experiments to fix quasi-empirically or at least *ad hoc* the limits of genuine painting and the true criteria of artistic quality. (Similarly, nineteenth-century science expunged theology from itself by subjecting theological remnants in science to a specifically scientific critique.) Thus, although radical critique is often thought of as a prerogative of postmodernism, it is arguably the heir of a specifically modernist politics of knowledge.[7]

The classic analytic philosophy of education elaborated by Hirst and Peters was never announced as a form of modernism, but may readily be seen in this Greenbergian light. Hirst's Forms of Knowledge thesis clearly shares the same concern with the autonomy of differing kinds of intellectual pursuit and (at least implicitly) with the intellectual decadence consequent on infringements of that autonomy. (However, arguably Hirst did not share Greenberg's belief in self-critique as a motor for the intellectual and social entrenchment of disciplines.)

Peters' Transcendental Argument may be seen as a modernist attempt to entrench educational theory as a partially autonomous discipline by establishing the limits of value scepticism in the intellectual field. Interestingly, the Argument is typically presented in the form of a notional dialogue, and thus an implicitly political form: what could we say to someone who wanted to question the value of all or any intellectual pursuits?

Third, the moral views of Hirst, Peters and their colleague Robert Dearden, which informed their views of both the educational process in general and moral education in particular, were grounded in an unambiguously modernist belief in the autonomy of ethics. Such a belief constituted a clear but ambiguously acknowledged position in the politics of knowledge: one which repudiated the legitimacy of moral stances grounded on non-moral premises, particularly ideological arguments from the Right and (more so in those days) the Left, while questioning the very notion of a politics of knowledge itself. So, in abandoning belief in the foundations of knowledge, we put in question the central tenets of the analytic philosophy of education and with them its politics of knowledge.

DEMOLISHING FOUNDATIONS, BUT STILL TALKING SENSE

Those thinkers we have aligned with postfoundationalism may not share political commitments in the social sphere; but arguably, all have been masters of modernist philosophical critique and strategic players in the modern politics of knowledge. As we have suggested, in critique, positive and negative commitments are inextricable from each other: for validity and against error, for scepticism but as a tool of emancipation. Thus, there has been a demanding dynamic in postfoundationalist thought. If foundations of knowledge provide the basis on which one might "speak the truth to power," then the search for them is of paramount importance. But the search is bogus unless governed by a commitment to validity and therefore also to critique. Yet the search has failed, on every front: in the theory of meaning, the theory of truth, the theory of knowledge and in philosophy of mind. This might be taken to mean that one *cannot* speak the truth to power. But on the other hand, it might rather mean not that one cannot do so, but that securing foundations is the wrong preparation for doing so. Perhaps it is simply the commitment to critique itself, the critical position within the politics of knowledge, that authorizes dissent in the real world of politics? To test this possibility, we must first ask why the search for foundations has failed.

We noted in Chapter one that both structuralists and analytic philosophers had concluded that experience alone cannot determine what meanings we use.

Meanings cannot be thought of as ontologically independent of human beings, such that we first discover them and then have to name them. Linguists find it impossible to do semantics on such an assumption. Similarly, while philosophers have proposed many theoretical or actual entities as those ontologically given meanings which our words merely name—physical objects, sense data, mental images, personal representations, private experiences and so on—nonetheless each candidate fails as logically inadequate or inappropriate to its proposed role.

It is often said rather that meanings are constructed, not found but made. This is not strictly wrong but it can be seriously misleading in a number of ways. First it might seem to suggest either that the construction of meaning can typically be a deliberate exercise (as in rare and unusual circumstances it may be, like naming a new physical constant in science); or that it can be a matter for an individual or small subcultural group (as if all language could be idiosyncratic or as if a *patois* could be completely opaque to other speakers of the mother language). But we saw, in examining structuralism, that meanings are intrinsically interrelated with each other. In itself this puts constraints on the construction of new meanings. The new physical constant, for instance, needs to be comprehensible in relation to prior scientific knowledge and activity and its attendant vocabulary. Similarly, a personal idiom or subcultural jargon has no meaning even for its supposed users unless it can be somehow "cashed" in the terms of the wider language. As Wittgenstein put it, introducing new meanings to a language is perfectly possible; but it involves a lot of scene-setting and attention to background knowledge. Like the structuralists, he saw language as a complex and many-levelled network of meanings; but in his belief, the map of language is a less orderly one—less Parisian, more like London.[8]

But these linguistic constraints are in turn just as much social constraints. For the negotiation of meaning is intrinsically bound up with decisions about truth. "Attention to background knowledge" (just mentioned) is in large part attention to what we accept already as true. But any claim to knowledge is intrinsically open to question; and this means open to question by other people in dialogue. "But surely," it might be objected, "that cannot be so. There are certain fundamental truths that can never be disregarded and never sensibly put in question." A brave assumption; but if it's correct, we need to find out just which these are. For the history of philosophy is littered with abandoned candidates for foundational ideas, from the existence of God to "this patch is red." Yet how are we to sift out the genuine foundations except by engaging in a practice of critical dialogue? And since critique is intrinsically an open process, an exploration of all possibilities without prejudice, it is also intrinsically social and dialogic. No thinker can seriously assume herself immune from natural human limitations. In critique, we necessarily look to the knowledge and insights of others as well. So there is no stepping outside the politics of knowledge.

In effect, then, philosophers cannot believe in foundations because a critical politics of knowledge precludes them. "Nonsense!" one might insist, "Suppose critique reveals that some foundational claims are right?" Indeed, critical examination might well conclude that some candidate claim for foundational status were right; but we would not know it to be right because it was foundational, but only because it had survived critique. It is not that there are no constraints on meaning or knowledge, language or belief. Rather, the constraints are not foundations, ontologically prior to discourse, but the intrinsic constraints of critique itself, internal to discourse and intrinsically social.

Language is always actually or potentially enmeshed in dialogue, then. Even monologue, to the extent it is concerned with getting things right and therefore with balancing pros and cons, is an internal dialogue. But is language no longer to be thought of as transparent, but as opaque to reality? If language does not draw its meanings from some reality external to it, doesn't that mean that it can't refer to anything outside itself? And isn't such a view of language a disaster?

This is not the implication of postfoundationalism. The question of the transparency of language is a category mistake. It is not that we have no access to reality or that language cannot refer to something outside of it. The point is that our access to reality, which is genuine enough, is never unmediated by language or, therefore, by dialogue. Of course we can refer to things outside our language; but reference itself is an activity internal to language. This point is often misunderstood. There are always those who argue that since our vocabulary encodes the things we refer to, it also constrains what we can possibly refer to. This does not follow. Vocabulary is an enactment of our transactions with the world around us, which are nonetheless undetermined. After all, as we argued in Chapter one, we are not immured in a single language, even less a unique discourse.

The mediating function of reference goes deeper than this. Reference is not a two-way relationship between words and things, but a three-way relationship between speakers, things and hearers. A linguistic act of reference is a failure unless some hearer or reader understands it. The word "book," for instance, can only refer to the object in question if speaker and hearer concur in using it that way. Its use to refer cannot possibly be constituted by some asocial relationship between word and thing. Reference to reality must be socially mediated, otherwise it's futile.

Clearly, we normally talk as if reality exists independently of us, thus unmediated by us. This is no problem as far as it goes. But it does not follow that we need our language to be transparent to such a reality. Yet neither does it follow that language is opaque. We do not need, because we cannot use, an unmediated view of reality in order to talk about it. Our access to reality and its mediation in language stand or fall together. Language is not transparent; but it isn't opaque either.

So reference does not disappear from this picture and the possibility of meaningful agreement is central to it. It follows that truth does not need expunging from the picture either. Habermas has developed a consensus theory of truth which tries to explain the fundamental role of the idea of truth in a discourse without foundations. Lakatos insisted that it is only propositions that can be proven, not ontologically independent facts; but that didn't stop him talking of "proofs and refutations." Strawson pointed out that a fact is nothing other than a true statement and thus that facts were internal to language. But he had no wish to deny that there really are facts.

As Richard Rorty has seen the most clearly, to the extent that languages can be called constructed—human and social products, unconstrained by prior foundations—then appeals to the truth simply cannot tell us what kind of language we must talk: in his terms, what "final vocabulary" to use. But truth does not disappear from Rorty's view of language. It simply moves to the back seat (see Rorty's *Contingency, Irony, and Solidarity*, Pt.1) because talking about truth just doesn't help with the kinds of moral and cultural problems that concern him. That doesn't mean there is no difference in a Rortyan language between true and false statements or facts and errors.

We mentioned earlier the view that postfoundationalism is a kind of relativism; and we accepted in the previous chapter that certain forms of educational relativism are educationally dangerous. Where does this leave us? Surely the educational worry about relativism is a worry about objectivity: a worry as to whether there are any constraints on what it makes sense to say, to infer, to believe and so on. And as we can now see, postfoundationalism does not repudiate such constraints. Rather it relocates them as internal to discourse, dialogue and debate. Whether postfoundationalism is a form of relativism seems irrelevant to education. But this is not to say that postfoundationalism has no educational implications at all. With a conscious postfoundationalism comes renewed responsibility to the politics of knowledge, no longer seen as an excuse for the arbitrary, but a demanding intertwining of the normative and epistemic realms. The task is to sustain a progressive politics of knowledge: "progressive" in Lakatos' sense of furthering the pursuit of knowledge rather than driving it down a blind alley—cultivating a healthy discourse. Later chapters expand on different aspects of this politics in relation to education.

Now let's look back at Richard Rorty's idea of morality without foundations. Is it really so scandalous, so foreign to our apparent need for moral universals?

It may seem frivolous to suppose that we can solve moral difficulties just by redescribing people, or problems, or situations. But is not appropriate description at least necessary? What would our relationship to moral universals be like if we couldn't redescribe in such a way? We readily accept, in Kantian spirit, an imperative to treat others as equals, but wonder who qualify as "others." Babies suffering gross mental impairment, capable of nothing but suffering? Our cat? Our home computer? Or we complain that if the cat is a morally relevant other, then clearly not all moral others can possibly be our equals. We still need answers to Rorty's hypothetical objections—"They do not feel it as *we* would," or, "there must always be suffering, so why not let *them* suffer?" Without answers, we can only experience the imperative entailed by a universal principle as a kind of authoritarian *Diktat*—"Never mind why, just do it!"—which is no appropriate way to relate to morality at all. (Thus Kant's idea of the Categorical Imperative encumbered him with problems about the Good Will.) It's not enough just to be told that others are relevantly equal: we need to be able to *see how* they are like us.

But relativists suppose that redescription is impossible in any significant sense; that we are trapped inside a given language. Foundationalists, on the other hand, suppose that redescription is either superficial (just changing the words) or irresponsible (ignoring the underlying realities). Both put in question a kind of activity, redescription, which is arguably morally vital. But as we have just seen, the concept of truth does not disappear with the concept of foundations. And as we saw in Chapter one, it is just not credible to think of ourselves as immured in one language, much less corralled within one discourse. One *can* redescribe without disregard for the truth.

But if there are no foundations, what keeps us honest, on the straight and narrow? Our languages are necessarily shared languages. So we are constrained by the talk of other people, whether or not they agree with us. In particular, we are constrained by the need to share references. So not all failures to agree are just disagreements of fact or opinion. Some indicate more deeply that we cannot share some particular usage, vocabulary or repertoire of meanings with others. That renders them useless to think with.

And this is not a predicament we can choose or opt out of. We are not prior-formed subjects of knowledge who then opt into the constraints of speech, discussion, agreement or disagreement with others. On the contrary, unless and until we are bound into this tight skein of linguistic bonds, which extend vertically through history and tradition no less than horizontally through affinity and society, then we cannot think propositionally at all, far less think morally.

Thus, what we can think is bounded by the possibilities of shared language, but not by the possibilities of one particular language. So it is similarly bounded by the possibilities of human relationships, but not by the parochial possibilities of our own particular society. What does constrain the possibilities of social relationships, and thus of language, is the physical form of our embodiment. It seems to be this alone—this shared lifeworld of eating, sleeping, sex, death—that accounts for the primordial and extensive agreement in judgments which makes shared language possible for us and ultimately constrains what we can say. We can extend thought and language in some directions, but not in any direction at all—only those we can make sense of with other human beings. That makes for a difference between sense and nonsense, and *a fortiori* between true and false. For instance, as Wittgenstein saw, we cannot extend the use of language to talk about the phenomena of our own subjective consciousness without reference to any objective world. There cannot be a logically private language.

So who or what can we describe as relevantly "like us?" Most of us nowadays can describe at least the higher animals as sufficiently like us to make sense of animal rights (whether we approve the idea or not). But that is because we find we can agree that certain claims about animals are true: that they act consciously, relate to each other and to us socially, behave in non-mechanical ways and so on. At the time of this writing, the possibility of a conscious computer is being taken seriously. But will we ever be able to make sense of an idea of computers' rights? Does *any* kind of speech have the resources to find adequate similarities between ourselves and a plastic box on the desktop? We cannot know *a priori*, however unlikely the possibility seems. There is no pre-given foundation of moral status that just is or isn't linguistically applicable to computers; so no appeals to foundations will settle the question. But nor do we have to assume that anything is possible. We can only wait and see what our language lets us do. But that is all we need to do.

NOTES

1. Modern scholarship suggests that Plato may have mislead us on the role of the sophists, who might be seen in a more positive light as liberal moralists.

2. "He," of course, is a construction of Plato's, even where the Dialogues intend to be most faithful to the views of the historical figure. But we may infer with some confidence that such concerns and such habits in discussion were characteristic of the actual man.

3. For an introduction to trends in contemporary dialogic rationalism, see Myerson (1994).

4. Of course, the genre is still occasionally revived in later philosophy. Bishop Berkeley and Iris Murdoch have both used the form.

5. We believe the phrase is actually Foucault's.

6. See the three great Kantian Critiques: of Pure Reason, of Practical Reason and of Judgment.

7. If this is so often misunderstood, the misunderstanding probably stems from a misreading of Adorno and Horkheimer's thesis on the role of instrumental reason in the self-subversion of Enlightenment. It was never their position to *equate* modern culture with instrumentalism—Adorno, after all, is the preeminent modernist aesthetician—but to reveal the internal problems of instrumentalism as a salient aspect of modern culture and their potential to subvert the whole edifice. Habermas ties this subversive process yet more tightly than Adorno and Horkheimer do to the invidious role of capitalism in modern society, and sees this self-subversion not as the inevitable destiny of modernity but rather a false turn from which we may—just—turn back. A modern politics of knowledge in all fields remains, he argues, a critical inheritance to be cherished and improved.

8. Lyotard gets it quite wrong in *The Postmodern Condition* when he appeals to Wittgenstein as the source for the idea of language games as establishing "islands of meaning." That is exactly what Wittgenstein was trying to escape from. The "atomic propositions" of Wittgenstein's *Tractatus Logico-Philosophicus* are the ultimate islands of meaning; but they are logically impossible, as Wittgenstein came to see.

Chapter 3

The Ascription of Identity

By a name
I know not how to tell thee who I am:
My name, dear saint, is hateful to myself
Because it is an enemy to thee.
Had I it written I would tear the word.
—*Romeo and Juliet*, 2.2.53-57

Suppose that children are classified as follows: (a) mother tongue not English, (b) IQs above 120, (c) live in rented accommodation, (d) of color, (e) from single-parent families, (f) good at games, (g) included in this list, (h) weighing more than 65 lbs, (i) running in the corridor. We do not get far with this list before we are disturbed. The classification seems arbitrary. How, we wonder, can some of the terms be relevant? But who are we? Perhaps this is not the kind of school that we are familiar with. We think again. Should we take stock of our ethnocentric presumptions? Suspend our accustomed judgments? We are left with a puzzle. Where could such a classification apply?

Everywhere, perhaps inevitably, formal education registers identity through systems of difference. Teachers concern themselves with differences in nature and ability, and commonly with differences in learners' circumstances. They identify achievements and they identify needs.

This may seem a labelling of natural characteristics. Being a C-stream (slower learning) pupil or being naughty, like having blue eyes, is a natural endowment. The child has an essence and language can record this. Separation of language from the differences it registers keeps intact a veil of naturalness. Being C-stream can have little meaning, however, unless there are other streams. Thus, as we have seen, characteristics must be seen as not purely natural but dependent on the relationship of terms in a system of classification. Recognizing this is a step toward structuralism. Differences are then read off, as it were, from a vertical axis of possible characteristics, while the horizontal axis registers change. Through progress the learner acquires new characteristics, conceived perhaps as value added or distance travelled. It is nevertheless against the vertical dimension that the new characteristics are registered: learning is a "detour between two presences."[1]

Registration of difference tends toward standardization and normalization in a kind of reduction: learners are reduced to descriptions. Teachers are warned of the give-a-dog-a-bad-name problem, yet in systems of education where classification is dominant, how can such branding be avoided? With the logistics of large scale education systems, ascription becomes virtual inscription on the body of the pupils with stipulated codes of dress and behavior, seating arrangements and orders of procession. Beyond the rationale for such arrangements, these behavioral features become signs. Weighted with significance, they provide, ironically, the vocabulary for the rebellious teenager's defiant behavior: C-stream status carries kudos with delinquents.

Sometimes our confidence in classification can be unsettled. Confronted by claims of different cultural groups we feel a characteristic unease. Confronted by claims of different subjects within the curriculum, we search in vain for some over-arching framework and standard criteria. But the framework comes to seem partial if not partisan; recognition of difference seems incapacitating and bewildering. Ways of dealing with difference are to overrule, subjugate or simply deny it, strategies adopted with varying degrees of self-deceit. When we see clearly, what is different presents us with a question, requiring responsive sensitivity, charging us with responsibility.

The architectonic tendency, based on assumptions of stable structures, characterizes the modernist *episteme*. Consider dominant paradigms in modern philosophy of education. The restatement of the idea of a liberal education undertaken by R. S. Peters and his collaborators in the United Kingdom and by Israel Scheffler in the United States is characterized by a faith in clear and distinct ideas and in a universal human nature, with respective backgrounds in Descartes and Kant. High points in the British tradition are Peters' conception of the educated man, R. F. Dearden's ideal of rational autonomy and perhaps above all, the Forms of Knowledge thesis of P. H. Hirst.

The restatement of liberal education was in part a reaction to the development of progressivism and its promulgation in expanding teacher education colleges in the 1960s. Probably the most influential and important figure behind the progressivism of that time was John Dewey. On an initial reading, Dewey's work may be thought itself to institute a rival overarching theory—not of a universal rationality but of a natural self unfolding through growth. This common interpretation of Dewey, run together rather uncritically with the work of Friedrich Fröbel, is exposed in its inadequacies by Dewey's specific rejection of the idea of the child as unfolding. The crucial factor, a theme that will recur in this chapter, is the way that growth is to be understood. Against the idea of an immanent whole in Fröbel's thinking and the restrictive conception of growth to which it leads, Dewey writes: "Since growth is just a movement toward a completed being, the final ideal is immobile. An abstract and indefinite future is in control with all that that connotes in depreciation of present power and opportunity" (Dewey, 1966, p. 57). Following Richard Rorty's revival of interest in Dewey's work, Wilfred Carr suggests that:

In true Deweyan fashion, *Democracy and Education* can now be "reconstructed" as a postmodern text that speaks to and for the Enlightenment vision of emancipatory education in a way which anticipates the emergence of many postmodern ideas: the open-ended formation of the human subject; the contingency of democratic norms and values; the futility of utopian ideas about a ready-made fixed self; the realisation that there is no corpus of "objective" knowledge that stands outside the historical context which endows it with meaning and significance. (Carr, 1995, p. 89)

Dewey's language sometimes emphasizes a movement toward increased control or mastery, sometimes an appreciation of the fluid nature of the social world. The split between the idea of an unfolding immanent human nature and the idea of growth that Dewey champions is of key importance in what follows.

It is important for the way we see ourselves. "I don't speak in seminars because I'm shy." Is this an honest recognition of one's true nature? Or is it bad faith, the comfortable acceptance of a supposedly fixed characteristic insulating us from responsibility? How we see ourselves extends into how we see our activities and projects. In the fashionable concern with ownership in education, however, there is only the palest reflection, if not distortion, of this. Ideas of belonging and responsibility become confused with property ownership and consumerism. What is then owned is externalized as an objective thing, standing over against the subject.

Vertical systems of difference through which ascription functions give the illusion of successive presences, where mastery arrests play and the very conditions of responsibility. What is concealed when temporality is masked in this way? Think of yourself at the present moment, and the way you might be described. You will perhaps think of your name, nationality, appearance, age, job, domestic situation and so forth. Descriptions that typically come to mind suppress certain very general existential structures, structures only seen with a complete change of perspective. Is it melodramatic to ask: How is our mortality to be understood? We must ask how far the ordinary circumstances of our lives make sense at all without this horizon of finitude. "Meet me at Blackwell's at 3:30" loses urgency but also meaning itself if time is available without limit. With no ultimate limit, time as lived ceases to be. This opens up the necessary temporality of our being and indicates the taken-for-granted structure of finitude within which those ascriptions of identity make sense. We are always within structures of *in-order-to*, necessarily futural: while you are reading this, any moment of your reading has its momentum toward what follows after, even as it reaches back to what has gone before. The present involves past and future. Isolate the present and it vanishes.

In 1957, some thirty years after the publication of *Being and Time*, Heidegger spoke of "the active nature of identity between man and Being" (Heidegger, 1974, p. 41). There is a reciprocity between man and Being that can be characterized as an "event of appropriation" (p. 36). This appropriation reaches into the very concept of world, for what the world is is not independent of man's thinking. We live in a world of rocks and trees, towns, telephones, love affairs, law suits. But the natural world is something we can only conceive from *within* the perspective of this elaborated complex human world. Consider the fate of the natural in the following scene.

A class of adults is reading *Full Moon and Little Frieda* by Ted Hughes. The poem describes the writer's infant daughter standing outside their house and suddenly noticing the moon, huge and very low. She cries out "Moon! Moon!" and the moon has "stepped back like an artist gazing amazed at a work/That points at him amazed" (Hughes, 1982, p. 113). Why does the child utter these words? To communicate or command attention? But surely the child would say the same if no one was listening. How is the moon connected with romance or mystery? What *is* the moon? For one student, at least, the answer to this last is obvious: the moon is a mass of rock. He is suspicious of the fact that his teacher could think anything different. Of course, the student is not wrong about the moon but he is in the grip of a certain metaphysical picture, which allows no space for mystery or the ineffable or perhaps for a child's (and an adult's) wonder. The moon is a mass of rock. All else is fantasy. And this stark contrast of the language of "objectivity" and fantasy leaves nothing in between. Yet it leaves scarcely credible the scientific impulse to find out about the moon.

Positivist anxiety lingers in the wings unless we can achieve a more subtle understanding. This will involve unsettling certain assumptions about the integrity of the human subject and the way this stands over against a world of objects. The active nature of identity of which Heidegger speaks involves reciprocity and mutual appropriation: "The event of appropriation is that realm, vibrating within itself, through which man and Being reach each other in their nature, achieve their active nature by losing those qualities with which metaphysics has endowed them" (1974, p. 37). Heidegger leans on the opening phrase, "the event of appropriation," a key term, impervious to paraphrase as the Greek *logos* or the Chinese *Tao*. What can be made of this talk of vibration and the achieving of active nature? Tacit and emergent, this opposes the stability apparently endowed by the prevailing metaphysics. This appropriation comes to shape ideas of identity and of difference. There is the endless possibility of things, possibility that is arrested where the prevailing technology with its calculative thinking holds sway. Covering over difference with its "objectivity," the modern world is trapped in a particular frame; what is needed is a releasement toward things, a *Gelassenheit*, in which difference emerges.[2] This releasement would be less self-conscious reverie than absorption in practice: the world might then be understood as coming to be in a holistic articulation with our coping behavior.

How does the moon come to be *qua* moon? How does the child come to be without the moon? The student's "objective" response covers over the strange potency of the child's naming of the moon, which both identifies the moon and places her in relation to it, a creative reciprocity figured in the mutual staring of child and artist-moon (poem and poet). Metaphor here suggests the metaphysics. If the world emerges in the light of human response, so too human beings come into their nature through their world's becoming. There is no human being prior to this, nor any world—only some materiality that we conceive by abstraction from that world. Appropriation is dynamic: what man and Being are is never finally determined. It is not just that any description will necessarily be incomplete but that description in terms of characteristics sets the account off in the wrong direction. It is more than a matter of misunderstanding: under the influence of the prevailing metaphysics appropriation's active nature is itself suppressed.

Progressivism picked up the Deweyan idea of man's active nature and, in the popular interpretation, gave this a particular (behavioral) hue. It is clear in Heidegger, however, but also true for Dewey, that active nature is misconceived if construed in terms of consciously planned activity, a calculative and structured thinking as opposed to something more fluid—a tacit and responsive adjustment to one's circumstances and emergent projects. More contentiously, situational concern in Heidegger's account of authenticity develops from the recognition of the circumstances one *finds oneself* in to an alignment with one's cultural heritage (1962, 2:5). Yet this is no conventional conservatism. As Heidegger later puts it, "Tradition prevails when it frees us from a thinking back to a thinking forward, which is no longer a planning" (1974, p. 41). Tradition is live and fluid; only on its strength can our future be authentic. Pervasive foundationalism suppresses this active nature frustrating our efforts to see what is problematic; a certain accustomed philosophical approach further entangles us. It is not just that the Archimedean standpoint or foundationalism are to be rejected: we need to question the idea that there must be a center to our thinking, the stabilizing element in the structure. And this must take us beyond Heidegger.

Derrida sees Heidegger as offering a picture that by being defined in opposition to the prevailing metaphysics is ultimately bound to it. How does Derrida lead us beyond this centered thinking? He writes:

Structure—or rather the structurality of structure—although it has always been at work, has always been neutralised or reduced, and this by a process of giving it a center or of referring it to a point of presence, a fixed origin. The function of this center was not only to orient, balance, and organize the structure—one cannot in fact conceive of an unorganized structure—but above all to make sure that the organizing principle of the structure would limit what we might call the *play* of the structure. By orienting and organizing the coherence of the system, the center of a structure permits the play of its elements inside the total form. And even today the notion of a structure lacking any center represents the unthinkable itself. (1978, pp. 278-279)

What can be said of the play of language to take us beyond points of presence and fixed origin? Any idea or principle or strategy or word that Derrida now adopts may take on the role of master-concept and take root in that way of thinking that is the problem—a danger inherent also in writing about Derrida that erects the language into a "position." How can we proceed?

Take a pair of terms, identify the dominant one, then take the side of the minor term and see it infiltrate the dominant, dismantling the hierarchy. At least, making it tremble. The minor element works its way through the whole. Most poignant and productive perhaps is Derrida's deconstruction of speech and writing.

Throughout Western philosophy writing has normally been understood to be subordinate to speech, in a hierarchy that extends upwards to thought, with its ideal in logic. Thoughts are transmitted through spoken words, and these signs can in turn be converted into written words. Thoughts exist independently of, in a sense prior to, their expression in words, and speech exists independently of writing. No writing without a background of speech, no speech without a background of thought. Logic is the secure point that holds the structure in place. Thought is progressively contaminated by mediation (and this typifies the metaphysics of presence). Socrates does not write. As Plato puts it in *The Seventh Letter*, "any serious student of serious realities will shrink from making truth the helpless object of men's ill-will by committing it to writing" (1973, p. 140). No responsible parent will ever commit his thoughts to writing, he says, no thinker in earnest will "sow his seed in the black fluid called ink" (p. 98). Speech is the legitimate son; writing the bastard. As unprotected orphan, writing may fall into the wrong hands. The threat to security encroaches on the very source of that security, the immediate self-presence of thoughts in your head. There is this faith in the immediacy, the presence, of the voice. Your silent voice, your voice in the head, seems to epitomize your being.

These indeed are essential characteristics of writing. But Derrida shows how the crucial aspects of these characteristics apply also to speech, that is, to language as a whole. A word is quite unlike a thing in that it can be repeated endlessly, unlike a thing in that no act could destroy it. Romeo cannot "tear" his name. There cannot in principle be a single occurrence of a word because built into its structure as a word is the possibility of its repeatability, with all its possibilities of misunderstanding. Words can always be taken out of context, they can be cited, they can occur in plays. Overheard conversations, inadvertent puns, unhappy uses—there are multiple ways speech can go astray. Nor is this ruled out by the apparent immediacy of direct speech. There is no language for which this is not possible; the possibility of this breaching is necessarily there. Words come to us with histories, beyond anything we can know. The printed word is like the footprint, a trace of what has gone before. So also our speech uses signs that can never be our own, under our own control, entirely. Our words leave us to be appropriated in contexts we can never fully foresee, interpreted in ways we can never fully control. A phrase is quoted, dislocated, out of its home. But there is no ideal home free from this breaching. Words say more than we can mean, and mean more than we can say; call these breaches and snags dissemination. And what could a totally secure language possibly be like? Disturbing this ancient hierarchy unsettles common sense. The security of speech was an illusion about our thinking and being, the innocence of speech always already corrupted. What repressions must hide in the voice of philosophy ridding itself of the play of writing?

Marking a difference in writing that is lost in speech, Derrida coins the term "differance" (*différance*). Not a word, not a concept, differance gives classification the slip. To unsettle the master-concepts governing so much of our thought differance must not itself become a master-concept: it is to be thought under erasure. Differance differs from its familiar homophone only in the graphical mark: it is a difference in writing. Spoken, it carries an ambiguity which writing resolves: we are made to pause, attention brought back from habitual usage to the operation of the language.

Differance works against any idea of simple matching of name to object. As our discussion of Saussure in Chapter 1 demonstrates, meaning is differential: the word comes to be according to systems of difference. But a second emphasis takes us away from Saussure, where the structure of language from which language usage draws is in a limited sense static. The distinction between *langue* and *parole* leads one to think in terms of a vertical axis of stability and a horizontal axis of change. But structural elements in language are always in play. There is a power within these differences such that their full meaning is forever deferred. It is precisely this sense of deferral that Derrida, exploiting the sense of *différer* as both "differ" and "defer," brings into play: differance implies the differences that are incorporated into the language we use but without their crystallization in stable structural relations; meaning is not static and never fulfilled.

Contemporary consumption with its brandnames and logos manifests this deferral of meaning. It is evident in works of art. A celebrated art image such as the *Mona Lisa* may feature on a poster or paper bag advertising the Louvre. Moustachioed after Duchamp, in multiple frames after Warhol, on television the image may turn and wink. The picture's meaning extends, as does the part it plays in the culture. Che Guevara's writings become sweatshirt slogans, *Nessun Dorma* the 1990 World Cup music. Beyond these most dramatic of examples, this deferral applies generally to works of art. The work has a stable meaning, it is assumed—the author's intention, something internal to the text; the critic sets about uncovering this meaning. A history of a work of art, however, shows something rather different at work. Charles Dickens' novel *A Tale of Two Cities*, which deals with the French revolution, is now read at a time when the word "revolution" has been shaped by a century of revolutions. The history of England and France over the past two hundred years affects the ways in which London and Paris are thought of, even when reference is to their past. Moreover, the text has acquired accretions of meaning through its various interpretations and transformations on stage and screen. The work never has an entirely stable meaning. But rather than this being a cause for regret, indefiniteness is essential to a work of art's life. Indeed, this play is essential to the very functioning of signs. Never saturated with meaning, a sign (word or work of art) is open to dislocation, interpretation, appropriation, repetition. Meaning is never punctually present.

Yet the title of a work, *A Tale of Two Cities* or *Romeo and Juliet* for example, functions in a twofold way: on the one hand, cryptically and suggestively, requiring the supplement of imagination and response; on the other, its short self-containment seeming to encapsulate, defining the horizon, arresting the work in a unified whole. Like the aphorism, it offers rich openness to interpretation and reappropriation even as it separates itself off with the semblance of closure. So also with other names, and proper names especially. This is iterability writ large and the space for an equivocation between divergent understandings of ourselves. Romeo's alienation from his own name exposes the gulf between the naturalism of understanding people in terms of personal attribute and lineage and the existential awareness of lived experience. "Romeo" encapsulates Romeo's identity. It is a name *par excellence*, a part of our iconography. Like any name it will survive its bearer. It is Romeo's tragedy that he cannot tear his name, cannot separate himself from the grids of meaning that locate him in a relationship that is doomed:

Dates, timetables, property registers, place-names, all the codes that we cast like nets over time and space—in order to reduce or master differences, to arrest them, determine them ... to be in harmony with our rhythms by bending them to objective measurement, they produce misunderstanding, they accumulate the opportunities for false steps or wrong moves. (Derrida, 1992b, p. 419)

The possibility of tragedy, a condition for being human, depends precisely on being out of step but necessarily implicated in this inhuman operation of names, and this no naturalism can fathom: "A proper name does not name anything which is human, which belongs to a human body, a human spirit, an essence of man. And yet this relation to the inhuman only befalls man, for him, to him, in the name of man. He alone gives himself this inhuman name" (Derrida, 1992b, p. 427). A proper name points to the bearer of a string of characteristics and a place in a chronology without remainder. Yet this is an impossible containment of words, of texts, of human beings in which false steps and wrong moves, breaches and snags, must appear. When names are conferred on attributes and activities, the securing of identity that they effect is less reliable than it seems. Recall the branding of the C-stream. Company logos confer corporate style while brandnames offer a kind of purchasing of personal identity. New jargon phrases in educational practice redefine activities and agents re-presenting them in new structural formations. Fetishizing of signs coincides with new anxiety about presentation. Is this not an obsession with presence? Mass communication's aphorism is the sound-bite, fulfilling "the promise of a now in common . . . the desired sharing of a living present" (p. 421).

We can know nothing. Nothing can be relied on. All values are empty, and exposed as such by deconstruction. It is all just a matter of words. Getting Derrida *wrong* in this way may be a symptom not only of a different philosophical sensibility but itself of a kind of nihilism. Far from any crude reductivism or debunking of values, Derrida's work brings together an acknowledgment of the influence of the past with a sense of responsibility to the future. Ethical choices come to be seen not as matters of deliberation based on stable and calculable values but as themselves creative and interpretative. In *Specters of Marx* (1994), the trace structure of language reverberates through the way that the past and the texts of the past impress their marks on us, are with us in a way that is beyond the natural, and leave us in their debt. Untimely texts of Marx destabilize the present and reveal responsibility *to come*: foundations tremble as the voice of

Hamlet's father's ghost comes to us out of time from under the stage (dull promontory) on which we stand. Contrast Nietzsche's Last Man, the bourgeois: his reckoning of values loses sight of the higher and reduces things to relativity to his needs. Not so long ago educationalists and teachers worried about judgments that were value-laden and practices "shot-through with values." It would be encouraging if the more recent preoccupation with values education fully departed from this. But values are seen too often as bolt-on elements in a person's life and education; ethical "auditing" holds the mirror up to practice with the tendency tidily to reckon up. Dominated by the stability of ideas and the fixed scale in evaluation, these practices harbor a naturalism that surreptitiously excludes what is higher. Responsibility is then reduced by etiolated understandings of citizenship and family values; different versions of that anodyne conception of value that, with its subjectivism and bland consensus, hides an ultimate nihilism.

Differance, dissemination and the logic of the trace show that meaning is in excess, and this disarms nihilism. They point toward a decentered thinking. How can this cast light on our identity?

Dissemination, Derrida has said, is loss of the father. What might dissemination say about the growth of the child? From the child's acquisition of language to the adult's continuing education, entry is into a thinking that is never totalizable. The logic of the sign puts thought always in part beyond reach, always still in play. Resistance to this involves an attempt to arrest play and bring thought (and one's "self") under control. Looking for a center, if not an origin, a trunk from which branches can spread, it promotes structure and planning in education, with all their reinforcements of performativity. It totalizes its conception of the learner in sets of needs or outcomes, or composite pictures of the educated man. It thereby forgets—probably never knows—the necessarily secret aspect of the sign and its availability to unforeseen uses, a secrecy that as a matter of principle could never be fully disclosed. It is blind to the bearing this has on the learner, and to its bearing on what is learned.

This play of thought challenges purely linear thinking—thinking that grows like a tree, develops from a center—in ways that are realizable in the curriculum. Juxtaposition of a canon of great books with contrasting texts, one paradigm with another, initiates into tradition even as it puts this in crisis, activating the critical potential of discipline. The canon is not rejected but given pedagogical and cultural vibrancy. This growth is different from those predictable controlled teleologies that Dewey resisted.

The more insistent decentering in the work of Gilles Deleuze and Félix Guattari, at odds with this conflictual vibration between paradigms, affirms a smooth space and smooth time. The tree/root metaphor is attacked explicitly. The primary security provided by the grounding of the roots connects with a linear and vertical pattern, epitomizing progress and authority. The root structure constitutes the archetypal pattern of our genealogy. Upright and erect, the securely grounded tree suggests a standard for others—Europeanism with man as the gold standard. Standard metaphors, the metaphoricity barely shows.

But displace this metaphor with another type of growth. Contrast the root and the tree with the rhizome. Potatoes are rhizomes and so is couch-grass. Humbler parts of nature in contrast to proud trees, rhizomes shoot under the ground in a cloning and lateral spreading. They might form a staple diet; they are survivors, like their counterparts in the animal world, the ant colony and rats; even the burrow with its extensive tunnelling and multiple entry-ways is rhizomatic. The acentric form suggests not building but dispersal and extension:

It is odd how the tree has dominated Western reality and all of Western thought, from botany to biology and anatomy, but also gnosiology, theology, ontology, all of philosophy . . . the root-foundation, *Grund, racine, fondement*. The West has a special relation to the forest, and deforestation; the fields carved from the forest are populated with seed plants produced by cultivation based on species lineages of the arborescent type; animal raising, carried out on fallow fields, selects lineages forming an entire animal arborescence. The East presents a different figure: a relation to the steppe and the garden (or in some cases, the desert and the oasis), rather than forest and field; cultivation of tubers by fragmentation of the individual; a casting aside or bracketing of animal raising, which is confined to closed spaces or pushed out onto the steppes of the nomads. The West: agriculture based on a chosen lineage containing a large number of variable individuals. The East: horticulture based on a small number of individuals derived from a wide range of "clones." (Deleuze & Guattari, 1992, p. 18)

Transcendence in the West, spiritual immanence of the East. Indeed, transcendence is referred to as a "specifically European disease" (p. 18). Its East reaches back to a European ancestry; but the West becomes paradoxically its own Orient, "its rhizomatic West, with its Indians without ancestry, its ever-receding limit, its shifting and displaced frontiers" (p. 19). Its book is different: *Leaves of Grass*.

If the tree is located, the rhizome is nomadic. The nomad moves from point to point along accustomed pathways, the points subordinated to the paths they determine. The *nomos* originally was a distribution in an open space, not a parcelling out and allocation of that space. The *nomos*, in this earlier sense, "stands in opposition to the law or the *polis*, as the backcountry, a mountainside, or the vague expanse around a city" (p. 380). The nomad exists in a smooth space in contrast to the striated space of the city with its walls and enclosures. Nomad thinking disturbs identity, enabling a different access to thinking itself, to teaching and learning. That stasis of stable identities, successions of presences, gives way to a flow, as of a river that you cannot step into twice.

Heidegger's authenticity comes back to a nostalgia for the center—for the home, the culture, even the German language itself. Nostalgia is a homesickness, a need for roots. Honoring and drawing strength from those roots, authenticity becomes possible but not without the pain of loss. Other conceptions of authenticity, if they avoid the kind of grounding that these roots imply, do not dispense with a certain conception of the real—correspondence with a true self or the centering of authorship. In a kind of overthrow of ontology, rhizomatic thinking effects an affirmation that "sweeps one *and* the other away, a stream without beginning or end that undermines its banks and picks up speed in the middle" (p. 25).

This chapter begins with a list, and lists, Iris Murdoch remarks, are instruments of power. Remove the coherence of items in a series and the power of the letter sequence with its interstitial blanks haunt our awareness. Foucault recalls his uneasy laughter at the celebrated passage in Borges that

quotes a "certain Chinese encyclopaedia" in which it is written that "animals are divided into: (a) belonging to the Emperor, (b) embalmed, (c) tame, (d) sucking pigs, (e) sirens, (f) fabulous, (g) stray dogs, (h) included in the present classification, (i) frenzied, (j) innumerable, (k) drawn with a very fine camelhair brush, (l) *et cetera*, (m) having just broken the water pitcher, (n) that from a long way off look like flies." In the wonderment of this taxonomy, the thing we apprehend in one great leap, the thing that, by means of the fable, is demonstrated as the exotic charm of another system of thought, is the limitation of our own, the stark impossibility of thinking *that*. (Foucault, 1974, p. xv)

There is no common place within which to situate these categories, nor those at the start of this chapter. The lists disturb, "breaking up all the ordered surfaces and planes with which we are accustomed to tame the wild profusion of existing things, and continuing long afterwards to disturb and threaten with collapse our age-old distinction between the Same and the Other." The different categorizations within which the categories would make sense are jumbled in heterotopias that "dessicate speech, stop words in their tracks, contest the very possibility of grammar at its source; they dissolve our myths and sterilize the lyricism of our sentences" (p. xviii).

What education could ever apply our classification? Amused discomfiture resonates with a more familiar bewilderment at education's burgeoning performativity, its names and classifications. Dates, timetables, registers and returns, codes to master difference, nets over space and time. Disparate categorizations: too much information, information that does not fit. Times out of joint. Out of time.

NOTES

1. Derrida speaks of a certain conception of history in these terms (Derrida, 1978, p. 291).

2. Heidegger elaborates the significance of *Gelassenheit*, especially as a response to technology, in *Discourse on Thinking* (1966).

Chapter 4

Literacy Under the Microscope

Literacy is important: far too important to be left to chance. All around the developed world governments recognize the importance of raising children's reading standards, and determine also to address the problem of the substantial numbers of adults that are functionally illiterate. The search for new programs and methods to arrest the decline is widespread. In the United Kingdom the new Labour administration promises to focus closely on "the basics" and to eliminate illiteracy altogether early in the new millennium.

Governments, in making literacy their concern, naturally must make it clear what is to count as literacy, and for whom. We cannot achieve what we have not defined. Hence the National Curriculum for England and Wales carefully stipulates what is to be expected of pupils at various stages of their education. Here are two of the English Reading Level Descriptions from the Department for Education (1995, p. 19):

Level 2

Pupils' reading of simple texts shows understanding and is generally accurate. . . . They use more than one strategy, such as phonic, graphic, syntactic and contextual, in reading unfamiliar words and establishing meaning.

Level 3

Pupils read a range of texts fluently and accurately. They read independently, using strategies appropriately to establish meaning. . . . They use their knowledge of the alphabet to locate books and find information.

Accuracy and fluency: who in their right mind can be against these? And clearly the reader must establish the meaning of what she reads. Otherwise she would have to go back and try again. Once she has established the meaning she can move on—to the next sentence or to the next book, or maybe to some other activity altogether, such as honing her mathematical skills via a computer program. All of this is simply common sense. And it is only common sense too to put a system of testing in place so that we may know exactly what children have and have not achieved, in literacy as in other areas of the curriculum. Inspectors bring finely-tuned instruments into schools to discover where the teachers are failing the children; in what has been called the greatest exercise in public information in the United Kingdom for fifty years, detailed league-tables are constructed in which every school has its precise place. The effort and expense is justifiable in terms of the need to account for the use of public money. Microscopic examination of all aspects of education ensures there is no hiding-place for failure or irregularity.

In response, out in the schools every effort is made to ensure children learn to read. In all sorts of ways the kindergarten and infant classroom show how meaning is established, nailing words firmly to the world. The window shows tadpole heads on matchstick bodies, each with the name of a pupil. Inside the same names appear on stacked trays. The blackboard is helpfully labelled "blackboard," similarly the computer and other equipment. The word, as the children should be able to see clearly enough, is the name of the thing it is attached to. You can even peel it off and talk about the word itself: does 'book' have at its heart two eyes reading it? Does 'tall,' with its three high letters, make you think of three giraffes? This is daring, in our utilitarian times, and can only be attempted when and because fundamentally meaning is established, secure and certain.

What of the books themselves? The reading book which the children are using, and which the teacher is careful to hear them read, shows Peter and Jane looking at a police car. The text declares: "In the street they see some of the police. Two of them go by in a Police car. Peter and Jane can read POLICE on the car." Lest there should be any doubt about the solidity of this transaction, about the reliability with which meaning is established, one of the policemen has smilingly caught their eye—caught them looking at the police—and, by the skill of the illustrator, he catches our eye too. They see the police, and we see them see the police. Not only are they seen to see the police, but they are seen by us to be seen to. Teacher will see if the children in class are reading successfully, and presently someone will come to see if she is competent in doing so. All is transparent: light passes uninterruptedly through teacher, reader and the children in the book. Situated as it were at the heart of the panopticon, whoever monitors all this can see all the way through to the police who, as is only proper for the guardians of order, guarantee stability, meaning and understanding. Lest the police should seem a merely contingent, earth-bound source of security, the most sovereign source of light and enlightenment shines over all: the book, 5b in the Ladybird Key Words Reading Scheme, is entitled *Out in the Sun*.

How *naturally* language seems to be used in this text! Children who learn to read (learn to read accurately and effectively) in this classroom are well prepared for what Margaret Meek calls "the 'topic' book, the 'story of the post office', the dinosaurs, the Normans" (1992, p. 180). These are real things, real creatures and places: Peter and Jane, for all their reassuring police sponsorship, still have about them the disturbing aura of fiction. In return for the benefit of reading about reality perhaps there is some cost to be paid in "the consequent drying up of the imagination in those whose reading becomes limited to books designed for learning to read followed by those which promote a particular kind of reading to learn" (p. 180). Perhaps if children are reading to learn they are hurrying to leave reading in favor of some other business altogether: in order to become members of the Learning Society for example, accumulating useful skills and having them accredited. But this is to anticipate.

In another classroom, somewhere, another teacher is reading John Burningham's *Come Away From the Water, Shirley* (1977) to a group of small children. She shows them the pictures as she reads. Shirley and her parents are on a trip to the seaside. On the left-hand pages deck chairs are set up, sandwiches eaten. Shirley is told to keep away from a stray dog. On the opposite pages something different is happening. Shirley and the dog set out in a small boat. They are captured by pirates. Shirley is forced to walk the plank, but the dog intervenes with a judicious bite at the pirate captain's leg and after a battle the two of them escape. "Your father might have a game with you when he's had a little rest," declares the left-hand page, over a picture of father snoring beneath a newspaper. On the opposite page Shirley and the dog dig up a treasure chest which they have found by using a map they took from the pirates. Teacher reads the text with very little comment. Sometimes she draws attention to some detail of the pictures, such as the difficulty mother seems to be having putting up her deck chair, or the jolly roger flying from the mast of the pirate ship. She does not ask: "Do you think this is really happening, or is Shirley imagining it all?" The children do not seem to have any problem with the book. If you could stand, invisible, behind the teacher, you would see what you might be tempted to describe as pleasure and recognition in their eyes as they look across each pair of pages. But are they learning to read?

We might talk as if a cultural and educational divide begins here: between those who will grow up to relish the constructedness of texts and their multilayered ironies, and those who will read the label on the box in order to match it with the shelf on which it is to be stacked; between those whose imaginations will be allowed to flourish and those who, at best, will read simply to learn. That way of putting it does at least remind us that issues of status and power arise starkly in different conceptions of literacy. Other matters too, which take us back to issues of power by a longer route, need to be considered here. It is questionable whether literacy is best conceived centrally in terms of "accuracy" and a solidity of meaning that is to be "established." Jacques Derrida and some of those who have followed his ideas help us to see that language cannot be supposed to operate as naturally or innocently as it may seem to in the case of the children in *Out in the Sun* and similar "readers," or in the well-labelled classroom. All postmodern philosophers, it has been said, "repudiate the dream of an innocent language" (Wellbery, quoted in Peters, 1996, p. 9): a language so free from opacity, or from complicity in structures of power/knowledge, that we can see straight through it to the meaning beneath.

Derrida challenges, in a vivid and unsettling way, the supposition that there needs to be something outside of language to serve as a warrant for its meaning. Thus he denies that speech is somehow primary and directly related to meaning, while writing is secondary and derivative and unreliable: a prejudice that he identifies as "phonocentrism" and traces back through Western thought to its classic sources in Plato's *Cratylus* and *Phaedrus*. "Cratylism" posits a close relationship between language as sound and the referential function of language, as if the connection between the baby's sound at the breast and the bilabial nasal consonant in most languages' words for mother (*maman, mater,* etc.) formed the model for all meaning. Writing, in contrast with the apparent directness of speech, becomes opaque once it is released to make its way in the world. How are we supposed to know what sentences written perhaps a hundred years ago, and long since severed from their author's intention, were supposed to mean? They may become corrupted and twisted (as Plato's own writings have been used to justify all manner of things which there is no reason to think he would have approved).

Derrida's arguments against phonocentrism are complex and at first sight counter-intuitive. He notes that a sequence of marks—that is, any linguistic expression—can only signify if it has iterability, i.e., it can be repeated. In this it is no different from writing. There is no essential connection with the speaker's intention or state of mind such that when the connection is severed meaning is lost. Descartes' "clear and distinct ideas" do not stand as the guarantors of meaning. Messages, after all, can be conveyed by people who do not understand them. This is why Derrida would have us break with the idea that there needs to be some kind of guarantee if language is to have meaning, the kind of guarantee that might seem to be supplied if a speaker's words are somehow warranted by the fact of his own self-consciousness and from his knowledge of what he is signifying or referring to.

This structural possibility of being weaned from the referent or from the signified (hence from communication and its context) seems to me to make every mark, including those which are oral, a grapheme in general; which is to say, as we have seen, the non-present remainder of a differential mark cut off from its putative "production" or origin. And I shall even extend this law to all "experience" in general if it is conceded that there is no experience consisting of pure presence but only of chains of differential marks. (Derrida, 1988, p. 10)

Thus we must break with that "most constant, profound and potent procedure" (p. 66) of our habit of thinking by which we construct oppositions such as literal/metaphorical, transcendental/empirical, signified/signifier and conceive the first term as prior and the second "in relation to it, as a complication, a negation, a manifestation, or a disruption of the first" (Culler, 1987, p. 93). This is the *logocentrism*—the tendency to take the first terms of those oppositions as foundational—of which phonocentrism is one dimension.

These ideas place the children who see the police in a new light. Logocentrism is there in the desperate attempt to convey the highest degree of transparency between the text and its referent. Whence comes the meaning of "they see some of the Police"? From the fact that they clearly do see them, which is proved by their being seen to do so, which is guaranteed by . . . and so on, as we described above. But of course the language betrays its opacity nevertheless. "They see some of the Police" is a very odd sequence of words, since no context is supplied to make sense of it. Children do not wander around seeing things except in the sense that things impinge on their vision, a semi-scientific sense that is not appropriate here. They might look at, notice or glance at things, for various reasons. They might see the police if they are Martians for whom police are indeed one of the first sense-data that, goggle-eyed, they experience on earth, the police having naturally turned up to investigate sightings of strange creatures and flying objects. It would make near-sense if, about to mug an old lady, at the last moment Peter and Jane "see some of the police" and refrain; even better if there is a context in which some dramatic irony is at work such that they see some of the police but we, knowledgeable readers, are aware of other police around the corner whom they do not see. But there is no such, as one might say, nexus of events occurring on the horizontal plane. There is only the words on the page, and the logocentrism that imagines the quasi-reality of the picture gives the words meaning.

It may seem perverse to find phonocentrism in attempts to help children to read the written word. Yet what is often called the phonics approach to the teaching of reading (which is the approach that the reading scheme book involving Peter and Jane, with its simplified vocabulary, lends itself to), treats reading precisely as if it is at root an exercise in decoding into sound. That is, as a matter of taking the word *bus*, seeing that it consists of the 'b' as in 'bell' and the 'u' as in 'fun,' and so on, and thus relating the print to what we say when we say "bus:" exactly, in fact, as if the sign on the page derived from its relation to speech. And this is phonocentrism of a fully-blown sort. To say this is not to take sides in the so-called phonics debate[1] about how best to teach children to read. The issue here is not about how to teach children to read, but about how language comes to be meaningful. Derrida's charge of phonocentrism bears on this question in a number of helpful ways.

We can see the force of his charge by looking first at what may be called the communication model of language. It is common to find language discussed as if all writing (and all speech, come to that) aspired to the condition of unambiguous instructions to order goods from a mail-order catalog. It would, for example, be easy to show how reports and official documents on the teaching of English in schools have over recent years moved further and further toward this model (see Chapter nine). One sign is the repeated emphasis on "effectiveness." Communication that is not effective does not communicate. But what would an "effective" poem be? One perhaps where, as the student essays put it, "What Keats is trying to tell us is that . . ." as if there was an antecedent meaning in the poet's head, which could have been communicated in other, better (more effective) ways. If we are teaching children to read and write so that they can communicate, we are teaching them to read and write in order to do what can more directly and successfully be done through speech. This is to teach them that writing is only important insofar as it is for something else. Could it be that this implicit phonocentrism undoes what we think of as our best efforts? Or even that we do not value writing as much as we imagine we do? This suggestion may sound unlikely or even perverse. Yet it is not difficult to find support for it. Writers such as Frank Smith, for example, have documented the ways in which, as teachers, we require the child to do something else when learning to read: to stand up straight, concentrate, speak clear standard English. The teacher may even "take the opportunity during reading instruction to improve spelling" (Smith, 1973, p. 185). And much anecdotal evidence testifies not simply to poor practice in teaching to read but to what appears to be a deep-rooted fear of text, a strategy of picking off its units one by one, as if they were dangerous enemies. "I can remember having to stand at the teacher's desk and her covering up all the words bar the one you were reading. If you made a mistake you had to go back to the beginning *and the offending word was put in your word tin*" (Lynch, 1996, our emphasis).

Of course all sort of complex factors enter here to defeat what may be the teacher's best instincts. As Lyotard has shown, the new information technologies "shrink language (and meaning) to the 'binary logic of Boolean algebra' in order to reduce it to a 'commercial unit of information' that can be rendered sensible in account books" (Bain in Peters, 1995, p. 7). The assimilation of language to a species of infomatics, and the principle of performativity, which reduces what is worthwhile (or what can be legitimated) to what can be handled most effectively by modern technology—thus replacing truth or justice, Lyotard emphasizes, with efficiency—powerfully influence us to see encoding and decoding as the dominant (most "effective") modes of language use.

In any case, it might be asked, on what grounds can it be implied that the child poring over *Come Away* is reading, in some full or favored sense, while the one who encounters Peter, Jane and the police is presented with an exercise in decoding? Are there not rather different kinds of text here, different ways of reading? The first point to make in response is that *Come Away* certainly can be read in the same way as *Out in the Sun*, and is so read by the sophisticated pupil who reads "Look, Jane, see the bus. See the cars. I am glad we came out in the sun!" (or whatever) in a voice of bright condescension, as if addressing a simpleton. Such a pupil has noticed what kind of a text we have here, even if he or she is unlikely to be commended by teacher for doing so ("Start again and read it properly"). The second point requires returning to the ideas of Jacques Derrida.

Derrida rejects the notion that the meaning of language comes from something else, whether that is the signified to which the signifier is held to refer, the originating intention of the speaker or writer, or any other entity on which language might be supposed to center. In language there are only differences.

The play of differences involves syntheses and referrals that prevent there from being at any moment or in any way a simple element that is present in and of itself and refers only to itself. Whether in written or in spoken discourse, no element can function as a sign without relating to another element which itself is not simply present. This linkage means that each "element"—phoneme or grapheme—is constituted with reference to the trace in it of the other elements of the sequence or system. This linkage, this weaving, is the text, which is produced only through the transformation of another text. Nothing, either in the elements or in the system, is anywhere simply present or absent. There are only, everywhere, differences and traces of differences. (Derrida, 1981b, p. 26)

Meaning, then, is a function of the endless web of language itself, and not of the relationship between language and anything else. Because the connections in the web are without limit, meaning can never be finalized: there is no closure, no point at which meaning is established once and for all. Derrida coins the word *différance* to mean both difference (French *différence*) and the deferring of meaning; the pun only works in writing since there is no difference between *différence* and *différance* in speech. Derrida's wit may not appeal to all of us all of the time. But the form of the pun itself makes a serious point: we are tricked, if only momentarily, into considering whether the relationship between signifiers, rather than between them and the world, tells us something significant. And so "we treat the pun as a joke, lest signifiers infect thought" (Culler, 1987, p. 92).

It may be illuminating to revisit some of the above by way of a consideration of Edgar Allan Poe's short story, *The Purloined Letter*. Both Derrida (1987b) and Lacan (1973) have produced detailed "readings" of this, Lacan for his own distinctive psychoanalytical purposes and Derrida as a deconstruction of Lacan's appropriation of the story. While our own discussion is broadly sympathetic to Derrida's treatment there is no reason to suppose that he would agree with it. There is always, after all, something more to be said.

At the heart of *The Purloined Letter* is the visit of a brilliant but unprincipled Minister of State, known to us only as D---, to an "exalted personage" whom we may suppose to be the Queen. During his visit he notices on her table a letter: recognizing the handwriting and observing the Queen's confusion and evident anxiety to conceal the letter from the King (we are to suppose that the letter compromises the Queen in some way: it is from a person who would have no innocent business in writing to her), the Minister sees the advantage to himself of gaining possession of the letter. Accordingly he manages to drop a similar letter of his own onto the table and retrieve the Queen's in its place: this maneuvre the Queen sees but, in the presence of the King, she is powerless to protest.

The story opens with the visit to the narrator and his friend, Dupin, of the Prefect of Police whom the desperate Queen has asked to recover her compromising letter. Perhaps significantly the Prefect finds them in Dupin's "little back library or book-closet:" this is a story where the literary, and perhaps literacy and meaning itself, is vividly foregrounded. The police are at their wits' end. The Minister must be in possession of the letter, for the politics of the situation demand that he must be able to produce it at a moment's notice. The use of hired footpads to waylay and search him, as if for money, has established that the Minister does not carry the letter on his person. The police have made the most microscopic (the word is used several times) search of the Minister's apartment, probing cushions, books, the legs of chairs.

We opened every package and parcel; we not only opened every book, but we turned over every leaf in every volume, not contenting ourselves with a mere shake. . . . We also measured the thickness of every book-*cover*, with the most accurate admeasurement, and applied to each the most jealous scrutiny of the microscope.

What advice can Dupin give the Prefect? He advises him to "make a thorough research of the premises." At this point, as Johnson (1980) notes, the narrator deviates from his usual practice of directly quoting the principal characters of the story, even when doing so inflicts what may seem an unnecessary amount of detail on the reader (as in the preceding paragraph). Here Dupin tells the Prefect that he has no better advice to give him, asking

"You have, of course, an accurate description of the letter?"
"Oh, yes!"—And here the Prefect, producing a memorandum-book, proceeded to read aloud a minute account of the internal, and especially of the external, appearance of the missing document.

Here, where we might expect a description of the letter (and especially of its contents) that the story is about, we get paraphrase. And paraphrase does not do what it usually does, which is to take us to the gist of the matter, but functions, as Johnson (1980) observes, to hide the substance, from us. We return to the significance of this below.

A month passes, and the Prefect returns: the second search has proved as fruitless as the first. Despairingly, he says he would give fifty thousand francs to anyone who could shed light on the mystery. Dupin promptly offers to hand him the letter in return for a check of that amount. When the astounded policeman has left with the letter, Dupin explains how he found the letter. To put it briefly, he deduced that what the Prefect thought was difficult and obscure must be plain and simple. The letter must be quite obvious to anyone who looks in the right way: we only fail to see it if we look too minutely, as one looking on a map for the name of a small village will not read the letters of the county stretching across the map in large letters. Visiting the Minister, whom he knew well, Dupin noticed a kind of card-rack hanging from the mantlepiece, holding "six visiting cards and a solitary letter." The letter was dirty, crumpled and torn, bearing the Minister's seal, and addressed to the Minister himself. From the radically different condition of the letter from the one he was looking for, "together with the hyperobtrusive situation of this document, full in the view of every visitor," as well as the fact that the edges looked more chafed than necessary, Dupin concluded that this was the missing letter, "turned as a glove, inside-out, re-directed and re-sealed." He found an excuse to return the next day, and when the Minister went to the window to investigate the cause of a disturbance in the street (which Dupin had arranged in order to distract him at the crucial moment), he substituted a letter of identical appearance for the original purloined one.

This story helps to make vivid the earlier points about meaning, difference and presence. The letter that is purloined can be regarded as a signifier, but one that refuses to be reduced to a signified (as we might suppose that "bus" just comes down to the bus that it labels). As we noted, the actual contents of the letter are withheld from the reader by the device of paraphrase: the function of the letter as signifier does not depend at all on knowledge (or ignorance) of the contents (see Johnson, 1980, p. 139). Nothing either inside or outside the letter serves as warrant for its meaning. The very inside/outside polarity, and its applicability to the act of interpretation, are subverted (p. 128): the metaphysics of presence is rejected. In a similar way the polarity hidden/exposed is challenged or deconstructed. The Prefect of Police sees space in conventional terms, as something to be probed microscopically (accurately, carefully and patiently—the qualities of the "good reader") for what is hidden in it. But the letter, if it is hidden, is not hidden in that way. There are no *secrets* to detect. The letter is both hidden and not hidden, hidden by being as it were exposed, just as the name on the map is less obvious for being stretched across it in large letters. The word *purloined* itself evades the dichotomy stolen/not stolen (the Minister might say: "I did not steal it—you *saw* me take it! No deception was intended, as 'stealing' implies. In fact the power over you which my possession of the letter gave me *depended* on you knowing that I had it").

The literate reader understands something of the conventions or *frames* within which his or her reading takes place. Encountering the line from Kipling's poem *Fuzzy-Wuzzy*, "You're a pore benighted 'eathen but a first-class fightin' man," such a reader grasps that these lines are not offered as some timeless, context-free (frame-free) truth about certain persons of color: they are framed by the implicit speaker-in-persona, a drunken red-coat leaning to sentimentality. Further frames are the imperial attitudes implicit in the poem, the post-imperial *frisson* that may attach to a contemporary reading, the reading that refuses the sense of guilt thereby induced. All these frames are "provisional, pragmatic, heuristic and contingent" (Martindale, 1993, p. 14). Here is difference as deferral, the resistance to closure. There is no final, for-all-time reading to be achieved or sought.

Any frame can itself be framed, or as Derrida puts it, "frames are always framed" (1987b, p. 99). *This the literate reader understands*, on some level or another. Not even Peter and Jane come free of a frame, of a context, and it is to inculcate a kind of blindness, or illiteracy, to pretend that they do. They come framed by the conventions of a classroom *reader*, and the literate reader (we pass over this suggestive awkwardness)[2] accordingly gets his/her head down, either defensively or studiously, or takes refuge in burlesque, or otherwise responds appropriately. That is why there is nothing intrinsically harmful about such classroom readers—except that they seem to offer a standing temptation to pretend that the frame does not exist, that there is no frame.

How is *The Purloined Letter* framed? This story, which being about a letter is so to speak *literal* (yet the meaning of the letter was not in its contents) is prefixed by one literary quotation and ends with another. The latter, a quotation from a French dramatist, acts as Dupin's signature on the letter that he leaves behind in place of the purloined one, for he wants the Minister to know, when he discovers the substitution, that it is Dupin who is responsible for it. In a further twist, Dupin is thus signing himself with this quotation (in inverted commas, of course) not

'Dupin' but "'Dupin,'" and the prefixed quotation from Seneca, having resisted all identification by classical scholars, is not from Seneca but from 'Seneca.' Every frame can be framed, every sign can be put between quotation marks.

If the framing of the story is thus literary, then the inside and the outside have become hard to separate. The story began, as we noted, in Dupin's *library*; both he and the Minister are poets—eminently literary figures—which is how Dupin was able to gain some sympathetic insight into the workings of the Minister's mind. "Frames are always framed: thus, *by part of their context*" (Derrida, 1987b, p. 99, our emphasis). The boundaries of the story "crumble off into an abyss" (p. 100). It seems that, if we are to make sense of the story, we have to follow the very theme of writing (Johnson, 1980, p. 131), of literature. It is almost as if the signified of the story (so far from the signified being its *contents*) is literature, is literacy in the broadest sense. Our understanding of the story, then, does not depend on a microscopic, jealous scrutiny of the contents of the letter that is situated at the heart of the story, but on the continual placing and replacing of the story's borders or frames.

Krajewski (1992) remarks that both Lacan and Derrida have overlooked the 'Seneca' quotation that prefixes *The Purloined Letter*. Johnson's only remark on it is that it is from Seneca and not from Seneca. This quotation, *Nil sapientiae odiosius acumine nimio*, deserves a little more attention. Krajewski translates it as "Nothing is more detestable to wisdom than too much subtlety." Yet *acumine* has a more obvious meaning than "subtlety:" it is *accuracy*, Latin *acumen*, "a point to prick or sting with"—the very property of those "fine long needles" with which the police probed the Minister's apartment. To be wise is to know when a different approach is called for: it is to understand the limitations of accuracy.

To be literate is also to understand these limitations, and to be alert to what Derrida calls the disseminating play of the text, its constant escape from unity of meaning or privileged order of truth (such an order as the psychoanalytic, which is the basis of the Lacanian interpretation of Poe's story that Derrida deconstructs in his own reading of it). Meaning is like a letter which, sent into the postal system, may always fail to reach its destination. Derrida's discussion of Lacan's treatment of *The Purloined Letter* is entitled "Le facteur de la vérité," *facteur* being both the factor or determining order of truth and, more prosaically, the American mailman or British postman.

In another classroom another postman raises questions of truth, reality and 'framing.' This is the postman of *The Jolly Postman, or Other People's Letters* (Ahlberg and Ahlberg, 1986). A group of children and their teacher are reading this together. "Once upon a bicycle,/So they say,/A Jolly Postman came one day/From over the hills/And far away." There are smiles of recognition at the subversion of the conventional "Once upon a time." Opposite this doggerel, the page forms an envelope, addressed to Mr. and Mrs. Bear, Three Bears Cottage, The Woods. You can take out the letter it contains, in which Goldilocks apologizes, in poor spelling and with some crossing-out: "Mummy says I am a bad girl. I hardly eat any porij when she cooks it she s*X*ays." Other post includes a circular from Hobgoblin Supplies Ltd. for the Wicked Witch ("Easy-clean nonstick Cauldron Set, with free recipe for Toad in the hole"), a holiday postcard from Jack to Mr. V. Bigg the Giant (the hen that lays the golden eggs having proved every bit as useful as traveller's checks) and a solicitor's letter for B. B. Wolf Esq. ("Miss Hood tells us that you are presently occupying her grandma's cottage and wearing her grandma's clothes without this lady's permission").

Here what might be called the established meanings of the world of nursery-rhyme are disrupted by the prosaic world of solicitors, mail-shots and the need to apologize and make amends. Each world frames the other, and the text refuses to privilege either as the place where the reader can finally close the book. If literacy is crucial "to the degree that it makes problematic the very structure and practice of representation" (Giroux, 1993, p. 367), then the children in this classroom may be on the way to becoming good readers.

Presently someone will be along to see if they are reading accurately.

NOTES

1. In many parts of the English-speaking world the complex issue of literacy has been reduced to a pseudo-debate between proponents of the phonics approach to the teaching of reading (now generally thought to be traditional and therefore good) and proponents of so-called real books (progressive and therefore bad).

2. Does "reader" designate a text or a person? See Introduction in P. Kamuf (1991).

Chapter 5

Shifting, Shifted, . . . Shattered: The Ethical Self

Has postmodern philosophy changed the way the positions of the parent and the teacher are conceptualized? And, if so, in what sense? Does it have a message at all for the individual in education? Can it offer guidelines or does it open a fruitful general perspective for those involved in raising children? Answering these and related issues necessitates first an idea of the different ways knowledge and the subject may be conceived in postmodernism and the way this affects how ethics itself is interpreted. A variety of perspectives have been taken in postmodernism on the historical relativity of knowledge and its inextricability from relations of power, the repressive nature of the knowing consciousness, and last but not least, the conception of the ethical subject as "hostage to the other." These matters will be developed before turning to the possible promise of this approach for education and the educator.

The many blends of postmodernism, *pace* their mutual differences, share a concept of the subject different from that of the canonic philosophical tradition. Postmodernism is based on a critique of the subject as primordially a consciousness that knows. The epistemological subject in Descartes and in classical phenomenology is characterized by the intentional character of consciousness.

Recent French philosophy in particular has sought to undermine this picture by demonstrating that cognition is not the subject's most primitive encounter with the other and, by showing that this view of cognition is based on a flawed model, i.e., the model of knowledge as representation. The key figures in this debate inasfar as it is relevant to ethics are Foucault, Derrida, Lyotard and Levinas. Though stressing different points, they all embrace a hostility toward the private cogito and the difficulty of considering ethics as a relation between mutually hermetic consciousnesses. They are furthermore united in distrust of society and its institutions. They have all contributed to a shift of the concept of ethics, outlining either an ethos without a normative core (Foucault); a fractured vision of the social world as composed of a number of incommensurables (Lyotard); a vision of the subject as more vigilant and responsive to the Other (Derrida); and a conception of the Other as an anchorage for the command (Levinas). To put things in the right perspective, we shall first give a brief characterization of the traditional understanding of ethics.

ETHICS: THE TRADITIONAL PICTURE

One can distinguish roughly between a morality based on principles and one that elaborates a particular idea of the good life by indicating what kind of a person one should be. With its insistence on virtues, ancient ethics belongs to the latter. The ethical problem is conceived as twofold: it involves the need for action in a practical situation and demands that such action demonstrates awareness of general ethical values, the fundamental question being: "What should my life be like?" or "How can I make sense of my life as whole?" As Annas argues, it is "assumed that people of average intellect with a modicum of leisure will at some point reflect on their lives and ask whether they are as they should be, or whether they could be improved" (1993, p. 27). Here, an important assumption is made on behalf of the ethical subject, namely that the arguments and conclusions of ethics will only affect those who have come to them through worrying about real problems, only those who have paused to ask themselves how their lives are going. And it is also accepted that the love of the good itself is shown in self-conscious direction and development of one's self. Ethics in this form does not refer to a body of rules or prescriptions for right conduct as such, but rather to the self-forming activity wherein one seeks to develop insight by practicing the kind of inquiry that makes philosophical ethics possible.

Another version of ethics—mentioned above but not dealt with here at any length—is the ethic of design or arrangement (principles). Here what binds us, what we must seek, is that world which everyone would choose if they were not contaminated by their prejudices or parochial interests. Both kinds of ethic are thoroughly foundationalist and universalist and can be labelled rationalist.

The Romantic rejection of rationalist ethics helps us understand postmodernism. Two directions of critique may be distinguished: the first follows from a conception of vital inspiration as central to life, in which the rationality required by modernity is interpreted as rationalization, normalization and ultimately as an attack on life itself. Its overall aim is to unmask truths as countless local and contextual incidences determined by chance and power together, whilst also celebrating the particular. This attack on traditional ethics criticizes all institutions, communications and traditions as hidden instruments of conservatism, against which it advocates a glorification of vital desires, action to subvert the system and permanent avant-gardism. The second direction explores a more positive appreciation of reason's social embeddedness. It supposes that to understand the binding character of morality, we need not discover or design anything, because we already have an ethical home. We are already bound by the practices, codes and images that organize the historical life in which we are anchored. Authors such Oakeshott, MacIntyre, and Taylor belong to the latter project; to the former Foucault, Lyotard, and Derrida, among others.

The idea that ethics has one way or another to do with an activity of self-formation will be taken up by those postmodernists who seek their inspiration in the work of Nietzsche. To understand these authors, it is important to keep another characteristic in mind. Ancient ethics drew a distinction between different forms of dependency to which one might be subject: those that arise from one's own chosen projects and those that one does not seek but cannot avoid. For instance, your life can be self-sufficient even if your well-being is dependent on that of your children, providing that having and caring about children is an aim you have chosen for yourself. But the postmodern idea of a person starts from a different basic proposition; though people can never be completely free, they aspire to be free, and constantly withdraw from what they are at present in order to achieve yet greater freedom. In Chapter eight we will show how, for Lacan, my identity is formed by the other, who ascribes to me my identity and my desire. Here we will first focus on Foucault's concept of power to see how it changes the concept of ethics.

FOUCAULT: LIFE AS A WORK OF ART

In the modern period, moral conduct came to be articulated in the context of positive knowledge. Modernists denied that moral experience was either a response to religious revelation or a commitment to an aesthetic task. Foucault radicalizes this liberation by indicating how ethical reflection depends on knowledge. He also criticizes the practices of intellectual reflection, practical action and self-constitution that give rise to the exercise of moral-political discernment and decision, analysing the discursive and extra-discursive relations which govern their conduct in a given culture. His concern is with what knowledge does, what power constructs (rather than represents) and how a relationship of the self to the self is invented rather than discovered.

Foucault thought of ethics as that component of morality that concerns the self's relationship to itself. Histories of morality should not be exclusively focused on the history of codes of moral behavior. We must also pay careful attention to the history of what Foucault calls the forms of moral subjectivation, of the ways we constitute ourselves as moral subjects of our own actions. For Foucault, ethics proper, the self's relationship to itself, has four main aspects: the ethical substance—that part of oneself that is taken to be the relevant domain for ethical judgment; the mode of subjection, the way in which the individual establishes her relation to moral obligations and rules; the self-forming activity or ethical work that one performs on oneself in order to transform oneself into an ethical subject; and the *telos*, the mode of being at which one aims in behaving ethically. Foucault's interest in relations to oneself focuses on the government of the self by the self in connection with its relations to others, a relationship described in pedagogy, advice for conduct, spiritual direction, and the prescription of models of life. The ways in which we relate to ourselves (our "technologies of the self") affect the ways in which our subjectivity is constituted and our experiences are shaped, as well as the way in which we govern our thought and conduct. The Foucauldian position describes an ethos and a self-relation that is constituted by a complex historical inheritance, but an ethos without a normative core: an ethos based on the observation that one can always detach oneself from oneself, thanks to the fragmentation of the elements that constitute the self.

According to Foucault, subjects and selves do not belong to themselves, but to circulations of powers. Their destiny is not to belong to anything at all. The subject of desire is not structured by desire itself or force of will, but by the circulation of those powers that emerge as individuals are formed within given cultural circumstances. For Foucault, who is fascinated with the question of how our culture made sexuality into a moral experience, the moral subject forms itself and is formed by the body's desires. Foucault regards sexuality as the outstanding area for discipline and normalization.

In achieving a permanent possibility of escape from ourselves, we affirm our nonbelonging in the world which surrounds and constrains us. Foucault's thought is concerned with converting people to a better communal life. He interrupts not only our conventions but also our impulse toward coherence and our uncritical sense that our lives are shaped by nature or necessity. Seeing every state of being as a product of unstable power formations, he makes possible a critical dismemberment of every characteristic that seems intrinsic to us. When critical investigation interrupts those power formations, another kind of power comes into play. This power loosens the hold of other powers, and so the subject is opened up to a kind of nonbelonging that gives us distance from the values that direct us. Simultaneously, as we solve the problems internal to a given ethos, our answers raise further fundamental problems of a different sort.

The identities of human beings are unsteady then, not because we repress our true natures, nor because our true natures are repressed by our parents, our leaders, or our culture, but because we do not have true natures. Each of us is a nexus of relations formed in response to ever-shifting problems. Our identities are formed and reformed in relation to these changing problematizations. A subject will find freedom in the ability to reverse or to resist a situation. It is because she has no essence that the subject enjoys this freedom, which is a freedom of fragmentation: a freedom that arises in the constellation of differences that constitute a lineage of loose alliances, relations of resistance and mastery, and configurations of fluid interests. The freedom of fragmentation remains real in response to the constant transformation of problems. It puts in question the firmest of principles and established practices. The result is an ethic of responsibility for the truths one speaks, for the political strategies which these truths inform, and for those ways of relating to ourselves that make us either conformists or dissidents. For Foucault ethics involves understanding oneself as the subject of a critical practice of freedom which is not outside the games of truth. With such an understanding, we are able to oppose political institutions, states of domination and juridical notions of the subject.

One aspect of resistance is to refuse what we are, the other is to invent (not to discover) who we are by promoting new forms of subjectivity. Resistance has an analytic role: it exposes what a particular strategy of power is. Something unseen but unacceptable in an ascription of identity is disclosed (the taken-for-granted of a community, which totalizes our thinking) and exposed to risk. The result might be a new way of thinking, one in which totalization might not be able to grow again in the name of some other, better morality or a new cooperative endeavor. It is in this sense that one has to understand the idea of an aesthetics of existence; as referring to those intentional and voluntary projects by which men not only set themselves rules of conduct, but also seek to transform themselves, to change themselves, and to make their life into something like a work of art that carries certain aesthetic values and meets certain stylistic criteria.

Since Socrates a concern with the "care of the self" has always been part of what it is to be a philosopher. The view that such a concern should be expunged or kept to oneself is a late development. Over a long history, the ancient preoccupation with the self came to be seen as a matter of vanity, pride, self-interest or self-love. It was the opposite of selflessness or charitable relations with others and a private obstacle to the realization of a rational, public or collective good. Thus morality became a morality of asceticism whose maxim was that "the self is that which one can reject." This asceticism tried to determine what one must sacrifice of oneself to know what is good or right. It sought to define legitimate violence as well as pain and pleasure, and encouraged the turning of oneself into a being of the right sort, virtuous and dutiful. Further, the ancient task of taking care of or being concerned with oneself was obscured and replaced by knowing oneself.

But to take care of oneself, to regard oneself as a work to be accomplished could, according to Foucault, sustain an ethics that is no longer supported by either tradition or reason. As creator of itself, the self could enjoy that autonomy that modern man cannot do without—a position reminiscent of Nietzsche's "aesthetics of existence." One result of this conversion is, according to Foucault, the experience of a pleasure that one takes in oneself. Furthermore, the characterization of how one lives, one's style of life, indicates what aspect of oneself one puts under judgment, how one relates oneself to moral obligations, what one does to transform oneself into an ethical subject and what mode of being one aims to realize. And as the self's relationship to itself undergoes modification in every historical period, as the way in which one cares for oneself changes, so too will one's style of life change.

For Foucault, to reinvent ethical thought today is to ask again the ancient question of how to speak truly of our lives. It is a matter of understanding how our bonds, our freedom and our truth might enter into a contemporary critical philosophical activity. The central question in Foucault's ethic concerns the bonds we may have with one another, affective and political, the question of who we are and who we may be. In an interview he insists: "One must not have the care for others precede the care for self. The care for self takes moral precedence in the measure that the relationship to self takes ontological precedence" (1988, p. 7). In stressing subjectivity he does not intend to abandon a social or collective ethic in favor of an individual or private one. He wanted to rethink the great questions of community: how and why people bond together, how and why they are bound to one another, the question of passion, and the question of the *eros* of our identity. Foucault's subject is therefore not an individuality, an indivisible unit in which we locate our identity, neither is it a particularity, the exemplification of a common nature. It is not a single thing. Rather there are as many subjectivities as there are accepted forms of self-relation. Human beings each have more than one kind of subjectivity, more than one kind of social being. Individual and society are not opposed to one another as absolute entities; they are instead linked together in a common history, the forms of one being able to survive a change in the forms of the other.

In a critical community the self-sufficiency of its taken-for-granted is problematized; Foucault tried to characterize such a community in terms of the tradition that had linked the activity of the intellectual to philosophy. Such a community is a "free community," and the passion of the critical "bond" is a passion for being free. It would maintain the ancient ethical belief that the art of leading a noble or beautiful life was an art of being, or of self-creation. The experience of freedom is not the experience of an identity or of a natural or pre-given state, but an experience of the fragility of any taken-for-granted identity. Our identity is not the source of freedom or the goal it aspires to, but something constantly liberated or opened to question by freedom.

It is not in our basic individualities or communities that we are free, but the historical forms of our individual and communal being themselves which may be freed or exposed to the risk of new and unforeseen transformation. Freedom is not a state one achieves once and for all, but a condition of undefined work of thought, action and self-invention. To be free we must be able to question the ways our own history defines us; freeing and liberating ourselves is therefore never a completed or absolute process. Foucault's message seems to be that everything is dangerous. We have no unquestioned sovereignty or internalized discipline to inspire overwhelming conviction and ethical passion in us. His ethics invites us to the practice of liberty, to struggle and to transgress, which open possibilities for new relations to self and to events in the world. The search for a form of morality acceptable to everyone, in the sense that everyone would have to submit to it, seems to Foucault catastrophic. His concern is not with the supposed relativity of all values, but with the dangers of drives for unity, universality and wholeness. In other words, a concern for selfhood.

Foucault's question is not whether political action is possible. He was very clear that a bookish act of participation was no substitute for activism pure and simple and he held that the essence of radicalism is physical action. He never asked whether action was possible, but took part in political movements. Furthermore he never attacked the choices of others, but rather the rationalizations that they appended to their choices. Thus he refused to convert our finitude into a basis for new certainties. Veyne similarly argues: "A true warrior, lacking indignation, knows anger, *thumos*. Foucault did not worry about justifying his convictions; it was enough for him to hold to them. But to ratiocinate would have been to lower himself, with no benefit to his cause" (1993, p. 6). This seems to coincide with what Foucault meant by "an ethics no longer supported by either tradition or reason." In Foucault's position, the intersubjective relationship as the focus of ethics seems to have evaporated, or at least to have lost its importance. We will now look at two authors representing the other extreme.

LEVINAS AND DERRIDA: THE OTHER AND THE
CLAIM OF DIFFERENCE

No one has criticized the ontological and epistemological preoccupations of traditional philosophy more thoroughly than the Jewish thinker Emmanuel Levinas, preoccupations which in his opinion made it impossible to conceive what a true ethical relationship amounts to.

According to Levinas, philosophy was born out of the question: "Why is there something rather than nothing?" Philosophy's preoccupation is with the question of the origin of being; that is, how to account for the existence of things. But Levinas asks whether this is the only legitimate philosophical question, since in his opinion the decision of the first Greek philosophers to interpret "the good" in terms of "what is true" need not be accepted. It seems possible to him to interpret transcendence not as the ground of being but as something that addresses an appeal to me, that puts to me a radical question. When we are involved with reality external to ourselves, we are in a sense estranged from ourselves. If we define subjectivity as the autonomous definition of oneself, a person becomes a self by withdrawing from that estrangement. One becomes oneself in a reflexive return to oneself. The subject, who can only exist in relation to reality (in which it necessarily loses itself), discovers itself in a moment of self-conscience.

An ethics whose starting point is consciousness, for example, one that is based on a mental intuition of values or an ethics that begins with the meaning of being, cannot dictate restraints on agency. For Levinas, in an ethical encounter, the datum of the face emerges (see also Child, Williams, Birch & Boody, 1995), and what is essentially a form or shape is transformed into a moral imperative. According to Levinas, the subject loses all its entitlements when confronted with the face of the Other. By the same token, it also makes contact with its truest and most proper core. The revelation of the face brings to being a new stratum within the perceiver's own sensibility. It addresses the perceiver and solicits a relationship with her that compels her to see the Other as destitute. This is not necessarily an empirical matter; rather, the face has to be read as overturning power relations, as asking the perceiver to refrain from the exercise of power which, in its most extreme form, consists in the annihilation of the Other. What properly constitutes a subject cannot be understood except in relation to its fragility when confronted by the Other.

As Caputo argues, it should not go unnoticed that the ethics of Levinas is not only philosophical but religious (1988, p. 69). It is necessary to grasp this to be able to see and accept its full strength. Thus Levinas argues that it is only thanks to a prior unfreedom that we can be free at all. In accepting responsibility for the Other and the unfreedom which this entails, the subject realizes her own nature as an ethical subject. She must be willing to be hostage to the Other. Therefore what is demanded by the face of the Other is a radical altruism. The face of the Other makes me free because it confronts me with a possibility that I couldn't have chosen without it. If the Good were to show itself to us in its full glory, we would be enslaved, but the Good is good because it provides us with this opportunity. For Levinas the Other is an anchorage for the moral imperative, rather than the moral imperative an anchorage for Otherness. The Other cannot act as an anchor strictly speaking because the Other can never present herself as fully present; consequently the Other remains outside ontology. The word of the Other would have no power, however, if it didn't echo that which precedes it: God. The Other is able to reverse my inclinations, my attempts to appropriate her, only because she is more than I can see of her—the proximity of God in the face of the Other.

The issue of otherness and responsibility for the other is also preeminently present in Derrida's writings. Staten comments: "If there is any scepticism in Derrida, it is moral not an epistemological scepticism—not a doubt about the possibility of morality but about an idealized picture of sincerity that takes insufficient account of the windings and twistings of fear and desire, weakness and lust, sadism and masochism and the will to power, in the mind of the most sincere man" (1985, p. 126-127).

Bernstein claims that there is a way of reading Derrida's texts that shows his ethical-political horizon as surrounding and influencing virtually everything he has written. Subtly interwoven in his critique of the metaphysics of presence (logocentricism,[1] phallocentrism, ethnocentrism), the theme of responsibility keeps surfacing in his text. His writings are at times so powerful and disconcerting, Bernstein argues, because he has an uncanny (*unheimlich*) ability to show us that at the heart of what we take to be familiar, native, homely—there where we think we can find our center—there lurks, concealed and repressed, that which is unfamiliar, strange, and uncanny. But given his indebtedness to Heidegger, he seeks to expose what he calls the dominance of the entire metaphorics of proximity, of simple and immediate presence: a metaphorics associating the proximity of Being with the values of neighborhood, shelter, house, service, guard, voice and listening. Derrida seeks to show us that we never are or quite can be at home in the world—a matter related to his discussion of the *heimlich/unheimlich*, the canny or uncanny, to the question of our ethos or dwelling in the world. "We are always threatened by the uncanniness of what is canny; we are always in exile—even from ourselves. We may long and dream of being at home in our world, to find a 'proper' centre, but we never achieve this form of presence or self-presence" (Bernstein, 1987, p. 100).

Derrida's deconstruction opens up an ethics sensitive to the demands not of presence but of absence, not of identity but of difference. Unlike the mainstream of the metaphysics of morals, deconstruction does not invoke universal, rational or natural laws. It does not answer to them but assumes responsibility for them and investigates their extraordinary power to marginalize everything which seems particular, irrational or unnatural in their light. Deconstruction is set in motion by the responsibility to the rights of the different. Unlike mainstream thinking, it does not heed the call of Being, presence, and the same, but keeps its ear alert to the call of the Other. "Derrida systematically defends the rights of the different not the same, of the particular not the universal, of the exception not the rule, of everything which is excluded and marginalized by the rule of the same, of the *arche/principium/*prince" (Caputo, 1988, p. 65).

The height of responsibility, according to Derrida, is to wonder about the origin of that which calls for a response. In this sense deconstruction practices a radical *Gelassenheit* (letting be) which is bent not on assimilating the other but on letting the other be. Derrida argues: "The event being singular each time, to the measure of the otherness of the other, each time one must invent, not without concepts, but by going each time beyond the concept, without any guarantee nor certainty. This obligation can only be double, contradictory, and conflictual, since it calls for a responsibility and not a moral or political technique. . . . Each time, one must *invent* in order to betray as little as possible . . . *with* no previous *guarantee* whatsoever of success" (Derrida & Ewald, 1995, p. 288).

Each time it is necessary to reinvent the responsibilities involved, in order to respond to the singularity of the event. This is not done by ignoring previously developed concepts, but by going beyond them, as Egéa-Kuehne (1995) argues. Derridean deconstruction does not amount to submersion in nothingness (equivalent to the common charge of nihilism) but to an openness toward the other. Far from seeking to destroy the subject, Derrida only seeks to resituate it, leaving it more vigilant and responsive to the other. The result of this is "justice," the experience of aporia, of the impossible, of the undecidable. Deconstruction involves singularity, always demanded, never accomplished. "It concerns the 'other as other,' in a unique situation, irreducible to principles of duty, rights, or objective law" (Kearney, 1993, p. 36). Justice is, for Derrida, the idea of a gift without exchange, of a relation to the other that is utterly irreducible to the normal rules of circulation, gratitude, recognition or symmetry. That is why it appears to imply a certain kind of madness or mystique.

We turn now to Lyotard. It is not the subject in itself, nor the way the other presses on us, that Lyotard focuses on but the relationship between individuals who may belong to different subcultures.

LYOTARD: DIFFERENDS AND INCOMMENSURABLES

Lyotard posed the question of justice in the context of the radical conflict between incommensurable traditions. Starting from the heterogeneous character of contemporary society, which he refers to as our postmodern condition, Lyotard articulates a fractured vision of the social world composed of a number of incommensurable language games or genres of discourse, each with their own particular stakes and rules for discursive as well as non-discursive action. When these come into conflict, there arises what he calls a *differend*, a case of conflict that cannot be equitably resolved for lack of a rule of judgment applicable to both arguments. Lyotard speaks of our responsibility to recognize and expose *differends* through the construction of frames of reference in which the claims of those who have been denied a voice may be heard.

Lyotard tries to show what it is that obliges us to recognize the injustice of silencing those who radically contest our own position, what it is that moves us to respect the integrity of their concerns, their right to voice them and have them taken into account, despite the fact that we do not share those concerns with them.

He echoes Levinas' claim that one cannot experience the sheer alterity of another person, their presence as another like oneself but also totally other than oneself. The description of the other from one's own frame of reference, for instance, one's conception of the good life, could do injustice to the other. It is therefore one's freedom to act as one pleases that is radically called into question by Lyotard's position. We find ourselves in the midst of a *differend* in which the alterity of another calls us to account for how we understand things. In a form of justice sensitive to diversity, the question of the just and the unjust must permanently remain open. We confront the imperative of a radically open form of political debate. We are obliged to recognize that our standards are incommensurable with the standards of others and so do not permit any justifiable domination of one sphere by the other. As Lindsay argues: "The I's displacement marks an immediate obligation toward the other, even though the content of the obligation is not known. The other's advent is not an event of cognition, but rather of feeling; Lyotard defines the feeling of obligation as a feeling of *respect*. Thus a new universe is instituted, that of the ethical phrase. Saying yes to the indecipherable obligation imposed by the advent of the other fractures the I, dispossesses it, and opens the I onto the other" (1992, p. 399). According to Lindsay, ethical judgment itself becomes experimental, since it calls on us to make judgments without criteria, according to what we anticipate or imagine of the future ends and addressees of every judgment—a prescription for an honorable postmodernity.

Thus Lyotard's version of ethics recasts the political. The political is not that genre of discourse that includes all other discourses, a general metalanguage. Rather, everything is political in the sense that a radical conflict or *differend* can arise on the occasion of the slightest collision between different spheres. There is in his opinion no just society; but a just community might work in accordance with the imperative: live together in difference, but not indifferently, in respect for the irreducibly distinct other. The question he directs his attention to is the problem of how to act justly without pretending that one can succeed in justice. His ethics make no appeal to any essence of the human that might provide a paradigm for judgment, no description that might provide a rule for the formulation of prescriptions. He therefore advocates an unstable state of revolutionary prudence. It consists in knowing that there is no golden rule that can allow us to subjugate engagement in events to a metadiscourse on history. Resistance thus becomes endless and no consensus can establish a new world order.

Compromise and respect for difference do not involve establishing some common identity or universal subject to serve as an arbitrating instance, a vantage point from which differences might be tolerated. Instead a number of ruses or tricks are identified. First, acts of resistance are context specific and always singular. Second, acts of resistance occur all the time. Third, without predictable content or form, affirmations of resistance display respect for the other and cannot be seen as merely the negative finality of deceit. One is confronted here with a refusal to justify direct action in terms of a means to an end. Acts of resistance should be their own justification. The heteronomous determination (or limitation) of the will of the subject through a recognition of the other takes the concerns and interests of the other into account. One places the ends of one's actions in question through a submission to the appeal of the other in which these ends are called into question. On the social level this revolutionary prudence is paralleled by an appeal to dissensus instead of consensus.

PROBLEMS WITH THE SHIFTED ETHICS OF POSTMODERNISM AS RELEVANT TO EDUCATION

The postmodern repudiation of any moral quest, the refusal of a theory of human nature, its very hope-freeness, is of course a positive ethic in itself. Practical know-how, *phronesis*, preempts objective truth; concern for future action replaces worry about foundations and rules of thumb replace universal principles. In that time-space, anything other than provisional and delimited legislation seems vanity. Is there no opportunity left for ethical legislation, except in the nostalgia-soaked hideaways of academia? Bauman (1994) argues that we are now confronting the unimaginable: not the questioning of one set of legislated principles in the name of another set, but the questioning of the very legislating of principles as such: the unthinkable prospect of society without morality. Is this indeed the only and correct conclusion?

With Foucault it is clear that what he understands by ethics differs from the traditional formulation. The charge that he elevated an aesthetic of existence over all other intellectual and moral virtues, putting the self rather than the world and its inhabitants at the focus of ethical concern, is still heard. And his unrelinquished commitment to a social or collective ethic does not dispel the doubt that his ethical insights are foremost and primarily concerned with subjectivity and subjection. Foucault believed that our subjectivity is not an aspect of any intrinsic nature, and suggests that the question of the subject cannot be separated from the question of knowledge and power. While he recognizes the necessity of rationality, he wants to analyze its limits, dangers and historical effects; for the kinds of scientific knowledge we accept about ourselves are related to our forms of government and self-government.

One may wonder whether we are, as ethical subjects, destined to a life of struggle which we also want to avoid, and why struggle is preferable to submission. Why ought domination to be resisted? Such questions seem impossible to answer without appeal to some or other prior normative considerations. In other words, it seems impossible if one accepts Foucault's critique to accept the ethics of modernity unproblematically and yet at the same time Foucault seems unwilling to recommend any alternative. But what values are affirmed in resisting domination? What is gained by the criticism and rejection of repression if no alternative can be demonstrated? And is Foucault's deemphasis of the agent's role, particularly in an ethical context, also not puzzling?

What does this seem to imply for the promotion of freedom in education? Insofar as we come to see ourselves as individuals by internalizing procedures of self-identification—games of truth that structure our subjectivity by obliging us to declare who we are—education should help us resist the tendency to naturalize these procedures or make them seem inherently evident. Education should support a refusal to restrict ethico-political choices to the dictates of scientifically regulated norms and a regimen of cost-benefit calculations, and foster the courage, skill and patience to shape creative and liberating alternatives. Freedom is practiced by interrogating our games of truth. Through the exercise of freedom, a refusal to identify in a deep ontological way with fabricated subject categories, one learns and is led to rely on oneself alone to make sense of one's experience. Freedom requires one to be critically pragmatic.

If Foucault's insights seem to cause problems because of his focus on subjectivity, the problem with Levinas' position is quite the opposite. The demand that we do justice to each and every subject seems one we will never be able to live up to. And this position also presupposes a religious perspective not everyone is willing to accept.

Derrida and Lyotard confront us with partly analogous problems. The presuppositions of their arguments seem incompatible with what they, no less than others, actually do. Benhabib recalls White's observation that no postmodern thinker would give blanket endorsement to the explosions of violence associated with, say, the resurgence of ethnic group nationalism in the Soviet Union or with the growth of street gangs in Los Angeles (White, 1991). Yet, according to Benhabib, it is not at all clear that Derrida and Lyotard have a normative discourse available for condemning such violence. She is not implying that theorists of difference are responsible for degenerate forms of politics, nor that philosophical positions can be criticized for their imputed, real or imaginary political consequences in the hands of others; nor that one should judge, evaluate or question the commitment of theorists of difference to democratic ideals and aspirations. "What I will be arguing instead" she says "is that Jean-François Lyotard and, to some extent, Jacques Derrida, privilege in their writings on the political *a certain perspective, a certain angle, a certain heuristic framework*, which itself has deep and ultimately, I think, misleading consequences for understanding the rational foundations of the democratic form of government" (Benhabib, 1994, p. 5).

Both Lyotard and Derrida preoccupy themselves with the originary or foundational political act. A certain view of language is connected with a certain politics. Lyotard's emphasis on incommensurability between discourses informs a philosophical politics quite different from the politics of politicians. But, Benhabib argues, the thesis of radical incommensurability of genres of discourse is no more meaningful than the thesis of the radical incommensurability of conceptual frameworks. If frameworks, linguistic, conceptual or otherwise, actually are so radically incommensurable with each other, then we could not actually know this. She reproaches Lyotard and Derrida for disregarding the institutional mechanisms whereby constitutional traditions enable democracies to correct, to limit and to ameliorate moments of unbridled majority rule, exclusionary attributions of identity and the arbitrary formation of norms. Derrida cannot have it both ways, she argues: "on the one hand he criticizes and condemns nationalism, racism, xenophobia and anti-Semitism, and on the other hand, he undermines the conceptual bases for holding on to those universalistic moral and political principles in the name of which alone such critique can be carried out" (Benhabib, 1994, p. 21).

Similar criticisms are made by McLaren (1994). Because Lyotard largely disregards what the individual has in common with other human beings, the difference between people is pictured in a discourse of power. The otherness of the other has to be radicalized in Lyotard in order to safeguard a place for her, McLaren argues. There is a danger that Lyotard's uncritical celebration of multiplicity and heterogeneity could be used in the politics of multiculturalism as an excuse to exoticize otherness: to support a regressive nativism that locates difference in a primeval past of cultural authenticity. It is also troubling, says McLaren, that Lyotard's view of the subaltern subject repudiates all attempts to name such a subject, even provisionally, on the grounds that any form of naming is an act of appropriation and ultimately an act of violence—a position that can lead to both political and pedagogical paralysis. To name otherness suggests a tolerance of difference rather than an engagement. Lyotard's project thus lacks the substantive elements necessary for guiding our choices toward these ends.

Does the postmodern project in the moral domain necessarily lead to value nihilism and educational immobilism? McKinney argues that any principle that might give us direction is just as likely to blind and repress: "This conviction that we are doomed to choose, with every choice resulting in the omission of and harm to other values, is the essential truth of a postmodern ethics" (McKinney, 1992, p. 400). The only advice this kind of ethics can offer is to keep the debate as fair as possible (free from manipulative interests); it is thus more procedural than content-oriented. Intimate solidarity is always only a local and exclusionary affair: though many mourn the loss of the old consensus about public virtue, that loss is a gain for those who were excluded in the past. McKinney argues that we must give up relying on a form of *phronesis* that only works if we all agree on the same moral paradigm. Following Caputo, he argues that the modern megapolis requires "civility," a kind of metaphronesis; that is, the skill to cope with competing paradigms. The corresponding ethic: "is thus grounded in suspicion, since we know that every good proposal eventually becomes 'inflexible and repressive'" (McKinney, 1992, p. 404), though this is not necessarily inimical to the support of institutions and communities. The need to arrive at consensus, and to institutionalize it as the alternative to paralysis and despair, is urgent. Nevertheless, we must always be willing to relinquish a way of life that is no longer working—as all ways of life inevitably and eventually do cease to work. But when it comes to deciding whether to defend an institution, McKinney simply recommends that we get as many kinds of people together as possible and let them hammer out an answer. Other authors go a step further than this rather modest advice, further beyond the suspicion and distrust which in some sense always seems inherent in postmodern ethics.

On the one hand, a repudiation of foundations can be seen as an advantage for morality centered on a concern with ethical motives. The rehabilitation of our moral sensitivity preempts a concern for moral disinterestedness. However, an emphasis on the psychodynamics of behavior may also include a rejection of universalism as morally irrelevant and morally counterproductive. It is right to cultivate loyalty to our own historical place, our country, a particular context of embodied meanings. But ethical narratives are not interesting just because they are authentic. They need a further reference to shared experiences if they are to be interesting and not merely eccentric. Perhaps our unique place is ethically interesting not so much because it is ours, but because it is here that we can begin to understand something of what, in a general sense, can be called good. What binds me to this place is not purely its historical particularity but something universal (for instance, the achievement of freedom, the common good). Incidentally, doesn't the abstract universalism of rights always remain a preliminary condition for any social attachment? Morality seems to be in need not only of an anchoring in the warmth of my nest, and acceptance of what is, but also of a minimum tension between "is" and "ought." As De Wachter argues: "An ethos is only ethical if it refers to more than its own body of symbols, if it also is modelled by its own uncertainty, if it abandons the nostalgia for its own code, if it is conscious of more than its own consensus. The good then is both the object of experience and transcendence" (1994, p. 85).

Accordingly, he argues that a narrative is ethically interesting when others can learn from it, when it refers to experiences that can be shared, and when it contains a promise of universality, but reminds us at the same time that only a story that is deeply embedded in the contextuality of authentic experience can be morally instructive. Without a minimum of decontextualization, without a minimum of alienation, without the subtle introduction of a universalistic principle to contrast with the obviousness of the self, this content is never truly ethical, De Wachter argues.

According to Benhabib (1994), what we need is an articulation of the normative bases of cosmopolitan republicanism in an increasingly decentered, fragmented world, depicted in an anti-metaphysical philosophy: a new *jus gentium* that can transcend the self-centered narcissism of nations and force them to recognize the rights of others like them. The philosophical choice that Lyotard confronts us with between an account of language as subjectless and the Cartesian myth of a perfectly self-transparent subject, is therefore unhelpful. It is particularly unhelpful if we want to account for the creation of new meaning, escape from cliché, and articulate new modes of saying and doings things, all so essential in reconfiguring the social world.

While we can agree that any and all structures of meaning may be deconstructed and reshaped, it is difficult to accept that we should view conceptual structure as hopelessly unjust or terroristic in itself. The law of difference can allow that any narrative constructions or stories we tell about ourselves, the world and others are always open to redescription, so the self is never bound within a single, or even necessarily coherent, narrative. The tools of narrative are not the property of an individual, but the product of history, culture and community, which are themselves not homogeneous. Unremitting deconstruction of any and all subjects will produce an ethical paralysis. So it is the prioritization of difference that seems problematic, along with the underlying idea that individual uniqueness opens us all to exploitation and sets us necessarily against each other.

The poststructural critique of language and adoption of the law of difference do not preclude the existence of the subject. A reading of poststructuralism need only imply that the self is not autonomous, not wholly self-creating or single-minded and coherent. Moreover, in realizing that we are never a member of a single community, and identifying ourselves sometimes as members of marginalized communities, we can find tools to imagine a world other than that of liberalism. Recognizing each of us as potentially radically plural makes alternative discourses an open possibility, but requires no reference to some unpresentable that makes us who we are, a fiction that overlooks the possibility of infinite redescriptions made possible by identifying new communities. Even if there is no single description of the human condition, taking the law of difference as our guiding principle and treating contingency as an absolute does not leave us impotent or speechless.

When the subject is characterized only by the mark of difference, the postmodernist loses the political game. The goal of the politics of difference could rather be to encourage self-respect and self-knowledge among individuals whose identity has previously been silenced, devalued or erased because they belong to some group devalued in the ruling ideology. Individuals can then work as members of various communities and insert their needs into the larger social structure, undermining the complacency of the existing social and political "we." Politics seems as much in need of sameness and unity as of difference as a basis for group identification. There is nothing progressive in itself about change, particularly if it obstructs oppositional politics by repudiating the formation of community and of coherent subjects, both of which are necessary for the identity formation of otherness.

QUERIES AND EXPECTATIONS, PROMISES AND DELUSIONS FOR THE EDUCATOR

Postmodernist authors have correctly criticized the stress on performativity in the educational system and the scientization of the human sciences. It is another question as to whether the postmodernists promises of emancipation will be able to illuminate or, in the end, only delude. Some postmodernisms in their radical mistrust of society and its institutions lose their grasp on the possibility of social change and may create chaos. In stressing the individual's obligation to shape her own life and give meaning to it, we may lose sight of that which alone can give life meaning. If one accepts the critique of Benhabib and others concerning the implications for society at large, their perspective might disclose a more fruitful way to deal generally with the educational system. Curriculum content, accountability, pupils' options and so on and so forth—all these matters might be interestingly looked at from an amended postmodernist position.

Having indicated the characteristics of postmodern ethics and the problems it confronts us with, we now have to turn to the predicament of the (individual) educator who finds herself amid value pluralism and abandoned by grand metanarratives. Does not education necessarily invoke some deliberative process? But isn't rational deliberation precisely what is criticized by postmodern authors? If education still stands, how has it too been shifted?

Particularity

It is difficult to see how Foucault's idea of freedom, an unremitting flight from the self, can play a substantial role in education—though it rightly predisposes us against the over-zealous educator who tries to mold the child's subjectivity according to a preconceived form. It suggests that our responsibility toward any individual pupil does not depend on who she is, what she is or what she can already do, and that we must leave her future as open as possible, always taking notice of her desire, resisting the tendency to determine (psychologically or otherwise) what she can or may do. Yet abandoning any norms completely would deny to a teacher any critique of the way a human life can be led. To argue that action needs no theoretical justification, and that justification could only be rationalization, repudiates the possibility of reflection before one's action and is logically inconsistent. Again, taking Lyotard's and Derrida's insistence on otherness to the extreme may in its turn lead to educational immobility. The exhortation to go beyond previously developed concepts not only generates a logical problem (How else can we speak than with fragments from the past?), but presupposes that change is necessary, while offering no justification for this assumption.

A way out of this blind alley might be found if we accept the position that the educator cannot but offer the child at least a possible way of living a human life. Without the initiation into intersubjectivity, a subject cannot find identity. The illusion that intersubjectivity makes the subject unfree is based on a mirage of absolute freedom. The idea that intersubjectivity imposes on the other because it denies her possible radical difference, is also based on the mistaken disregard of what human beings have in common with each other—minimally, the prerequisite of being recognized as human. Finally, if one accepts that the individual is responsible for her actions—even if one assumes the subject is passive concerning her basic values—one must also accept that the subject has some ethical bedrock, some guiding criteria. How could this be denied, if the intersubjectivity is characterized not only by language but also by action? The real violence in ethics and in education seems to be indifference toward the other, denying her any status as human. Thus the "closure" Derrida refers to turns out to be essential if one cares for the other. Maybe this is—to use a Wittgensteinian image—a fly-bottle one needs to be inside. If one wants to take some action for the benefit of someone else, there is only that person and this society to start from. To put this more generally, something between complete transparency and total obscurity may offer a more viable alternative for a concept of the subject, of ethics and of education.

The following quotation from Wittgenstein's *On Certainty* indicates a more subtle concept of the subject which might prove interesting: "I, L.W., believe, am sure, that my friend hasn't sawdust in his body or in his head, even though I have no direct evidence of my senses. I am sure, by reason of what has been said to me, of what I have read, and of my experience. To have doubts about it would seem to be madness—of course, this is also in agreement with other people, but *I* agree with them" (Wittgenstein, 1969, # 281). Wittgenstein seems to insist that the person's own judgment is based on intersubjective criteria but nonetheless expresses her own approval of others' application of the criteria in this particular case. This kind of position, based on a different concept of intention compared to Descartes or to phenomenology, is further developed by Harry Frankfurt. While Frankfurt recognizes that we are not free simply to believe what we choose, he does not deny that we can distance ourselves from our own assumptions and make significant judgments as to what we (want to) do (though not from an Archimedean point, not from nowhere). What then could follow for education?

Education is probably not possible without some determination of the nature of human being. The person of the educator seems to play an important part in that. The sacrifices parents make show the importance they give to raising their children. It is displayed in who they are, by what, in their eyes, it is right to do. In the discussions they have with each other and with others, they decide what it means to educate. There are certain things that are acceptable to them and others which cannot be considered. Their personal achievements and failures are often connected to the demands of those they shape through their education. Their behavior is furthermore marked by their parental attachments: one certainly differentiates between one's own children and the children of others, and in deciding what is best for one's children, decides what it is to be a good parent. Similarly, in their behavior toward children it will become clear what educators stand for. Attention to the particular is the essence of what they have to do. They will indeed act differently if their own children are concerned. And though aspects of their behavior are subject to objective moral judgment, an important part of what they do will rest on the basis of personal commitment. Education is a personal relationship to a real person, helping her to develop her individuality vis-à-vis others within a particular situation. Finally, it seems clear that education is socially embedded in a particular community into which one initiates the pupil or student.

Integrity and Hypocrisy

To be present as a person means to be present as one really is, not as how one prefers to be perceived, or thinks one should be perceived. The educator invites the child to see the world as she sees it, a perception that determines what is good from the educator's perspective. The denial of the importance of the personal in education neglects, among other things, the very things that make life meaningful. The relative coherence found in the life of the adult is offered to the child as an aid to achieving her own coherence. Alongside care, integrity appears as a necessary condition and deceit an assault on any process of meaning-giving. Defeat will nourish suspicion and unless the child can acquire her own integrity she will have no life worth living. The educator is therefore not a hidden manipulator, but elicits appropriate behavior through her own integrity. Only if she makes clear the weaknesses of her own position while making explicit what she stands for, can the educator successfully appeal to those to be educated. Integrity also seems important in finding a balance between what one experiences externally and internally as good in leading a decent life. It is necessary to make clear what the concept of integrity refers to as it is by no means unequivocal. One way to do this is by contrasting it with its converse, hypocrisy. Surely we don't want hypocrites for educators.

Crisp and Cowton (1994) differentiate four different forms of this particular vice. The hypocrisy of pretence exists in any kind of pretence to virtue. The hypocrisy of blame indicates moral criticism of others by those with moral faults of their own. Where one fails to live up to one's own espoused morals, the authors speak of hypocrisy of inconsistency. Finally there is complacency, taking morality seriously in very unimportant ways but ignoring its demands where their fulfilment appears costly. Evidently, all four kinds are undesirable in educational contexts. The strand that runs through the various kinds of hypocrisy is not, however, the lack of integrity, but a failure to take morality seriously. If one does take it seriously and demonstrates an active and genuine concern to be moral, it becomes clear, they argue, that a metavirtue is involved, a concern to be virtuous. Not only do we want educators to have this concern, we also want to see it passed on to their pupils and students.

With the help of the concept of integrity something more can be said. Integrity could mean a number of different things in the wide range of educational contexts. Calhoun (1995) discusses three pictures of integrity. The "integrated self" view conceives integrity as the integration of parts of oneself (desires, evaluations, commitments) into a whole. A person who cannot or does not decide which of her desires to pursue lacks integrity. Obviously, this is not what one wants in an educator. But again one can ask, is decisiveness enough? Though indicating some important, necessary conditions of integrity (for example, not just following the crowd), this reduces integrity to volitional unity and thus obscures the fact that persons can have good reasons for resisting the resolution of conflicting commitments and for ambivalence regarding their own desires. (This is often the case in educational contexts.) The integrated self picture of integrity does not qualify any further the kinds of reasons that can motivate persons displaying this kind of integrity. Simply acting according to one's own reasons seems, however, insufficient. Moreover, some sorts of reasons seem incompatible with integrity: for example a primary concern with comfort, material gain, and pleasure, to the expense of one's own judgments as to what is worth doing.

The focus of the "identity" view is fidelity to those projects and principles that are constitutive of one's core identity. This comes down to having a character and being true to it, again something we want in an educator. But, Calhoun argues, identifying oneself with a desire does not entail that this person also endorse that desire. We expect persons of integrity not only to stand up for their most deeply felt commitments, but to treat all their endorsements as worthy to be those of any reflective agent. Acting on the deep impulses that define our psychological sense of self seems to have little to do with integrity, since agents may repudiate their deepest impulses.

Maintaining the purity of one's own agency (especially in compromising situations) characterizes the "clean hands" view of integrity. Here a person places the importance of principle and purity of conscience above consequentialist concerns. This picture also needs completion, though some such kind of integrity is without doubt important for educators. It points to something else, to the significance of formulating and exemplifying one's own views. Those who don't do so exchange conscientious action for gain, status, reward, approval, or escape from penalties, loss of status or disapproval; or they exchange their own views too readily for those of others more authoritative, more in step with public opinion, less demanding of themselves, and so on.

Calhoun argues that each of these three pictures of integrity ultimately reduces it to less than it fully involves (respectively, to coherent agency, to sustained identity and to the conditions for having a reason to refuse cooperating with some evils.) The three accounts also see integrity as a personal rather than a social virtue. Guarding one's integrity must be largely self-protective: for the sake of one's autonomy, one's character and one's agency one stands by one's own best judgment. But as Calhoun argues, this approach fails to provide an adequate explication of what it means to stand for something; it cannot make the relation of the person of integrity to other people central to integrity. The educational importance of bringing a relationship to other persons to the forefront of our account cannot be overestimated. We will develop the notion of standing for something as central to the meaning of integrity. Thus it will be seen that the principles and values which, in one's own best judgment, are worthy of defense refer to what we are interested in, concerning the just life and the good life.

The person of integrity is precisely the person who thinks that it matters to stand by one's judgment as to the good or the just. As a social virtue, integrity is tightly connected to viewing oneself as a member of a community that makes judgments of value and to caring about what that community endorses. Value is attached not to the "ownedness" of a view, but to something else which includes formulating and acting on one's own views as an integral part. "Having and acting on identity-conferring commitments is thus valuable, not because of the sheer fact that they are one's own, but because having and acting on deep commitments is part of any admirable, flourishing life worth living, and *that* kind of life is what has value" (Calhoun, 1995, p. 255).

Persons of integrity believe their own judgments matter, or ought to matter, to fellow deliberators. This shows why misleading others infringes one's integrity, in itself rather than for its effects on the hypocrite. It also helps show why we care that persons have the courage of their convictions. At the same time integrity calls us to take seriously others' doubts about our convictions.

Conceived thus as a social virtue, integrity can also be a corrective for an ethics of care, which though pointing to an important aspect of ethics, nevertheless still seems to be inadequate. The care perspective involves seeing oneself as connected to others within a web of relationships. But because this involves giving support to someone else's goals, the choice of whom to care for, and whether to continue a caring relationship, become significant moral matters. If one becomes engrossed in someone morally corrupt oneself, argues Davion (1993), one may become morally corrupted. Before becoming engrossed in another and displacing one's interest onto that person, one must judge them worthy of one's concern. Furthermore, because we cannot have caring relationships with most people in the world, we need other kinds of grounds for our obligations to them.

Trust

Besides particularity and integrity, an important characteristic of the educational relationship is trust. In contrast to reliance, trust does not require reasons. On the contrary, trust seems to provide the framework necessary for reasons to make sense. As they grow, children learn both to distinguish between objects that can and can't satisfy their needs and how to evaluate their own desires. In both cases, parents play a crucial role in teaching their children the appropriateness of certain reasons for particular actions. The preparedness of a child to do what her parents ask her to do relies on nothing more fundamental than the fact that her parents ask her to do so. It is only because we have a fundamental preparedness to accept what others teach us that we can learn to understand reasons for actions, the difference between good and evil, what is relevant and not, and so forth. As Wittgenstein argued: "I believe what people transmit to me in a certain manner. In this way I believe geographical, chemical, historical facts etc. That is how I *learn* the sciences. Of course learning is based on believing. If you have learnt that Mont Blanc is 4000 metres high, if you have looked it up on the map, you say you *know* it. And can it now be said: we accord credence in this way because it has proved to pay?" (Wittgenstein, 1969, #170).

Just as doubt comes after belief, the criteria for the truth of what we are taught cannot be questioned during the teaching itself if the teaching is to succeed. Hertzberg (1988) argues that a situation involving trust is one in which I may come to believe something simply because I trust the person in question. When I trust someone she personifies goodness and because there are people toward whom I have such an attitude, I can understand goodness and reasons. Following Wittgenstein who discussed epistemic (1969, ## 34, 170, 509, 672) and existential (1993, p. 383) trust, Hertzberg calls trust a primitive reaction. While not consciously deliberated by the child, this reaction is basic to intersubjectivity itself and plays a crucial role in the initiation of the child into society. Its destruction, as for instance in nearly all cases of incest, makes life a tragedy for the victim.

Baier (1994) argues that women cannot see morality as essentially a matter of keeping to a sort of minimal moral traffic rules, designed to restrict close encounters between autonomous persons to those we choose for ourselves:

Such a conception presupposes both an equality of power and a natural separateness from others, which are alien to women's experience of life and morality. For those most of whose daily dealings are with the less powerful or the more powerful, a moral code designed for those equal in power will be at best nonfunctional, at worst an offensive pretense of equality as a substitute for its actuality. But equality is not even a desirable ideal in all relationships—children not only are not but should not be equal in power to adults—and we need a morality to guide us in our dealings with those who either cannot or should not achieve equality of power (animals, the ill, the dying, children while still young) with those with whom they have unavoidable and often intimate relationships. (p.116)

From this perspective education can be conceived of as accepting the child as a gift, and so as recognizing her, as opening up for her and seeing this situation as an opportunity to give shape to a human life so that she can develop as completely as possible. Education is an answer from one individual person to another in a particular situation. Because of this particularity, care, integrity and trust are of the utmost importance.

If one believes that subjectivity does perform a foundational function in the context of modernity, what kind of subjectivity can perform that function now? Ferrara (1994) argues that the notion of authentic subjectivity is to contemporary modernity as the notion of autonomous subjectivity is to early modernity. Contemporary universalism needs to be described by reference to the model of reflective judgment. If autonomy refers to an agent's accountability in her choice of a course of action, authentic conduct is somehow connected with, and expressive of, the core of the actor's personality. Talk of authenticity refers to the affective dimension of rationality and the rational dimension of affect. But there are two kinds of authenticity: antagonistic and integrative. Antagonistic authenticity either expresses something in opposition to the demands of society and culture or sees social expectations, roles and institutions not as merely constraining or repressive, but also as creating the symbolic material out of which authentic selves and authentic conduct can be generated (cf. Rousseau, Schiller, Herder, Kierkegaard). The antagonistic model invites us to view all attempts to bring self-experience to a synthesis with suspicion. The two versions involve different conceptions of the modern differentiation of the value spheres: on the one hand breaking free of established normativity, on the other reconciling all the constitutive moments of the self under the aegis of a unique life-project.

It will be clear that the idea of authentic identity only makes sense within a context of intersubjectivity. An agent cannot articulate a project concerning who she wants to be on her own. Such a project must constitute a particularly illuminating example of what can be done in a certain social predicament. Furthermore, authentic identity presupposes a moment of recognition on the part of another. Authentic identity will thus mean pursuing a project in which a willed uniqueness is expressed and the wish for others to recognize this unique person whom we want to become. The agent is willing to take the risk that her intended identity will not be recognized. Finally, there is a central role here for reflective judgment (cf. Kant), which presupposes the ability to think for oneself, to be able to think from other people's perspectives and to think consistently. Recalling the intersubjective origin of identity, the need for recognition and the intersubjective nature of reflective judgment should dispel the impression that authenticity is yet another restatement of the philosophy of the subject.

If the educator is characterized by her willingness to stand for something and simultaneously willing to care for someone, then the philosophy of authenticity, thus conceived, should also help the educator out of the problems that the Enlightenment project and of some of its critics have pressed on her. While her integrative authenticity should rescue her from despair, it should also correct the possible immobilism occasioned by the interpretation of some postmodernist authors. If knowledge is based on "agreement of judgments" (cf. Wittgenstein, 1953, I, # 242), not only does education look different, the educator does so too. And for the person receiving education, not only is there more room, there are also more rooms. Still she remains in the house of Being.

NOTE

1. *Logocentrism* refers to the dominance of a certain kind of calculative rationality, for instance in means-end reasoning.

Chapter 6

Giving Someone a Lesson

Key words: gift, given, delivery, economy
Aims of this chapter: The aims of this chapter are to provide you with a clear understanding of teaching and learning in conditions of postmodernity and to acquaint you with the sorts of skills that you will need as a teacher in such conditions.
Objectives of this chapter: At the end of this chapter you will be able to:
- produce a lesson plan with clearly specified objectives
- explain how to organize and run a learning environment
- list the competences needed by the postmodern teacher
- explain how to deal with the unexpected in the learning environment

In the 1950s the playwright John Osborne, commenting on the conventional form of drama then dominating the London stage, coined the phrase "the well-made play." A well-made play would have a drawing-room setting; it would concern the fortunes and misfortunes of the well-to-do, its milieu and preoccupations predictable. From a clear though cumbersome exposition it would develop a well crafted story, nicely resolved with loose ends tied up. Osborne railed against the complacency and sterile conventionality of such dramas and their dislocation from reality.

What would a well-made lesson be like? Student teachers are typically required to document their practice with detailed lesson plans. This preparation, it is implied, is a key to good teaching itself. What is the character of this practice? Teaching and learning must be determined in accordance with learning outcomes and objectives. Let us see this as an economy of exchange. The efforts of teacher and pupils are directed by these outcomes. What is to be learned is made clear to the students while these processes must in turn be transparent and available to scrutiny. Teaching and learning in this manner dovetails with inspection and accounting and with the efficient use of resources. The teacher becomes a learning resource. This economy of exchange is suggested also in the vocabulary of "stakeholders," "learning entitlements," "vouchers" and "contracts." Efficiency and effectiveness become eminently rational criteria in this smooth-running system of circulation.

One can trace roots of this conception in behaviorism, in legacies of Taylorism and Fordism, and—now perhaps more evident than for some time—in the economic circumstances in which education operates. Beyond this, however, a whole metaphysical picture is at stake with implications for the way what is learned is conceived and for the idea of good teaching. What is learned is quantifiable. The teacher is a transmitter of learning content. Delivery and communication become key concepts in this process.

The good teacher does not require "barmy theory" but a set of competences. *Competence* becomes a common noun in a kind of aggressive reification: a practical skill that gets results. The teacher needs communication skills. At one time the good teacher was expected to present a lesson didactically from the front of the class. Now, as a facilitator, she manages learning, and this should be increasingly independent. Packaged learning makes possible the tailoring of a curriculum to the individual's needs. In place of mastery of a subject, the teacher needs skills to exploit the new technology of the learning center and to teach students to learn-how-to-learn. Content, reduced to information, is separable from skills of presentation and delivery.

The student now has ownership of her work, proceeding at her own pace according to her specific needs. She must be active and collaborate in her learning, and to access the diverse opportunities that life and learning present to her she must acquire a range of competencies; indeed this is what education is about. She plans her life by planning her education, knowing that learning must now be lifelong. She acquires flexible transferable skills, skills that enable her to travel light. Assessment comes to determine all activities on a course, delineating the curriculum and efficiently channeling the teacher's effort. What is to be learned appears in manageable, clearly defined tasks, providing regular reinforcement for the student. The total requirements of a subject are then easily surveyed while quality control gains rigor.

Such practice proclaims commitment to student-centeredness. Yet the ease and efficiency of the delivery that is sought, the lightening of the burden of content in favor of skills, suggest a distortion of the progressivism that was the source of that principle. The curriculum is not so much student-centered as resource-centered, its efficient control limiting possibilities of spontaneous growth of interest and absorption in content, with all the risk and unpredictability that that can entail. The student is a customer who follows her desires, who can easily avoid content that is difficult or challenging. Where what is learned is subordinated to outcomes and usefulness, intrinsic worth will be surreptitiously eclipsed. It is a different idea of education that she acquires.

Our caricature must not obscure the real benefits that it nevertheless depicts. With mass provision especially, matters of accountability, equity and the effective use of public money are understandably addressed in rational systematic terms. Moreover, the picture is softened by other developments—the reflective practitioner, a commitment to empowerment—if these are not colonized by managerialism. And surely, it might be maintained, it is anyway the outcomes that most concern the student. What can education give her? We shall see.

Where economy of delivery is paramount and teaching is theorized as fixed recipes, the variety of good practice can be suppressed. The wise teacher cultivates a range of approaches appropriate to different circumstances and injects vitality. The difference among teachers reveals variety of a different kind. One engages in meticulous preparation so that lessons run with clockwork efficiency. Another lacks organization but enthrals the class through enthusiasm for what is taught. Another lacks these qualities but is sensitive to children's needs and exceptionally able to gain their confidence. These qualities differ in value according to circumstance. With a levelling or uniformity of teaching styles this variety is lost.

Are these differences to be understood in terms of oppositions between student-centered and subject-centered practice, between experiential and book learning, between facilitation and didactic teaching? This chapter avoids the hardening of these oppositions, seeing this as a sclerosis in educational thought and practice. It will try to reveal a fluid complexity that current theory and practice overlook. It will further the consideration in this book of aspects of language and practice that seem minor or peripheral—if not odd or aberrant. In this it will follow lines of thought in recent writings of Jacques Derrida.

Let us move forward by attending to our words. What might be involved in giving a lesson or lecture? What is given in a lesson? What of the given in the geometrical proof? What of the *data* researchers amass? We will encounter risks where things do not go according to plan, and where we cannot always see what we are doing. We must face a partial paradox: contrary to our expectations of transparency and scrutiny, we may learn and understand more, as Aristotle intimates, where we cannot always see:

In his *De Anima* (421b) he distinguishes between man and those animals that have hard, dry eyes [*tôn sklerophtalmôn*], the animals lacking eyelids, that sort of sheath or tegumental membrane [*phragma*] which serves to protect the eye and permits it, at regular intervals, to close itself off in the darkness of inward thought or sleep. What is terrifying about an animal with hard eyes and a dry glance is that it always sees. (Derrida, 1983, p. 5)

How strong our faith in the optical dimension! But it may be necessary to close the eyes the better to attend. Beyond the up-front visibility of our behavior, expressions denoting our common practices—giving a lecture, giving a lesson—carry cryptic resonances of ineffable secrecy. They suggest different possibilities of education.[1]

Can we deliver? Today, it is asked if the manager or, *pari passu*, the teacher can deliver. It is no surprise that reviews of education in the United Kingdom have latterly been entrusted to Sir Ron Dearing, the former director of the postal system (hence an expert in delivery). But just as letters are delivered so also is a good speech. Socrates was an expert in delivery, a midwife to the birth of knowledge. But how is delivery different from giving? What after all is it to give?

What do the following have in common: on the one hand, to give a ring, a bracelet, to give something to drink and to eat and, on the other hand, to give an impression, to give a feeling, to give a show or play? The latter are all expressions that appeal irreducibly to the idiom and in principle therefore they have only a limited translatability. What is common to and what is the connection between "to give the time" and "to give a price" (in the sense of the auction bid: "I will give you so much for it"), between *donner une facilité* [to facilitate, as in a facilitated payment plan] and "give an order," between "give information," "give a course, a class, and a seminar," "give a lesson" (which is something completely different) and "give chase," "give signs," and so forth? Each time a structural difference of the given presents itself: It can be an apparently natural or material thing (water), a symbolic thing (a ring), a person (to give one's daughter or son in marriage, to give a child, to give a king to one's country), a discourse (still another order of the gift: to give a lecture, to give an order; once again the nature of the discourse alters each time the structure of the gift). Each time, then, the structural difference of the gi*ven* seems, and we do say *seems*, to transmit to the operation of the gi*ving* an irremediable heterogeneity. (Derrida, 1992c, pp. 49-50)

What is it to give a class or lesson? What is given when one learns? What is the gift of teaching? Let us begin with what is given.

The learner never begins at the beginning. Something has always been done before, something is taken for granted, a practice is already underway. When the child begins arithmetic, she has already played with bricks or sweets and already counted. What, after all, is it to begin arithmetic? A whole background of experience is taken for granted—a certain physiology and physical abilities, the syntax of a certain language. The teacher is already on the way and the child must begin by copying. The child must repeat without understanding in order to enter into the practice. Once the child is on the way, understanding can dawn. Is this education? In some languages a distinction is drawn that separates this elementary training. Wittgenstein speaks of *Abrichten*, a word used also for horse-breaking (1953, # 5). In training we begin by copying—perhaps by being forced to copy—given behavior. What we begin with is given, with a disproportion between what is taught and what is learned.

If this is initiation into a form of life (understood in terms of integrally related language and practices of a fairly unsophisticated kind), similar implications hold for cultural initiation at more sophisticated levels. How does the autonomy of the learner relate to such an initiation? What are the limits of this initiation? The idea that initiation into a culture is a tidy process to which there is a completion is alien to the very idea of culture, itself deeply interwoven with the idea of a liberal education. That there are developmental stages does not fundamentally alter the point: the cultural context is given with all that that entails. Rational autonomy is empty in abstraction from the cultural context: for that context gives principles their sense. This giving of culture is necessary for education. Consider Stanley Cavell:

What I require is a convening of my culture's criteria, in order to confront them with my words and life as I pursue them and as I may imagine them; and at the same time to confront my words and life as I pursue them with the life my culture's words may imagine for me: to confront the culture with itself along the lines in which it meets in me.

This seems to me a task that warrants the name of philosophy. It is also the description of something we might call education. (1979, p. 125)

The necessary convening of the culture's criteria reveals a level of culture that is not open to choice but that provides both grounds and capacity for choice. Not that one's culture is a unified or stable thing. Even the idea that one has a culture is suspect because, especially in the complex patterns of contemporary existence, most people find themselves in a complex weave of different cultural strands. In and through such a weave autonomous beings emerge. Wittgenstein puts this more provocatively. If our early learning must be a kind of obedience, "culture itself is an observance. Or at least it presupposes an observance" (1980, p. 83e). It involves attention and conformity with what is done, its development presupposing a large measure of prior acceptance. Wittgenstein's language here has a religious tone.

For some such remarks may prove troubling, even annoying. They defy the desire for an understandable beginning to things, for a rational foundation for what we do; they reject the kind of detachment, spectatorial rationality and universalizability that have characterized a certain philosophical tradition. Foundationalist modes of thinking, such as logical empiricism, fail on this view to recognize the background. In Heidegger's terms the background involves a *Vorhabe*: we need to appreciate the way circumstances *have us*. Backgrounds enable human beings to be. The background is that which preserves, its reality something to which a religious attitude might be directed, a different focusing of our contemporary cultural practices, a kind of reverence perhaps (Dreyfus, 1980, p. 23). Such an attitude would be a resistance against the nihilism engendered where the objectifying tendencies of modernity eclipse or disperse these practices. That there is a background must be acknowledged, as must its particular (fragile and contingent) forms.

Teaching and learning presuppose the given. What is passed on is given. Simone Weil considers waiting on truth against active pursuit and planning:

We do not obtain the most precious gifts by going in search of them but by waiting for them. Man cannot discover them by his powers and if he sets out to seek for them he will find in their place counterfeits of which he will be unable to discern the falsity. . . . In every school exercise there is a special way of waiting upon truth, setting our hearts upon it, yet not allowing ourselves to go out in search of it. There is a way of giving attention to the data of a problem in geometry without trying to find the solution, or to the words of a Latin or Greek text without trying to arrive at the meaning, a way of waiting, when we are writing, for the right word to come of itself at the end of our pen, when we must reject all inadequate words. (1977, p. 73)

In geometry we work with the given, toward truths that are analytic unfoldings of the given. In translation we wait for the word to come. Moving from receptivity to creativity, we do not acquisitively seek but go by the way of dispossession.[2] *Es gibt, ça donne*, what gives? (in colloquial American English)—these expressions speak of a kind of giving that does not identify a giver. (Heidegger: *Es gibt die Zeit, es gibt das Sein.*) The path that we must join, the background

that has us, we are back with the idea of the given. Consider Kierkegaard's advice
on preparing sermons:

When you go for a walk you must let your thoughts flutter randomly, letting them have a
go now here, now there. That is how to arrange one's housekeeping. Themata are the
accidents that the week should deliver to you in abundance. But the more you see to it that
the dividends are uncertain, the freer, better, richer they will become, and the more
striking, surprising, penetrating. (1996, p. 454)

This housekeeping is an economy where outcomes are left to take care of
themselves. What would it be to give in this way: to give a lecture, to give advice
and guidance, to give comments on essays, to give credit?

We began by considering delivery. As Heidegger earlier recognized, the idea
of delivery has the effect of separation: the action is independent of the content,
just as a vehicle can be used to carry a variety of different goods; the deliverer
and the recipient are independent, relating to one another on a quasi-contractual
basis. There is an association of ideas captured by the German *Zustellung*
(delivery), *Vorstellung* (representation), and *Nachstellung* (safeguarding):
everything is conceived in terms of a problematics of representation and the
subject-object relation. For Heidegger the idea of delivery suggested the atomic
age and the delivery of missile systems.

How can giving be different from delivery? There are subtle gradations and
modulations here. If we substitute delivery for giving in the quotation from
Derrida earlier in this section, these begin to come into view. In the giving of a
ring or of food, delivery introduces an anonymous third party in a role different
from that of the giver. In the more idiomatic expressions, "delivery" sounds out
of place, however seamlessly the idea of delivering a speech adapts to teaching.
The apparent sameness effected by delivery's separation of action from content
covers over the irremediable heterogeneity that arises from the categorial
difference of the given in different cases. If someone gives a ring, a gift is
received. If a revolver is given in to the police, however, this is no gift. Neither
are those who are given a lesson in possession of a gift. What is given in the first
two cases is a material object. In the lesson, in contrast, the given is complex: the
particular material or content that is passed on, the background of assumptions and
practices against which this content can make sense, the style and energy of the
presentation . . . the good teacher gives something of herself. Are content and
method discrete? They seem to defy the separation that the idea of delivery put
into effect. Rifts in the passage between these different inflections of "to give"
reveal its unavoidable idiomatic complications.

Let us try to draw out a broad distinction in giving, setting aside for the
moment more subtle gradations. On the one hand, there is the kind of reciprocal
giving with which festivals and other aspects of our social lives are marked. We
give presents. Objects are presented; parcels are opened often with a moment of
surprise. The reciprocity consists in a kind of exchange where the costs involved
are carefully judged to maintain a balanced circulation, an economy of goods and

good-will. The metaphysics of presence incorporates a metaphysics of presents. On the other hand, there is alms-giving, where those who receive are in no position to reciprocate. Though this cannot conform to the pattern of gift exchange, there may be another kind of return—in the gratitude of the poor, in the esteem one earns from others, in self-satisfaction, perhaps in the promise of heaven. Such expenditure remains within the circle of calculation of the economic system. It is in refining this realm that Zygmunt Bauman identifies the "liminal" concept of the "pure gift:" "Judged by the ordinary standards of ownership and exchange, the pure gift is a pure loss; it is a gain solely in moral terms, the very terms that the logic of gain does not recognize. Its moral value actually rises as the loss deepens" (1990, p. 91). But if this is purity it may still not escape the currency of hubris. How could giving be free from this?

For there to be a giving without reciprocity or exchange of any kind it is necessary to break out of the circle and this will lead into the realm of paradox. The gift must not present itself as a gift, must not be a present. There must be unawareness so that gratitude does not reciprocate for the gift. There must be forgetfulness so that there remains no sense of pride or debt. This points to a kind of giving without reserve and without return—the seed-pod bursts, dehiscence of the sign. Just as the linguistic sign can never be just a functional vehicle for the communication of stable meaning from transmitter to receiver, so here this same logic of dissemination reveals possibilities of giving—possibilities arrested where a certain linguistic economy takes hold of ethics. It is a kind of dissemination with effects that must exceed anything that could be known, exceeding any presence. The paradox is that, in this best kind of giving, what is given must not be recognized as a gift because recognition returns us to the circle of reciprocity. As Derrida puts it: "let us recall here the principle guiding us in this reflection on the gift: To reduce the latter to exchange is quite simply to annul the very possibility of the gift" (1992c, p. 76). The implications of this go beyond giving to cause the institution of morality to tremble: "The link between morality and the arithmetic, economy, or calculation of pleasures imprints an equivocation on any praise of good intentions. In giving the reasons for giving, in saying the reason of the gift, it signs the end of the gift" (p. 148). In recent writings Derrida has moved toward more religious themes. The following text from the Gospel of Matthew becomes a kind of key: "But when thou doest alms, let not thy left hand know what thy right hand doeth: That thine alms may be in secret; and thy Father which seeth in secret himself shall reward thee openly" (Matthew 6: 3-4). These lines, opening onto questions of secrecy, responsibility and conscience, lead the way in this discussion of giving. There *is* something paradoxical: giving with this obliviousness, if we pursue it to this limit, seems not to be giving as we typically understand it. It may be that this conception helps to lay bare a narcissistic giving, where hypocrisy furthers the circle of exchange. Or does it just seem absurd? That the right hand should not know what the left is doing licences inefficiency and incoherence, overturning transparency and accountability. Yet in resistance to the transparent rationality of demands for efficiency and effectiveness, can the teacher attend to this?

If you love only those who love you and to the extent that they love you, if you hold so strictly to this symmetry, mutuality, and reciprocity, then you give nothing, no love, and the reserve of your wages will be like a tax that is imposed or a debt that is repaid, like the acquittal of a debt. In order to expect an infinitely higher salary, one that goes beyond the perception of what is due, you have to give without taking account and love those who don't love you. (Derrida, 1995a, p. 106)

To expect this "infinitely higher salary" is to seek no salary at all. This comes off the scale into an *an*economy of giving and receiving. We must take the idea of the given back to the discussion of language and difference in Chapter three.

Human beings come into their nature through the way their world comes to be, through the convening of their culture's criteria. The mutual appropriation that brings this about is achieved through the workings of language, paradigmatically in the giving of names. Language gives this, not a gift to be unwrapped and contemplated as object. The giving is a dissemination in which effects go beyond what could ever be seen. This language is not simply a set of tools under control: "Language gives one to think but it also steals, spirits away from us, whispers to us [*elle nous souffle*], and withdraws the possibility that it seems to inaugurate; it carries off the property of our own thoughts even before we have appropriated them" (Derrida, 1992c, p. 80). *Es gibt . . . es spukt* (Derrida, 1994, p. 172). What language gives is good and bad. In what is given there are those idiomatic strange crossings of meaning: *donner la mort* (to put to death, to take life), to give birth (and hence to make mortal), to give knowledge where this is a poisoned fruit, to dose with medicine where this is also poison. To give someone a lesson is to teach but it is also (idiomatically) to punish: how this opens onto fields of undecidability—of initiation (training or education, indoctrination or enlightenment), of discipline (behavioral or academic), of responsibility (conformity or freedom)—in which any conscientious teacher must determine her practice!

In part what is given in teaching, in the initiation into a culture, is a gift that cannot be refused. What we come to know in this way precedes the possibility of our autonomy. Closer to us than we can readily acknowledge, it is familiar, occasioning a kind of love, as perhaps for things close to the heart. Later we will ask what it is to know by heart, and how education can involve *eros*.

Evaluation

The learning outcomes listed at the start of this chapter have, it seems, slipped our grasp. The elaboration of technique they promised has come to seem progressively irrelevant. The clear picture has gradually clouded, yet necessarily so if the implications of the postmodern are to be realized. In the end, if planning is to be maintained this must not be without irony and paradox. If curriculum planning is to reflect good education, the clouding of this reflection is the breath of a kind of life.

Do you think this chapter has met its objectives? You have been given a lesson. Now you are able to move on.

NOTES

1. Derrida implies that there is a loosening of the concept of the hidden to the detriment of the understanding of mystery and of the ineffable with the transition from the Greek *kryptos* to the Latin *absconditus* (Derrida, 1995a, pp. 88-91). The kind of loss effected by this helps to lay the way for the presumptions of surveillance in contemporary educational practice.

2. In *Four Quartets* T. S. Eliot writes of "the way of ignorance," "the way of dispossession" and "the way in which you are not." These ways lead to what we do not know. These are ways we need to take (Eliot, 1968, p. 29).

Chapter 7

Telling Stories Out of School

The general population across the English-speaking world has come to mistrust educational experts. Take curriculum as an important example. Widespread misgivings about curricula come in many forms. One of the best known is that clutch of anxieties and antipathies surrounding the canon. But much else is happening in curriculum studies, including constant reevaluation of teaching methods, which disorients and unnerves ordinary people. So it is interesting to ask how curricula get established in modern societies.

A quick answer could refer to professionalized processes of curriculum development, design and evaluation, backed by a vaguely defined body of curriculum theory: the latter a mix of contributions from better established academic disciplines, in particular psychology, sociology and philosophy, and a rationalized body of educational "craft knowledge" or common sense, manifest in such techniques as content analysis, teaching skills, computer assisted learning theory (CAL) and educational media theories.

But this is only part of the story. Those who establish curricula within institutions have values and principles of their own which may not be those of curriculum developers. They are obliged to evaluate curricula not just for teaching effectiveness but also appropriateness. Curricula must be defensible in terms of the relationship—ethical and political—that they establish between the institution and the needs, wants, aspirations, obligations or rights of students or pupils. In short, the curriculum must have a legitimacy in the context in question. Without acknowledged legitimacy, the curriculum may not survive or even become established.

In this chapter, we want to use some ideas normally associated with poststructuralism to examine the nature of legitimation within the educational sphere: in particular, the concept of narrative, as developed by Jean-François Lyotard,[1] and its relationship to power. Such an analysis suggests that two different modes of legitimation are currently operative in education.

INSTITUTIONS AND THE PROBLEM OF LEGITIMACY

Most curriculum literature fits either within the genre of a rationalist and linear paradigm—of a stage-by-stage process from theorization through content development, curriculum design, pilot implementation and evaluation to established change, each stage in the hands of dedicated professional specialists—or within a genre of critique of such rationalism. But this means academic critique; so while it may abjure "rationalist" commitments to method, linearity, provider authority, value-neutrality and objectivity, it remains itself a *rational* critique of rationalism. Reasons are advanced and debated for repudiation of this or that feature of curricular rationalism: and the reasons are offered for peer assessment.

There is indeed at least one area of the education system where curricular legitimacy seems to derive from its perceived and agreed rationality, if not from rationalism, and that is higher education (at least until the recent intrusion of managerialism). The subject differentiation of university departments is a matter of more or less rational debate. And within departments (and sometimes across them), the content of courses is determined by collegial consideration of academic priorities, of intrinsic importance and pedagogic necessities.

Detailed design of a course invokes similar considerations and a rational process of curriculum development is increasingly likely to draw on a rationalized body of canonic curriculum expertise. This itself presupposes the prior institutionalization of curriculum studies, their established presence in higher education in terms of the rules, conventions, expectations, roles and purposes of its institutions. Both specific curriculum developments in higher education and the canonization of an applicable curriculum literature involve the usual academic processes of rational critique (such as peer review and critical response). And therein lie their legitimacy. They transcend the arbitrary and can offer institutionalized justifications of themselves.

Now of course school curricula can be developed in very much the same kind of way and within the same kinds of institution. And professional curriculum organizations outside higher education can share many of the ways of working of the universities. But contrary to appearances, school curricula have never *derived their legitimacy* in the same way. For whatever claims they may have made to a rational genesis and development, these claims have never sufficed for long to defend them from non-academic criticism and indeed rejection, either from within the educational establishment or from outside it. Correlatively, it may seem that where curricula have survived and prospered, it has been for reasons other than their value as products of institutionalized rational debate. Think of the public controversies surrounding New Maths in the 1970s, conservative attacks on new history curricula (in Britain) in the 1980s, the creationism controversy in the United States, the dogmatic trimming back of multi-faith religious curricula and the partly emotional and nostalgic campaigns against modern curricula for the teaching of reading.

In all these reactions, there are typically popular, demotic and even populist interests, values and commitments in play, of a sort that have been marginalized in "rational" curriculum development; beliefs that have not been and probably cannot be readily captured or justified in educational theory and have sometimes appeared, from a professional perspective, as mere prejudices, those of the uninformed public against the educational experts. Yet while these predispositions are non-academic, they are certainly not irrational or even non-rational. We think for instance of a commitment to "getting on in life," learning your "place," learning to be "one of the lads" (a "regular guy") or a "young lady," acquiring basic citizenship or knowing how to get by in the day-to-day (cookery, woodwork/DIY, basic health knowledge) or pride in your country and Christian values. In a political sense, curricula that fall foul of such reactions have lacked social and therefore political legitimacy and have tended to 'come unstuck' in the long run.

What is of interest here is not so much that these non-academic values have been in play so much as the manner in which they come into play. For they are not just non-academic but often positively anti-academic. In principle, it might be possible to draw these values into intellectual debate about education, by aiming to define them more closely, rank them as values and follow through discursive arguments as to how to integrate and balance them within the curriculum and derive their practical implications. Indeed, education academics have sometimes attempted to do precisely that.[2] But there is something about such efforts which is surely just besides the point. What is fundamental to these demotic verdicts on education is that the very attempt at legitimation by institutionalized rational critique is rejected in them. The whole point is that people who typically subscribe to these opinions do so as a strongly preferred alternative to the very possibility of expert deliberation. "Never mind what the experts think *and never mind why they think it*. This is what *we* want from education."

Why is this? Is it in itself a wholly irrational response? And is there anything educational academics could do about it and might be justified in doing? Is it helpful or illuminating here to fulminate against unbridled ideology or incoherent prejudice?

Let's start by noting that the public at large does not take educational academics at their own estimation of themselves. While academics might claim rationally grounded expertise, the public looks at the seemingly sorry consequences of expert intervention and draws accordingly sceptical conclusions. It infers that academic educationists just aren't, on the whole, truly expert and so disregards them. (It has no opportunity to invigilate expertise with rigor, itself an academic or quasi-academic job anyway.) The public may settle for limited ambitions in educational practice which it can understand and tolerate. If society aims for the Heavenly City of curricular rationality, it may yet finish holed up in some educational slum.[3] And once claims to academic expertise in education are seen as mere pretensions, the profession of educational theory comes to seem the vested interest of an entrenched academic *apparat* or priesthood.

Academics may readily chafe against such a process, which we may well find ill-informed and largely unfair. But we cannot dismiss it as merely irrational. The common curriculum in which children are to be educated as competent and responsible citizens is obviously a matter legitimately answerable to a wide variety of social interests. This historic shift against rational curriculum planning is grounded on reasons, which themselves invite a reasoned reaction. Charges of ideological blindness against an "unreasoning" public are likely to sound like feeble special pleading. Nonetheless, no one who is committed to thinking scrupulously and critically about education can simply bow the head before this inimical state of affairs.

If we concede some kind of rationality in this demotic sovereignty over educational practice, a puzzle arises. How can any kind of thinking resist incorporation within academic discourse, yet still retain the character of a rational response? One might have expected that whatever is rational must in principle be open to intellectual appreciation, appropriation or critique; but it is not clear in the case of demotic demands on education that this is so.

Primarily, philosophers think about rationality in terms of what makes for a rational argument. And disinterestedness has usually been taken to be important for rationality. Consequently, philosophers have tended to disregard the social preconditions and limits on argumentation, taking them either to be extraneous, if not invidious, to rationality or the proper concern of some other discipline, sociology perhaps. But when it comes to *rational action* and its role in society, the picture looks rather different. If rationality is to be effective in social life, then it is essential that it be institutionalized in some way or other; that is, that there be socially accepted and entrenched assumptions, forms and mechanisms for cultivating, sustaining, refurbishing or rejecting examples and exemplars of rational thought and action.

Why so? If there were no conventional canons for the acceptance of thoughts or actions as *prima facie* reasonable, every argument would stand open to radical and profound critique, involving return to first principles, before it were accepted. And without such critique, its acceptance would seem arbitrary and thus irrational. The pressure to exhaustive critique would be unrelenting yet practically impossible to accommodate. Consequently, there has to be a well-elaborated matrix of entrenched and taken-for-granted beliefs and values, patterns of inference and, in particular, conventional methods for generating and discriminating new beliefs or values. But to say that there are such matrices of the taken-for-granted, socially recognized and sustained, is to say that there are institutions underpinning rational thought and action in society.

The reason why the demotic beliefs and attitudes that concern us here cannot be assimilated into academic discourse is because the two are institutionalized in quite different ways. Academic discourse is institutionalized in particular forms of social organization. Demotic beliefs are institutionalized in what Lyotard famously refers to as narratives.[4]

To see why this is so, consider academic discourse first. As Habermas has pointed out, theoretical discourse can only flourish within a social setting that safeguards certain forms of democratic openness; open as to participation (under limitations of competence), opinion and respect for the needs of individual participants.[5] It is incorporated and embedded in such social forms as the university, the academic journal or society or the seminar or conference. The overriding necessity for rational intellectual discourse is to be unfettered by convention, personal prejudice and power, and thus ring-fenced in some way against them. The intrinsic aim of such discourse is for debate to follow where argument leads, irrespective of practical consequences.

Consider by contrast the task of demotic thought and action in a sphere such as education. What keeps the social enterprise of education ticking over in a more or less orderly fashion? One might well say the exercise of pure power: either the legitimate power of the state or its officers (headmasters, national advisory bodies, inspectors, individual teachers and so on), or the more doubtful power of the educational entrepreneur—the think-tank propagandist, the industrial spokesperson, the text-book publisher—perhaps manipulative, perhaps unreflective, perhaps opportunist. Clearly there is a lot of truth to such an answer. However, exercises of power can only succeed within a context of the accepted and taken-for-granted. The scene on which any educational activity takes place needs its own coherence and perspicuity to the educational actors and agents. But rigorous and continuous intellectual critique is ill-suited to secure this coherence and perspicuity. Narrative constitutes a different mechanism for institutionalizing the educational taken-for-granted. A narrative does not prompt the actor to return to first principles or plunge her into the problems of critique at every turn but offers readily available and popularly understood answers. Narrative understanding is more readily responsive to the demands of "Action now!"

Moreover, popular public support and understanding of education needs some kind of institutionalization if it is to confer legitimacy on education. Education departments in higher education cannot satisfy this need. Because higher education is institutionalized as a social formation, it is too sectional for the State readily to grant it authority in education.[6] (This is why rational critique plays only a weak role in the legitimation of school curricula). But narrative is suitable as an alternative institutional form; and arguably, it is narrative that legitimizes school education. To see that this is so, let us consider the formal characteristics that Lyotard ascribes to narrative.

NARRATIVE AND THE SOCIAL BOND

It is a commonplace that current educational attitudes in much of the Western world tend strongly toward traditionalism. Lyotard ascribes five features to narratives (1984, pp. 19-23) which, in effect, define them as thoroughly conservative institutions; and they plainly play important roles in the transmission of social traditions. In looking for a non-rationalist alternative to the concept of ideology to explain conservative aspects of the postmodern condition, Lyotard (himself a socialist philosopher) turns to the resources of anthropology.

The narratives he takes for his model are quite literally the fables, myths and legends that are ritually told and retold within "primitive" societies. These in a sense, are institutions too but of a different kind to universities, conferences, journals and seminars. They are institutions inasfar as they are socially constructed, accepted and reproduced and have definable and sustained roles within society. And it is precisely such popular stories as myths, fables and legends that Lyotard has in mind when he writes of narratives (1984, p. 27)—a point which is often and mistakenly overlooked where Lyotard is addressed in educational theory.

But one might query what relevance these could possibly have to an analysis of any modern society. Certainly we have our myths and legends. But surely they do not have the same important role in our societies, nor are they transmitted in the same ritualistic ways. Where are the camp fires we gather around to retell them? Who are the shamans who tell them to us? Indeed, an important part of Lyotard's story of postmodernism concerns the modern conflict between narratives and "scientific knowledge" (rational critique), which concerns us here. But he argues that narrative does persist and plays very important roles for us; though now it manifests itself in more complex and dispersed ways. We shall presently consider the dispersion of modern narratives, but first we must consider its original "camp fire" characteristics.

First, "popular stories themselves recount what could be called positive or negative apprenticeships: in other words, the successes or failures greeting the hero's undertakings" (Lyotard, 1984, pp. 19-20). These stories have the social function of describing those paradigmatic competences (successes) that are valued within the society, so that particular actions and activities can be evaluated. They also distinguish particular people, real or legendary, as role models and underwrite the institutions within which these people function.

The relevance of this to education is surely patent. We need education to show young people what is expected of them and to inculcate an understanding and degree of respect for the institutions within which they will have to function (work, the law, finance, the family, constitutional politics, religion). And surely we do achieve this partly through telling stories. On the one hand, there are the obvious literary stories they get in school. Even the stories of small children may have this function—*Postman Pat* (a glimpse for the very young of the world of work), *Spot's Birthday Party*[7] (about the institutions of parties and friendship) and so on. But we also hold up exemplars to schoolchildren in adverts and careers leaflets, distinguished visitors at school prize-givings and fêtes, school trips to workplaces and cultural sites, and so on. These often include narrative elements—talk about real or imaginary characters, fictional or historic events. Major narrative heroes of the educational past have included the Good Apprentice, the Highly Trained Professional, the Responsible Citizen and (yes) the Competent Housewife.

A second characteristic of narratives is more abstract. Lyotard tries to emphasize that scientific discourse, by contrast with narrative, is constituted through a very restricted class of "speech acts" (p. 20). In ordinary speech, we do a great variety of things when we make utterances. We don't always or perhaps even usually just describe things or retail facts. We also make promises, greet people, swear, complain, admonish, beg, make love or joke. Science does only a limited group of these things; on the surface at least it confines itself to statements of fact, of principle or of inference and to calculations and pictures or diagrams. Narratives, by contrast, may include anything from the whole range of speech acts, and not just reports of fact or descriptions: sometimes in the form of reported speech ("He whispered sweet nothings in her ear") but also directly in address to the reader ('Call me Ishmael!').

Specialized forms of life, such as science, tend to involve narrowly limited kinds of speech act. But conversely, a kind of speech that is not so limited, such as narrative, need not be closely bound to particular forms of life. This has two consequences for education. On the one hand, because educational narratives are unspecialized, they can more readily secure an appeal to the whole spread of social groups, as they must if they are to secure legitimacy for particular educational practices. But, by the same token, we glimpse here the intrinsic conservatism of the narrative mode. Of their very nature, appeals to narrative cannot be appeals to the authority of particular social groups, least of all expert cultures. An appeal to an educational narrative precisely cannot be an appeal to the views or findings of academic educationists.

The conservatism becomes more evident if we skip to Lyotard's fourth and fifth claims (pp. 21-23). He draws attention to the ritualized form of retelling narratives in primitive societies. Primitive narratives are repeated regularly and preferably intact. There is a rhythm to their telling. (Think of the rhythm of religious feasts and their associated narratives). Even internally, primitive narratives may have a rhythmic structure. But what is the point of this? Rhythmic repetition involves an uncritical surrender to "the beat." And it is conducive to the transmission of social (though not cultural) traditions that the process should be uncritical. It needs also to be repetitive to accomplish the reproductive task of inducting new cohorts into the tradition, as young adults prepare themselves for parenthood by rehearsing the legitimating narratives of education.

Lyotard makes a paradoxical point about all this. Tradition mediated by narrative is not, as we tend to think, a matter of consciously tying ourselves to our history. On the contrary, "a collectivity that takes narrative as its key form of competence *has no need to remember its past*. It finds the raw material for its social bond not only in the meaning of the narratives it recounts, *but also in the act of reciting them*" (p. 22, emphasis added). Why is this? He invites us to "Consider the form of popular sayings, proverbs, and maxims; they are like splinters of potential narratives, or molds of old ones, which have continued to circulate on certain levels of the contemporary social edifice" (p. 22). It is their plain repetition by diverse people that provides the reassurance as to the aims and understandings others hold and that provides the basis of social solidarity within the tradition. By contrast, to attempt to remember our history is to try to remember it correctly; and that in turn opens up the very dimension of critique, of doubt about questions of historical fact which narrative understanding marginalizes.[8] The very value of narrative for institutionalizing popular understanding of education derives precisely from its marginalization of critique and thus, of serious history.

On the other hand, we tend to think of science as an ahistorical pursuit. Yet again, paradoxically, scientists do need to have regard at least to the history of their recent past, in order to avoid earlier mistakes and to bear in mind unsolved problems. Some regard for history is a necessary characteristic of any developmental project (such as science and, as we will presently note, the Enlightenment Project). But in sustaining the taken-for-granted, narratives usually conceptualize society in non-developmental ways (though again, we shall note that some grand narratives have differed here). If traditions do indeed develop and evolve, traditionalists are rarely at pains to emphasize or applaud the fact.

Lyotard's fifth comment emphasizes the opposition, important to us here, between popular assent and expert authority. "It is [hard] to imagine [society] handing over the authority for its narratives to some incomprehensible subject [or teller] of narration. The narratives themselves have this authority" (p. 23). To know the narratives of a society is not in any way to have expert knowledge. On the contrary, a social narrative is by definition something that any well socialized member of a society can retell without having to research the matter, just as one's language is what one can speak without recourse to a dictionary. Where we identify particular narratives in this chapter, we can give no scholarly references for them. The reader must recognize or fail to recognize them from her own social experience. And it is just this instant perspicuity that distinguishes educational narrative from educational research and accounts for their power.

Let us pause here to reflect on the course of the argument so far. We have noted that as a society we do not readily accept institutionalized critique as the source of legitimation for curricula in mass schooling. We have wondered what other form of institutionalization of rationality provides this for us and have suggested that it is narratives that do so. In effect, we have mounted a familiar argument in an updated way. We have argued that tradition has an ineliminable role in education. But so far we have appealed to narrative simply to explain how traditions give legitimacy to the activities and actions of particular institutions or people. We want next to try to show how traditions establish the social bond in society. To show this is to suggest how they knit the practice of education into its social context other than in terms of its purely instrumental role.

How do traditions maintain their hold on society? The traditionalist seems to suppose that this depends on individual acts of will on the part of members of society. He will present this not as a rational autonomous choice but rather as a kind of surrender to something larger than himself which he may barely understand. Nonetheless, the traditionalist wants people to *assent* to tradition, else it cannot function. Exhortation and complaint are typical modes of traditionalist writing. Similarly, non-traditionalists too easily treat traditionalism as a form of irrational attachment. But arguably there is a specific form of rationality intrinsic to tradition, and which secures its social potency more effectively than any sheer emotional appeal. For rationality is not something one assents to, but a mode of existence we are located within and cannot transcend. A rationality is a kind of way to make sense of life and has thus a determining influence on our very social relationships. Do narratives have such an effect? The theory of narrative elucidates a kind of thinking that is looser than critique but not arbitrary. It has its own qualified but potent rationality, its own canons of correctness. And narratives simultaneously function to secure a social bond.

Any kind of speech act involves a speaker and a hearer and presupposes a specific social relationship between them. But speech acts also do something else: they reconstruct existing relations, by confirming them, by constructing new ones or reconfiguring the network within which particular relations are located. Lyotard reminds us that a specific and particular relation is constructed between the speaker and the hearer of a related narrative. On the one hand, it is the nature of social narratives that anyone is authorized to repeat them to others merely in virtue of having heard them. This is not an empty authority. To say "You just made that up!" is to refuse authority to a person telling a tale. Nonetheless, it is an unusually freely available form of authority, inasmuch as anyone can have it and anyone is capable of achieving it. Conferring this kind of authority is like giving away money, the authority to buy.

Authority is the word Lyotard uses (p. 20); but perhaps that is not the central concern here. When a hearer becomes a speaker and retells a social narrative, she becomes to that degree a representative of the society to which that narrative belongs. And to that degree, she herself belongs to the society. The more such narratives she is in a position to recount, the more deeply embedded in her society she is, and the tighter the social bonds that bind her. Narratives are instrumental in constructing that paradigm postmodern concern: belonging.

Belonging is not created by a person's commitment to a tradition, not simply a matter of a felt affinity. Nor is it simply a matter of how we classify her or the tradition to which we allocate her. Her belonging is created by an actual social bond, created in the interpersonal act of telling and listening to a narrative. Such narratives can and sometimes do incorporate either the speaker or hearer as an actual character in the story, thus further redefining and so reinforcing the social bond. This is important in connection with the role of narrative in education. One may tell a narrative to a young person and insert them themselves into it as a character. For instance, "There are difficult times ahead for jobs for youngsters in this town, and you're going to be in trouble unless you get your act together!" This grim prediction takes the form of a narrative: a small story about the future, which includes the addressee as one of its characters and constructs a correlative social bond. Educational narratives don't just tell us where we belong, they put us where we belong.

It is tempting to construe the belonging created in the telling of narratives as a non-rational matter. But arguably, the transmission of narrative knowledge constitutes rationality itself here. On the one hand, belonging cannot be, by definition, an arbitrary matter. There has to be a relevant difference between those who belong and those who don't. But it is not at all clear what would constitute a more rational way of constructing a relation of belonging than telling people the stories intrinsic to the social group. Sharing narratives is the rational way to include people in the relevant social group; that's the way to do it, because only in narrative can we address the history of the group and thus its deepest roots rather than just its current and perhaps adventitious shared characteristics. (Remember how Christians, Jews and Muslims sometimes refer to themselves as "the peoples of the Book." They define themselves in terms of biblical narratives, and narratives which partially overlap.)

Belonging accompanies identity. One belongs to a group as someone with a particular identity. And narratives provide potent means for ascribing identities to people or enabling the hearer to define herself. Here's an example of an important British narrative, a fragment of dialogue from a popular song: "We'll meet again, Don't know where, don't know when; But I know we'll meet again Some sunny day." Dame Vera Lynn's great song of the Second World War functions precisely as a narrative in British popular culture. Every time it's sung, and it's sung often, history seems suspended. Its singing can create a powerful illusion of being back in those war years, even for those not born then. Of course, there is nothing esoteric about it either. It does not play any abstruse language game open only to initiates. But most importantly, those who were young in the war can relate to it easily as their song, indeed as their story. It evokes powerfully their predicament and emotions at that time, the inevitable uncertainties of war and the hope and optimism that helped them endure, which explains Dame Vera's status today as a national institution. (As narratives are institutions, so too Dame Vera plays an institutional role. This song and this singer are inseparable.) It does indeed recount a kind of heroic apprenticeship: the cheerful stoicism of the ordinary loving couple in the face of war. (We may compare it to Homer's story of Penelope waiting faithfully for Odysseus, a master narrative of Western civilization.)

Thinking about this little narrative demonstrates how narratives are used to define identities. In thinking of it as "our song," people can relate actual incidents and circumstances of their own lives to it as examples of what it talks about. "Don't know where, don't know when"—"Yes, I never knew where they were sending my Fred off to; and then he'd turn up on leave, just out of the blue." "Lucky there were no nasty surprises for me, eh love!" The song talks later of "the people I know," which invites everyone to insert their own cast list. And of course, the "sunny day" actually did arrive for most people, and is etched in their memories.

People of that generation can define an important time in their own lives by using elements of their own history to fill in the blanks in the song; and in doing so, they define themselves in relation to a national narrative and as members of the nation. This is a potent activity. The sense of belonging is the sense of a right to belong: an ethical sense of bondship, obligation (not least of remembrance), gratitude and so on. The song is sung at events that celebrate these relations: reunions and ceremonies of remembrance. And when it is sung (still by the redoubtable Dame Vera), listeners join in unison. Thus the bonds of belonging and the definition of identity are reconstituted and reaffirmed. If this is not a contemporary narrative, then what is?

We begin to see the connection between narratives and power. Narratives belong to particular social groups. They are the property of anyone who can define themselves in relation to them. So members of those groups are empowered to decide how and to whom they will retell the narratives (either as "This concerns you" or "This doesn't concern you"). It is intrinsic to narratives that they marginalize particular people as not members of the group, and marginalize certain kinds of knowledge as irrelevant to or incompatible with the knowledge shared by the group. Thus identity and belonging are intertwined with power, the power to marginalize. This link is at the root of the usefulness of the concept of narrative in analyzing contemporary educational realities.

It's important to see the difference between the power of social narrative and the educational potential of literary narrative. With the latter, teachers are concerned with extending the imaginative scope of their pupils' understanding. But important as that is, the use of *social* narrative does something more fundamental and in a diametrically opposed way. Social narratives are there to relate to real events, real people, real feelings and historical predicaments: not to extend the imagination of their audience but to modify or reinforce their identity, not to extend the culture of the individual, but to fit her into a place, happy or unhappy, in the social structure.

So to discuss education in terms of narratives is not to deal in imaginative constructions but with real social relationships. It is to notice that these are not constructed in any abstract way by reference to values, ideologies, conceptual frameworks and so on, but by linguistic constructs—stories—whose retelling is a significant social act that modifies the network of social bonds; and that we all, inevitably, conceptualize our lives partly in a narrative way.[9] That is why narratives are powerful. The theory of narrative is one version, or one aspect of the general poststructuralist insight, derived from Heidegger, that "language speaks man," and relates to Lacan's contention that the things said to us and about us make us the people we are.[10] Narrative theory reminds us that the potency of language derives not just from what is said, but from the social activity of saying it.[11]

NARRATIVE IN MODERN SOCIETY

It is one thing to agree that narrative persists and performs a function in modern society, another to see it as important. Lyotard himself emphasizes the importance in the modern (and postmodern) worlds of scientific (and quasi-scientific) kinds of knowledge. (Those writers who equate the postmodern with the post-scientific are quite out of step with Lyotard.[12]) But scientific forms of knowledge are sharply contrasted with narrative. So is narrative still so important?

There are two questions to answer here. The first is how and where narrative might manifest itself. Does social narrative survive in any significant degree in our society? Secondly, if it does, does it perform any important task?

Certainly ours is not a society in which storytelling seems to be a central social institution, however important it may be in popular culture (film, soap operas, even adverts). It is hard to see narratives in action. But this is misleading to a degree. For, in modern societies, narratives become fragmented and dispersed. Recall how Lyotard described popular saying and proverbs as "splinters of potential narratives, or molds of old ones, which have continued to circulate on certain levels of the contemporary social edifice." It is in this kind of way that narratives persist for us: as collections of elements which crop up in different times and places so that the connections between them may go unremarked.

Nonetheless, any attempt to explain their individual significance would involve relating them to each other. For instance, "We'll meet again" might be thought of as a splinter of a narrative of love in war; which in turn might be thought of as an episode in a larger narrative of remembrance. In Britain, the narrative of remembrance is expressed in the Ceremony of Remembrance in Whitehall, in the buying and selling of poppies,[13] in any visit by a member of the royal family to any tomb of the unknown warrior at home or abroad and in a whole range of music, poetry and monuments associated with remembrance. These elements can be encountered on different occasions and not in immediate connection with each other. But they go together; and the surest way to show how they go together is to relate them each to a narrative about the two world wars, sacrifice to one's country, national gratitude, and the obligation and need to remember who we are and how we have survived as who we are. More generally, to understand the identity of a culture is still, in the last resort, to piece together their narratives and show their underlying coherence.

But what particular narratives have been operative in modern society and what have they been *for*? Lyotard famously coined the notion of grand narrative, of some kind of master narrative for modern society which marginalizes all others to tell of some central thrust to the modern project. Such narratives, he suggests, are metadiscourses—they are stories about stories, which attempt to show these others as just episodes in a larger story, and thus make sense of them (Lyotard, 1984, p. xxiii). Different narratives are not necessarily incompatible as different conceptual frameworks are often thought to be. On the contrary, they can be related sometimes like different episodes in a story, like plots and subplots or like a series of narrative sequels. (It is important for the conclusion of this chapter to note that such kinds of accommodation are possible between narratives.) Furthermore, grand narratives, being quintessentially modern, are typically stories of progress toward some further and higher end, "such as the dialectics of Spirit [in Hegel], the hermeneutics of meaning [in the unfolding of God's will, perhaps],[14] the emancipation of the rational or working subject [e.g., in Marx] or the creation of wealth [in the triumph of capitalism]" (1984, p. xxiii).

One of the most important functions of modern grand narrative, Lyotard suggests, has been until recently to legitimize science itself. As a non-normative form of knowledge, science cannot give grounds for its own legitimacy. And yet, as the central and determinative institution of the modern world, it clearly needs legitimacy. This legitimacy, Lyotard believes, can only be provided by some kind of narrative. But this in turn suggests (though it does not prove) that science can never obviate the narrative mode of knowledge. In a scientific society, the two modes of knowledge have seemed destined to coexist. Science requires its own narrative justification, and grand narratives of progress provide it. As such they have been fundamentally important in knitting together modern societies.

But, famously, Lyotard proclaimed in *The Postmodern Condition* the demise of grand narrative. "Simplifying to the extreme, I define *postmodern* as incredulity [sic] toward metanarratives" (1984, p. xxiv). Metanarratives, he claimed, had lost their power to confer legitimacy. We suggest that this collapse of grand narrative and its consequences can throw light on the democratic predicament of curriculum theory, philosophy of education in particular and educational studies in general:

their political weakness in the face of popular scepticism and the state of play in the wake of their demise.

To see further, we have to ask what specifically these grand narratives were. Lyotard refers variously to the Enlightenment narrative or the grand narrative of emancipation. Either way, he discerns two forms of this narrative, which we might associate respectively with the empiricist version of Enlightenment whose first home is Britain and the rationalist/Hegelian version in the German tradition. The two collided and conflicted in Lyotard's own France. The heroes or subjects of the two versions of the narrative are not the same. In the first version, the subject is "humanity as the hero of liberty" (p. 31), while in the second it is the subject of knowledge (the entity which knows) and this in turn is "not the people but the speculative spirit" familiar from Hegel (p. 33).

Lyotard argues that both forms of the narrative have proven self-subverting. And as we saw in Chapter two, in both traditions philosophical argument and reflection have led to that impugning of the idea of foundations of knowledge which has historically formed a cornerstone of any narrative of emancipation. If societies could be emancipated from authoritarian regimes, religious superstition or stifling social conventions it was because firmer grounds for the ordering of society could be somehow discovered in the pursuit of knowledge and understanding of justice. The firmness of these grounds inhered in their objectivity, their imperviousness to unreliable human will. But modern philosophers of all stripes have come to find the idea of such grounds untenable. This, we think, lies at the heart of Lyotard's account of the collapse of grand narrative.

But we have still not told the narrative. We shall confine ourselves to the first version which is familiar to an English-speaking audience, because this is the one that has been operative for us. As Lyotard puts it, this version of the narrative runs as follows, "All peoples have the right to science. If the social subject is not already the subject of scientific knowledge, it is because that has been forbidden by priests and tyrants. The right to science must be reconquered" (1984, p. 31). In other words, in a free society our arrangements should be grounded in expertise rather than in guesswork, superstition or the prejudices of the powerful. A vivid and important instance of this demand is the recognition of a popular right to the benefits of medical science. It is no coincidence that medical schools and teaching hospitals are so often associated with modern universities. More generally, the welfare state gained legitimacy from the grand narrative of emancipation.

It should be immediately clear how the development of bodies of supposedly expert knowledge in education can be fitted in to such a narrative and thus accorded legitimacy; how educational experts can think of themselves as actors in an appropriate narrative. Indeed, we can perhaps see the British tradition of Peters and Hirst, with its emphasis on the expertise and authority of providers, as an educational correlate of the welfare state, an element in the same narrative. This fit is yet more perspicuous in the light of further comments from Lyotard. "It seems that this narrative finds it necessary to de-emphasize higher education," he says (1984, pp. 31-32), since the thrust of the narrative is democratic rather than élitist. And accordingly educational theory in the English-speaking world has long exhibited more interest in schools than universities. He adds later, "The subject [of liberty] is concrete, or supposedly so, and its epic is the story of its emancipation from everything that prevents it from governing itself" (1984, p. 35). Thus it is an epic of autonomy, and Lyotard explicitly associates it with the thought of Kant. No coincidence, perhaps, that the classic philosophy of education of the British school owes so much to Kant, and so much more than does the British philosophical tradition generally, which would otherwise count as a surprise. Autonomy is central to British philosophy of education, both in terms of the autonomy of individuals and in terms of the autonomy of forms of life, such as the autonomy of ethics or the Forms of Knowledge (whose autonomy necessarily involves the social autonomy of their respective practitioners vis-a-vis each other).

But it seems undeniable that the narrative of emancipation is in abeyance if not moribund. This is not, of course, to say that liberty is no longer a watchword—quite evidently it is so more than ever—but rather that modern social movements look to the unconstrained workings of the market to secure liberty; and in doing so, they repudiate communal commitment to a grand narrative in favor of a play of individual choices which may have to do with idiosyncratic narratives or with none. The interesting question is how education fares in these circumstances.

LEGITIMACY AFTER GRAND NARRATIVE

Let us look first at Lyotard's own account in relation to higher education. If the grand narrative of emancipation falls into disuse or disrepair, what are we left with? Clearly a disparate array of heterogeneous activities—scientific, political, cultural—seem likely to lose any pattern or overall coherence once the thread that had bound them together is broken. To conceptualize the resulting formlessness, Lyotard reaches for the idea of a small narrative. Speaking of narratives in general, Lyotard says at one point, "Narratives . . . determine criteria of competence and/or illustrate how they are to be applied. They thus define what has the right to be said and done in the culture in question, and since they are themselves a part of that culture, they are legitimated by the simple fact that they do what they do" (1984, p. 23). If education and culture lose a guiding grand narrative, a plurality of small narratives are there, supposedly, to take its place. If different areas of discourse are disjunct from each other, nonetheless they each retain their own internal integrity. Among these many narratives, of course, are the many demotic narratives of education.

Once the unifying thread of grand narrative is snapped, the narrative is "dispersed in clouds of narrative language elements" (Lyotard, 1984, p. xxiv), as we saw with the socially scattered elements of the narrative of remembrance. "Conveyed within each cloud are pragmatic valencies [potentials for creating social bonds] specific to its kind. . . . There are many different language games—a heterogeneity of elements. They only give rise to institutions [such as

Dame Vera Lynn] in patches" (p. xxiv). Importantly, "the social bond is linguistic, but is not woven with a single thread" (1984, p. 40).

Lyotard uses this picture as a background to the phenomenon we now recognize in educational practice in the West, which we described in the first chapter as instrumentalism or managerialism. "The decision makers . . . attempt to manage these clouds of sociality according to input/output matrices, following a logic which implies that their elements are commensurable and that the whole is determinable. They allocate our lives for the growth of [economic and political] power" (p. xxiv). Under capitalism and also state socialism, the governing criterion for all decisions is that of efficiency. This criterion he calls "performativity," and it threatens to govern all decisions in society, whether normative or epistemic (such as those which inform the course of research). Performativity is specifically to be contrasted with those non-calculating and socially embedded criteria conveyed through narratives, both grand and small. Yet, we might add, it mobilizes small narratives against the grand narrative of Enlightenment. As we saw in the first chapter, popular common sense supports managerialism. They align with each other as forms of anti-theoreticism. The profound threat all this poses to education is vividly familiar to philosophers of education.

So far, so familiar. But this raises the question of what happens to legitimacy in such a state of affairs. Yet it is at just this point that *The Postmodern Condition* becomes less helpful, it seems to us, largely because of Lyotard's almost exclusive focus on higher education (quite understandable, since that was his brief).[15] Nonetheless, he might have seen things in higher education itself rather differently had his educational scope been more comprehensive.

Famously (again) Lyotard locates a source for resistance to the dominance of performativity—yet a support for legitimation by small narratives—in what he calls paralogy. For Lyotard, the performative society will necessarily find itself locked in a pragmatic contradiction. Modern industrial societies rely on science and the growth of scientific knowledge to sustain their internal stability through economic growth. They seek to predict and control and to enwrap science within this managerial project. But, pointing to modern work in philosophy of science, Lyotard argues that science is itself intrinsically unpredictable and indeed that this is even a source of its cognitive power. If this is so, then a performative society pursues an impossible goal: to control the uncontrollable by predicting the unpredictable (surely a serious and important insight). Ultimately, then, science must prove subversive to a performative society (which is not to say "to any society"). So might science provide a model for a new form of legitimation, a way of reinstating those concerns that performativity sweeps to one side?

Lyotard notes that the true task of scientists is not to assemble irrefragable facts or to construct deductive edifices which "prove" how things must go in the world, but rather to generate new ideas about the world which they encapsulate in stories about it; in other words, they tell narratives. Scientists generate new ideas by changing the stories they tell. Lyotard thinks of such shifts of narrative as new moves within scientific language games or as moves so radical that, if judged successful, they influence a change in the rules of scientific language games—and it is moves such as the latter that he calls "paralogies." Paralogy is a permanent possibility with scientific narrative. And Lyotard assumes that small social narratives operate in a similar way to scientific narratives, that they too are permanently open to paralogy and that social paralogies can similarly be valued for the challenge they may present to performativity. If scientific paralogy is to be valued in the postmodern world, why not social paralogy?

Unfortunately, however, he overlooks a major difference between social and scientific narratives: that the former do and the latter don't establish a social bond. Secondly, his analytic framework is vitiated by a failure to mark Wittgenstein's own distinction between language games and "forms of life." Often, where he talks of language games, Wittgenstein would have used the other term, and for good reason. Arguably, paralogy is not possible where narrative sustains the social bond, and such social narratives are themselves prerequisite to the practice of science.

First, Lyotard himself is at pains to emphasize the differences between narrative and scientific knowledge (1984, pp. 23-27); and this should have alerted him to the danger in sliding on a play in the word "story" to re-describe science as the telling of narratives. Whatever else scientific stories do, they don't establish or reconfigure the social bond. One cannot identify or describe one's own life in terms of scientific stories, about the interior of the atom or the ecology of the deep sea for instance, in the way one can relate to Vera Lynn's song.

However, if scientific narratives are no model for social relationships, social narratives remain important for science, whatever the fate of grand narrative. Scientists do need to be drawn together in social bonds for the enterprise of science to function at all. Without such bonds, paralogy itself is pointless. Why else would the scientific community adjust its rules to accommodate an eccentric move in its "language games?" It is not enough to say "because the new move is a good move." Not all such moves are good and good moves may not be immediately seen to be good; and in that case, the alternative would be more simply to expel from the community (or more simply ignore) the person who made the move. Conversely, the community will only adjust to the new move if they can see that its proponent can herself work with it fruitfully; otherwise it will seem merely wilful or eccentric.[16]

Accepting the new move involves maintaining a social bond with the iconoclast strong enough to need to keep her "inside the game." As we saw earlier on, the institutions which do establish these bonds in science are social rather than narrative—university departments, journals and conferences and so on. But can these particular institutions legitimate themselves without an informing narrative? As we have seen, Lyotard had earlier suggested that perhaps they can't; and that suggestion needs to be taken more seriously than he himself has done. Arguably, paralogy does not support the narratives underpinning science, even if it happens within scientific "stories" or language games; on the contrary, it is those narratives which sustain the possibility of paralogy.

But another difficulty presents itself against the proposal to rely on paralogy as an alternative tactic for resisting performativity. Lyotard's account of paralogy rests on the notion of a Wittgensteinian language game, which is intrinsically rule-bound. Wittgenstein uses the idea of a language game to show how meanings become constructed, sustained or altered. But language games require two forms of understanding. Internally, to understand such a game is to understand its rules. Externally, however, one also needs to see the point and purpose of any language game: the reason why people play it or why they need the vocabulary for which it constructs a meaning. And to understand that is to fit the game into what Wittgenstein calls a form of life.

In particular, science is not, *pace* Lyotard, a particular language game but a form of life that gives point and purpose to a myriad of scientific language games and their vast concomitant vocabularies. A form of life, such as science, is characterized by particular aims, values, conventions, expectations, personnel, "matériel," institutions and so on. It is not a language game writ large. A "form of life" does not construct, alter or sustain meanings but fits activities, thoughts and attitudes together in a more or less coherent pattern and allows us to change the fit where necessary or worthwhile. Indeed, forms of life are simply "what we do."

And just as forms of life are simply "what we do," so too, as we saw, narratives "are legitimated by the simple fact that they do what they do." Narratives fit into forms of life as internal explanations and justifications of them.

But if it is only against the background of forms of life that language games make sense, then forms of life are not rule bound in the same sense that language games are—to suppose so would surely invite a regress. And by that very token, one cannot speak of paralogy in respect of forms of life. There is nothing that counts as a new move or a rupture of the rules, because at this level of analysis there are no rules. Forms of life are open-textured, synthetic and eclectic. What is made possible within a language game (meaning) is not what is done within a form of life or explained by a narrative (social activity and its institutions), and vice-versa.

Yet arguably it is at precisely the level of forms of life that problems arise most pressingly in relation to the threat of performativity. Just as the telling and retelling of narratives creates the social bond, forms of life are the context in which problems of legitimacy arise in the first place. It is to forms of life that performativity poses a threat: forms of life such as the scientific, the social and the aesthetic (or indeed what we might call the modern, as opposed to medieval form of life) and not forgetting the life of sport or adventure or of charity which performativity also threatens to dilute, rupture, corrupt, suborn. But paralogy can perform no role of resistance here, because it has no meaning at this level. Only confrontation or accommodation between narratives can resolve problems of legitimacy and only the retelling of narratives and the reinforcement of social bonds which this involves can offer resistance to performativity.

In summary, if paralogies relate to language games, narratives relate to forms of life. And it is to forms of life that education relates in the first instance. The first question for higher education is how to sustain science (and other disciplines), and the second, how to sustain the social bonds that subtend science (and other disciplines). But for school education, the latter is the truly important question: how to construct, maintain and reconstruct the social bond in society at large. Had Lyotard looked to school education too, he might have seen this deeper link between it and higher education. For in both instances maintaining the social bond involves finding new narratives with which to do so.

EDUCATION AND THE SOCIAL BOND AFTER EMANCIPATION

Demotic narratives of education cannot be marginalized or trivialized. Yet currently they are suborned by the growth of performativity which will subvert in the long run the educational aims that they support. So can narratives appropriate to a critically serious education system be reinstated against the thrust of performativity while coexisting with popular educational narratives? Is there still any narrative adequate to sustain the discourse of educational experts? Can educational theory still be shown to belong to our society?

If the narrative of enlightenment which has informed education can no longer function as grand narrative, perhaps nonetheless it still has a place as one small narrative among others. The problem, as we saw above, is not its incoherence but our "incredulity toward metanarratives." Incredulity, as we saw, comes with loss of faith in foundations. But perhaps a postfoundational rationality can restore credibility, first by relinquishing the totalizing ambitions of foundationalist projects and second in virtue of the intrinsically democratic and non-dominatory nature of a postfoundational politics of knowledge. A more modest narrative for education would acknowledge the ethical and emotional costs of enlightenment, no less than the political and social dangers of prejudice and ignorance (including collapse in the face of performativity). It would itself demand a deeper sensitivity to other narratives and seek ways to fit together with them harmoniously—an ecological awareness, if you like. We might also ask whether emancipation is not also an aspect of many other small narratives. We might ask what potency they themselves will sustain in the longer run where society has no narrative of emancipation or enlightenment at all—not even in the form of a *petit récit*.

NOTES

1. Lyotard, 1984. Lyotard's structuralist sources include primarily the work of Vladimir Propp, a member of the Prague Linguistic Circle, and the structuralist anthropologist Claude Levi-Strauss (cf. Lyotard, 1984, p. 91, n. 74, 75).

2. John White's *Towards a Compulsory Curriculum* (1973) might count as an example of how to do so with academic rigor and completeness and within the parameters of the analytic philosophical approach of its day.

3. Such a view, of course, is elaborated in the critiques of the New Right, inspired by Hayek's onslaught on the evils of state planning. There is surely a connection between popular educational scepticism and a general disenchantment with planned social modernity in other fields, such as housing, health or the benefit system.

4. Lyotard, 1984, esp. sections 6, 8, 9 and 10.

5. See McCarthy, 1978, pp. 299-307.

6. Only a highly centralized democracy such as France can manage this.

7. Spot, a British children's favorite, is a cuddly puppy. His birthday guests include monkeys and alligators.

8. We are not denying that professional history may take the form of a chronological narrative. But it will not be a *social* narrative of the kind being considered here.

9. This insight is reaffirmed in psychoanalysis and psychotherapy, incidentally. In therapy, the patient both redeems her sense of self by affirming the uniqueness of her personal narrative while cross-referencing that narrative to social narratives and thus legitimizes herself as a valid member of her society.

10. This idea is elaborated further in Chapter eight on Lacan. And it underscores the relevance of ideas about "knowing things by heart," discussed in Chapter ten, ideas which themselves derive partly from Heidegger.

11. In this it makes some contact with the importance of linguistic pragmatics in Habermas.

12. Like Habermas, Foucault and Baudrillard in their different ways, Lyotard sees the postmodern condition as an exacerbation of modernity rather than its rescission. For Lyotard, science and technology are finally and unequivocally off the leash in the postmodern world, and unconstrained by alternative normative forces.

13. The Flanders poppy is the British national symbol of the losses of the First World War.

14. Hermeneutics was originally the discipline of systematic Biblical exegesis.

15. His essay was written at the instance of the Conseil des Universités of the government of Quebec.

16. Lyotard's view here is like that of Kuhn but with the social aspects eclipsed.

Chapter 8

The Responsibility of Desire

Children's lives are to a large extent led according to rules fixed by adults. Perhaps this situation is not to be deplored—they are, after all, not yet adults, not yet held responsible in the full-blown sense. Yet it remains hard to deny that their freedom is limited. People, and children as well, desire particular things, and what comes in the way of fulfilling these is experienced as restraint. In the relationships between teachers and parents, and teachers and children, *desire* works in different ways. There is first what they want for themselves and for this matter from each other, but there is also what they want the other to desire. And last but not least there are cases where it is not clear what exactly one wants from the other, where this can only generally be indicated as recognition for one's own desires. Educational theories have always had a special bearing on problems related to this matter. Some have argued that human beings become free precisely through education—that is, their initiation into what a human being is, conceived for instance as becoming free from animal-like tendencies, free to realize what is really human. It is there already in Aristotle's ontology, where the human being is conceived as *animal rationale*, a position spelled out even more explicitly in Kant's Enlightenment project.

In this traditional picture education is conceived as a relationship between the adult and the person being educated, which has as a specific aim the adulthood of the person being educated. The influence adults exert on children will bring them to the point where they can take up for themselves what is thought to be a fitting life-project. Adults, being representations of what is objectively good, are in the position to do that, that is, to educate, as they have already achieved adulthood. They are only considered to be representations, of course, and not the ultimate norm, which can only be what is objectively good. Adulthood will show itself by being in authority over oneself, that is, being able to bind oneself to what one has imposed on oneself, being able to maintain steady relationships both morally and practically and not being handed over to other people's judgments; or, to put this more positively, having personal access to value-standards. Adulthood will issue in being able to put oneself under a higher authority, that is, accepting responsibility to a moral order and thus being free in obedience to it. Finally, it is argued that the adult is taking part in social life in a constructive manner. The child, on the other hand, is helpless in a moral sense. She does not know what is good and therefore cannot take up responsibility yet. That, so it is claimed, will be provided by the adult. The child begs for her guidance. And only if such guidance is offered, if the adult (first the parent, and subsequently the teacher) decides what should be done concerning the child, will she be able to reach adulthood. Living a moral life has everything to do with knowing what is moral, and the child has first of all to develop this capacity—as yet she is only *potentially* human. Moreover, since being rational is conceived as undivided and being moral is grafted onto being rational, morality is in essence the same for all human beings. That one of the traditional preoccupations of philosophy of education is autonomy as an educational aim is easy to understand. As long as the child does not know what is objectively good, she is not autonomous—and how could she find that out unless she is told by others, and thus initiated in what it means to be a human being?

Another traditional interest of philosophy of education is the insistence on concepts such as authenticity. In dealing with that Cooper spoke of the importance of being involved in a particular educational content and not just in an "immersion in ways of thinking whose aim is to reach generalizations, to discover what items are instances of or data for" (1983, p. 67). For him, the supreme value we must confer, then, "is *the value of giving-value-to*; and what confers sense on life is *giving-sense-to* life. [Both are] the activities of individual human beings: indeed, they are the activities which manifest the supreme human capacities" (p. 116). Autonomy, authenticity, being able to give meaning to life as a person—it is in those terms that education was and still is conceived to a large extent. This traditional position raises a number of problems, some of them predominantly present in the child-centered movement.

The child-centered movement (*Reformpädagogik*)[1] criticizes the presuppositions of the traditional position. For child-centered theorists, childrearing can no longer be seen as a matter of activities pursued by adults in order to bring children to adulthood. Here the educator (the parent and the teacher) is, first of all, the adviser of the child, the facilitator of what she really wants. It is pupils who learn. They have to start from what they already know, and from what they perceive as their real interests, and master new material for themselves. It is the child, so it is argued, who is from the very beginning responsible for her learning. Because children know best what is good for them, parents ought not to impose their own values on their children. Instead they should respect their children's values. Child-centeredness introduces one of the issues central to education. For a number of progressive educators, particularly those influenced by Rogers in the late 1960s and 1970s, the concept of experience plays a crucial role (see, for instance, Gordon, 1975). There is an organic metaphor here (that is, a principle that works from inside) that assumes that the individual's understanding of herself, of others and of the surrounding world develops similarly to the seed of a plant. It is not from or on the intersubjective level that the person will discover what she really is, or wants, but in herself. The central metaphor here is the one of unfolding, as opposed to autonomy as the result of one's rational development, and this in turn is already different from the pre-Enlightenment conception of education as inculcation.

One of the questions that the child-centered movement raises is whether it is possible for an individual to discover within herself what she really wants. Others will go even further and argue that the child is not only to be conceived as free, but moreover that education always and necessarily sets unacceptable limits. They argue that parents misuse their power, and that this is tolerated, even supported, by society. For Alice Miller (1980), for instance, who accepts the primacy of the natural development of the self, the child will find in its own body protection against unreasonable demands, that is if parents succeed in not manipulating the infant in accordance with their own needs. For her, parents claim to love their children and want the best for them but instead of acting accordingly they misuse their power to impose their own values. That this extreme has its own pitfalls too is not very surprising. The autonomy that is presumed to be found within the subject is for various reasons indeed problematic. We underestimate the extent to which intersubjectivity is normative for us. Though progressivism in particular tried to articulate the idea of the "real self," analogous ideas are also found more generally within all those contexts where experience-based learning is stressed.

The tension between progressivism and traditionalism directs our attention to the evidently crucial matter here, namely how the subject is conceived, an issue which is linked with the question of how, both empirically and conceptually, it originates. We do not want to fall into the trap of the closed, even solipsistic, *cogito*, but in trying to avoid at the same time the evaporation of the subject we have to find a way to understand the subject as situated from the beginning at the intersubjective level, but also as able to be committed to what she does. This is indeed necessary in order to understand what responsibility amounts to. All kinds of other questions press themselves forward: How much autonomy is desirable and in what sense can it be an educational aim? Why is it not possible to avoid the influence of significant others? How is the subject's desire structured, in itself and in relation to others? The French philosopher and psychoanalyst Jacques Lacan[2] developed a theoretical position in which a number of these matters are dealt with in a highly sophisticated manner. This position sheds light on how others are necessarily always there, and on how their expectations are for the subject at the same time both unavoidable and liberating, that is, they enable her desire to find a pathway for expression. Lacan's subject is not the subject of the *cogito*, that is, the subject that consciously assures itself of itself in its representations. It is split, barred and divided by the signifier, separating itself from itself in the very act of self-representation and disappearing into the gap between the *cogito's* enunciation and its statement: in Lacan's words, the subject thinks where she is not, therefore she is where she does not think. Finally, Lacan's position illuminates not only how this is relevant to understand education and the origin of desire, but also how it structures what the educator does and more generally the relationships between human beings.

For Lacan, human beings are being spoken of, from the very beginning, even before they are born. They are fixed in a human order by those who relate to them. The infant is predefined by an intersubjective, symbolic network that predetermines much of her social identity and destiny. And for her parents, who expected and desired this identity and destiny, it is not a matter of indifference what their children do. The network of discourse also brings with it particular expectations. To start with there is a parental need to make sense of a baby's vocalizations. And as she interacts with her mother, language is mastered or, as Lacan says, language masters the child. It is through the Other that the first human communications are made; it is through the Other, too, that more sophisticated messages are sent once the child becomes proficient in her use of language. The measure of the baby's comfort depends on the feeding experience, during which time she and her mother seem merged. "I think he's hungry," a mother is often heard to say, trying to anticipate or understand the sounds her baby makes.

The act of feeding, which arouses feelings of love, may also trigger feelings of dependency and hatred. The mother may be late at times in responding to the infant's cries or inadvertently frustrate her in other ways. At other times she may be distracted or worse. These are examples of experiences that create the first evidence of ambivalence in the child's mind, causing her to repress certain feelings that conflict with her love for the mother. The code of language, through the unconscious, acts as a repository for the personal, tribal and social myths of her world. Through this code, she learns who to like and dislike, what illusions and identifications to cherish, and what verbal construction of reality to accept as real and true. The child slowly learns the discourse of her people, travelling from her natural state at birth to a more complex, cultural one. She locates herself in her family, neighborhood, and so on, and finds that she has a predetermined social identity. These insights lead to others. She learns to present herself as she has been recorded in language. The linguistic definitions of her self determine how others will see and respond to her even before they meet and know her. One recalls that the infant was located in the symbolic world before she was born. Her mother and father spoke of her and named her, her birth was a message to the world.

The infant enters a world of signs and symbols that are entirely separate from herself. Yet this world contains undifferentiated words whose meanings are ambiguous until they are used in actual speech. It is only then that the race or sex of a child becomes an advantage or an impediment, depending on the social situation of the family. Words may have several meanings, but these are clarified in the speech of the sender and receiver of messages. Language allows us to think of ourselves as part of a concrete, orderly universe. It can be easily understood that the language of parents fixes the child to her social and cultural place in the symbolic order from birth. Accepting these ideas, the infant can feel secure in her immediate surroundings and relationships. She can know what to value and what to turn away from, and how to deal with her own emotions and those of others around her. As parents provide a safe haven and interact with her, she learns the concepts of the Other and Otherness. This world of symbolic relationships and structures is defined by linguistic signifiers, chains of words that have their roots and meanings steeped in other signifiers that describe the Otherness of the world in an orderly, rational way. The rules of the family lead to the laws of human society. They determine how civilized persons will live together, spelling out in some detail what they may and may not do. A particular theory of language and how it is the home for the subject, its true intersubjective context, underlies Lacan's position.

To understand the full strength of Lacan's insights, his basic ideas about the subject will be elaborated. We will consider the formation of the subject and the symbolic order in which she finds her natural home. After having dealt with how responsibility has changed and how the law of desire grounds the Law[3] of human beings, educational practices are investigated from a Lacanian perspective. Finally, some general conclusions following from these insights for education and philosophy of education are drawn.

LACAN'S SUBJECT: A LACK OF BEING

Freud shows that the unconscious has its own laws, different from those of conscious reason. Essentially subversive, it is organized in the form of a constant questioning of the human subject which cannot be limited and tamed by the laws of good common sense. On its basis one finds the concept of "drive," for Freud not just a physiological or momentous impulse, but a constant quantity of energy organized by mental representations. On that force psychoanalysis has according to him nothing to say, it only shows itself through representations. Lacan radicalizes Freud's epistemological and psychoanalytical position, interpreting it as not so much as a matter of surging energy or a hydraulic metaphor of the instincts, but in terms of particular representations that will recur and recur. Psychoanalysis is itself, in his opinion, above all based on a fundamental split between the subject and the knowledge she has of herself. No longer a unified collection of thoughts and feelings (except as a fantasy, e.g., the infant's fantasy of being one with the mother), the subject is de-centered. Numerous references to this new concept of the subject, described as lacking, alienated, marked by an essential lack of being and so forth are present throughout his work. The unconscious and its corollary, unconscious desire, assemble all that cannot be part of the image a human being has of herself, focused on and used implicitly in the different human sciences. Indeed, it is generally supposed that a human being as a rational and self-conscious being has an adequate reason for everything she does or aspires to, that the representation of a particular aim leads to what one does. To understand someone's behavior is then to know the person's motives and what she is generally about. The implicit model is that of needs-satisfaction and the context is that of instrumental rationality. Only when one clearly knows what the aim is, is there a place for looking for the most efficient means. Through these motives and aims, human life is conceived naturalistically as based on self-preservation and self-interest—to satisfy lust and avoid pain—and everything else (politics, ethics) is fitted into this context. It is to such an all-incorporating functionalist explanation, where the human being is thus dominated by a loss of meaning, that Lacan is opposed. His way to deal with this problem leads to and through the study of language.

By distinguishing secondary (word representations) from primary (thing representations) processes Freud remains committed to the possibility of a language in which the meaning of the words can be determined once and for all. Where Saussure puts the emphasis on the parallel between signifier (the name) and signified (what is named), Lacan emphasizes the primacy of the former over the latter. Although the structural links between signifier and signified are arbitrary (though inextricable) for Saussure, there remains for him a signified. Lacan, on the contrary, conceives as the basic structure of language a number of different words without positive terms. Each term gets its meaning from its difference with other terms, but has in itself no once-and-for-all settled strict meaning. Lacan follows Jakobson, who described how the development of a discourse may take place along two different semantic lines. It is called metonymic when one topic leads to another through their contiguity. Words acquire relations on the basis of the linear nature of language, because they are chained together. The terms acquire their value because they stand in opposition to everything that precedes or follows. It is called metaphoric when one topic leads to another through their similarity, where one could as it were be replaced by another. The two basic mechanisms of language, metaphor and metonymy, make clear how meaning is produced. By metaphor, the possibility of fixation of meaning is indicated without which language (as a system of rules) would destroy itself. But as the bounds between sense and nonsense are not determined *a priori*, new meanings can appear by the process of metonymy (or shift of meaning). Signified and signifier are thus for Lacan two distinct and separate elements that are in a radical opposition and the bar between them is a formula of separateness, rather than a formula of reciprocity. Placing the signified under the signifier, he emphasizes symbolically the primacy of the signifier. To search for the signified now becomes vain, as it is always slipping out of reach and resisting attempts to keep it fixed. Only the signifier is available, revealed in the signifying chain, which is made up of signifiers connected to one another.

Lacan looks at the turning points of the discourse differently and not from a purely linguistic point: as the effect of a "meaning which escapes its own signification." Here metonymy (referring to the linear syntagmatic connection of one word to another) is used as the structure to indicate the subject's lack of being. The order of language replaces the subject's lack of being, from which the desire for the missing object arises. There are always other desires and other objects which present themselves as being able to fill up the lack of being. In the passage from one signifier to another (in metaphor, where one word substitutes for another word), desire finds a pathway for expression. Without dissolving entirely, desire runs through one metaphor and the next. Here a signifier substitutes for another only in order to articulate what cannot be said, that is the signified. At the basis lies the psychoanalytic insight that meaning is not to be found in *what* language says (in its statement), but in *the fact of saying* (in its utterance). It echoes the Hegelian demand for mediation, that is, the subject manifests herself in her truth only by exteriorizing herself, alienating herself in a common language, and having herself recognized by someone else.

Lacan's ideas will not only lead to a new way of interpreting clinical material, but all the notions of knowledge are turned upside down and gone is the never-ending quest for the meaning of the concept. The dependence of the subject is indicated, not so much as on an environment or a community, but on "a discourse in the universal movement" which founds the elementary structures of culture. The subject is a slave to the authority of language. How that can be understood will be made clear in dealing with the way the subject originates.

The Formation of the Subject

The formation of the subject (of the one who says "I") is explicated by Lacan through what he calls the mirror phase. The helpless infant, not yet objectively in control of her movements, jubilantly perceives in the mirror the mastery of her bodily unity, which objectively she still lacks. She becomes aware, through seeing her image, of her own body as a totality, as a total form or *Gestalt*. Different from the infant's objective state of fragmentation and insufficiency, there is the illusory feeling of autonomy and unity, experienced as a result of seeing her image in the mirror. This could be an actual mirror, but is of course more often another person who ascribes unity to the subject. "Look how big you are already," "Look what you can do," "I know you can do it," says the mother to the child—thus offering her an image of herself. The subject falls in love with her image and, in contrast to the auto-erotic stage, in which she has an erotic relationship to her fragmented body, she now takes the image of her whole body as her love-object. In the mirror phase the child does not experience the image as external. However, as the unity is formed outside of the subject, the human being turns out in essence to be separated from herself. The subject's identification with her own body as other than herself structures herself as a rival to herself. The separateness and the rivalry generate aggression. After all, the identification is violent: it spells out what the subject is but at the same time it indicates that it is not something else—something is thereby *done* to the subject. The concept of the mirror phase became the core of Lacan's theory of the human subject, in which all notions of unity and absolute autonomy are swept aside as mere illusions. It makes it clear that the identity of the child is accomplished (not preceded) by this stage. This structure remains present throughout human life and characterizes all human interactions. The relation to what is ideal in us, to our ideal-egos as well as our ego-ideals, derives from this fundamental violence or alienation. Thus it becomes clear that the ego, at bottom, is a self-idealization, and its identity inherently violent.

In using the mirror stage Lacan deals differently with the ego as conceived in Freud's topography. There its functions include voluntary movement control, memory, adaptation and learning. And likewise the super-ego (which comprises both a critical, self-observing and punishing function, and the setting up of ideal goals derived from the ego-ideal) is formed by internalization, through a complicated process of identification, of parental demands, prohibitions and ideal images. But according to Lacan there was not enough emphasis on the ego's function of *méconnaissance*—the refusal to acknowledge thoughts and feelings; instead the later Freud put too much emphasis on the ego's adaptive functions. In the mirror image she sees her form in an external image, in a virtual, alienated, ideal unity that cannot actually be touched. The disarticulation of the infant's movements and bodily prematurity are reversed for her in the fixity of a big statue of and for herself. The two aspects of its appearing (fixity and stature) symbolize the ego's mental permanence and at the same time prefigure their alienating fate, the statue into which a human being projects herself. The formation of the ego commences at the point of alienation and fascination with one's own image, which then organizes and constitutes the subject's vision of the world.

From very early on the infant is captured by the human form. The mirror stage inaugurates an identification with other human images and with the world the subject shares with them. With the primary conflict between identification with, and primordial rivalry with, the other's image, a dialectical process that links the ego to more complex social situations has begun. As far as clinical practice is concerned this implies Lacan's opposition to any idea that one should help the analysand to strengthen her ego, or to help her adjust to society in any way, or that one should help her tolerate unconscious impulses by building up her ego. It indicates how the ego's mastery of the environment is always an illusory mastery. As a result of the way it is formed at the mirror stage, the human subject will continue throughout life to look for an imaginary wholeness and unity, thus captivated and victimized by the illusion of autonomy.

In dealings with the Oedipus complex Lacan emphasizes the function of the lack of the object and lack in general. Freud's Oedipus complex indicates an organized set of loving and hostile wishes that the young child experiences toward its parents. In the so-called positive complex the child desires the death of its rival, the parent of the same sex, while harboring sexual desires for the parent of the opposite sex; in the negative complex the child loves the parent of the same sex, and hates the parent of the opposite sex. The peak period for the experiences is, according to Freud, between three and five years of age and it is considered to play a fundamental part in structuring the personality and the orientation of human desires. This basic structure of desire follows for Lacan from the law of the signifier, in that it signifies something only in relation to another signifier. Desire is always desire for another thing. The object of desire is the desire of the Other, to be understood as a desire for the Other and the Other's desire. The infant tries to identify herself with the mother's object of desire in order to be that object of desire, and in addition she has desires for her.

In Lacan's understanding of the Oedipus complex, the phallus, as the signifier of what the mother lacks, has a decisive role in the relationship between the parents and their child. The child does not enter the triangular (Oedipal) relationship and the Symbolic Order merely in relation to the satisfaction of her needs attended to by the mother. The relationship is also based on the recognition of desire, particularly the desire of the mother. Indeed, once the child has the capacity for language, there is a qualitative change in her psychic structure, that is, an alteration of all the pre-verbal structures (such as the perception of the fragmented body, the regulatory images from the mirror stage that captivate her, the *Gestalt*—oral, anal, Oedipal) to fit in with the language system. It is the father who introduces the principle of law, in particular the law of the language system. The end of the original unity of mother and child is precisely what leads to the subject's possibility of becoming a subject of desire. Without the Law, which deals with relations with others, the mother can autonomously, in a sense arbitrarily, deal with the child's wants. In the unmediated realm the other is not bound by any law and the child is a possible toy of her changing answers. The presence of a third person, one could say (literally or figuratively) the father, breaks this fusion-like unity open. He is also the one she desires. In this sense the child cannot be everything for her mother and she is not only there for her. The relationship between mother and child is mediated by a third who represents the symbolic law of the culture.

The mother (who lacks the phallus) provides the necessary care for the infant. She desires in the infant something other than herself: that she satisfy the lack which is the basis of the relationship with her father (who plays a prominent role in the symbolic order on which she depends). The infant is then caught in an imaginary relationship with respect to the mother and the phallus. Her desire can be structured by the desire of the Other only if she can identify with the mother's object of desire. She intimates to the mother that she can make up to her what she lacks and be, as it were, the metonymy of the phallus. In order to escape the all-powerful, image-inary relationship with the mother, and to enable the constitution of the subject, it is essential for the child to be drawn into the symbolic order. Lacan speaks of this intervention of the third person in terms of the "name-of-the-father." The father intervenes, either directly or through the mother's discourse, as the omnipotent and prohibiting figure, putting in question and forbidding the desire of the mother, laying down the Law and permitting identification with him as the one who has the phallus. The girl (symbolically castrated) can solve her Oedipal situation in receiving the phallus in fantasy (in the form of a substitute, that is, a baby as symbolic gift); and the little boy has to accede to the paternal position, legitimately in possession of his own phallus.

The Symbolic Order and the Unconscious

The separateness already indicated in the mirror stage is moreover affirmed when the child enters the symbolic, the social order of language and culture. Before the subject can act as a self, it is projected and absorbed in the universal order of language and culture. The child has to settle herself in this order. The symbolic order does not consist only of a system of different meanings (differences), but also of a complex network of discourse, conversations of the Other. The term *discourse* refers to what is said, to the conversation, to its content, to what is regarded as important. Because of that network, the subject is not only subjected to the formal system of signifiers, but also to the way in which these are organized in the discourses of others, in other words subjected to a historically determined meaning. A particular story foregrounds certain aspects of man's being in the world. It is revealing and concealing at the same time. It affirms and objectifies human being and world and identifies a particular human being; thus she can differentiate herself from others. The story defends itself against the reproach of not being true (in competition with other stories) and it provokes answers. It frustrates and alienates as all expression is metaphoric and therefore clouded by language. The child is absorbed as a part of a network of tales (discourse) told by others about him, some of them even before he was born: "It is a boy. Doesn't he take after his father?" This network consists of a number of prohibitions and commandments, desires, anticipations, obligations and value judgments to which the child has to accommodate herself. These discourses are contradictory and do not give a coherent image of herself. As a consequence the subject can never satisfy their demands. By identifying herself with the discourse of others, the subject achieves a relatively safe place in the confusion of more or less contradictory discourses. It is firstly through her mother and father that the structure of what is being told (the stories) will reach the child. The identity of the child reveals itself as the consequence of what others say about her and desire of her. It is indeed the Other, according to Lacan, who gives structure to one's desires.

The unconscious images, the discourses of the Other that cannot inscribe themselves in the subject, that cannot be accommodated by the subject, stay active in the mind and come to the surface in all kinds of symptoms unavoidable for the subject. They cannot be accommodated, are at war, with the already existing images in the subject. In this sense, the intentions of the conscious subject are always surpassed by the unconscious. Not only is the narcissistic subject (cf. the mirror phase) radically separated from the authentic subject (the one who says "I") and from the symbolic order, there is also an unbridgeable gap between the symbolic order and the authentic subject. The subject, the "I" who speaks of herself, is not the same as the "I" that is spoken of: the meaning surpasses her. The subject (the one who says "I") is not master of herself, but subject of the symbolic order: *Je est un autre*—"I" is another (Lacan, 1966, p. 118). The subject arises in relation to desire that is unknown to her. The Other is the real witness and guarantor of the subject's existence, as it is she who can recognize the subject. In the perception of the subject the Other is not affected by the same lack, and can be identified with the mother's original role in relation to the infant. The Other is where the subject is born, not only as a biological entity, but as a subject with a human existence.

From the moment of initiation into the symbolic order the subject can never reach any more what she in the end desires. That is what keeps the desire going. But it is also the symbolic law of the language and culture that makes it possible for the child to withdraw herself from the suffocating omnipotence of the Other. There is always the desire of the Other, who recognizes or does not recognize her desire, who approves or rejects, allows or punishes. Here and with the mirror metaphor Lacan reiterates (albeit critically) a Hegelian philosophical tradition in which subjectivity is achieved culturally through mutual recognition in the symmetry of reflection between self and others. To develop in a meaningful way the desire needs the recognition of the Other. Thus the desire of a human being, becomes the desire of the Other—"le désir de l'homme, est le désir de l'autre" (Lacan, 1966, p. 693). As the Other is also a subject, based on a lack of being, the mother's love cannot be absolute as she cannot fulfil this absolute demand for love made by the infant. The demand for love goes beyond the objects that satisfy this need. In this irreducible beyondness of demand, desire is constituted. Unlike Freud's version in the chain of conscious reasons, the Lacanian "unconscious" will not provide the answer we cannot find on a conscious level that leaves no gaps. The unconscious reminds the subject that reasons will never really do, it marks the ineliminable impossibility of understanding human desire in a definitive way. The structure of human desire (as a language) makes its opacity clear, that it can never be completely satisfied, that always something different is longed for. The human being's craving for happiness is embedded in a desire that is not interested in happiness. Notwithstanding her concern for herself, the subject is at the same time part of what is not concerned for her, the symbolic order. This truth of the unconscious, that human desire is not limited to what is good for herself, is something that the subject does not want to know.

Because the Other is (necessarily) deceiving her, the psychoanalyst's function is not to answer the subject's appeals and demands, but instead to act so that the answer comes back to the subject from the analyst as a question: What do you want from me? What the subject lacks or has lost is not present in the Other. And pleasure is bound to desire as a defence, a prohibition against going beyond a certain limit of pleasure (*jouissance*). This forbidden is what the unconscious strives to express. The linguistic bar between signifier and signified comes to take on a new meaning: the subject is barred (to pleasure) and can only express her desire for a forbidden enjoyment.

To summarize: the expectations of other people are contradictory, which explains the fact that they appeal to the subject from different positions. The subject must constantly search for what she has to do. Still she has to act. She is assimilated into a given symbolic system, according to Lacan, a rupture with the preceding stage in which the subject was not yet independent, and typically accompanies a unity with her mother. It is in this assimilation that meaning is shaped for the individual. The recognition of the Other and the recognition by the Other originate with this assimilation. The future subject only becomes a subject when and in so far as she participates in the reality of mutual recognition within a network of rules and discourse. The function of the Other is therefore a condition for the manifestation of the subject. As the child cannot speak, meaning has to be passed to her from an already existing language, nor can she desire without being absorbed in a network of specific and particular desire. These networks, meaning and desire, fix the subject within a particular culture. She is immediately caught up in the human order, structured by certain relationships, identified by language.

The Subject's Responsibility

The more the subject is conceived as autonomous, the more she can be held responsible; the more she is seen as heteronomous, the less responsible. Lacan's originality brings psychoanalysis and structuralism together. Both accept that the area of human responsibility is limited from the inside and the outside as these are both dimensions of the unconscious. What kind of subject are we thinking of? A subject that is not at one with itself, estranged from itself, but is multiple, many selves, unity shattered. The narrative that is told by the Other only temporarily ascribes her some unity. But there are many stories, many others, many different occasions to generate a story. The subject seems to have evaporated. And the Other? She is not necessarily someone who will give joy to the subject, neither is she someone to be cared for. The Other threatens the subject because of her identification of her, one of the possible narratives that can be told. Here the basic dimension seems to be one of opposition.

The subject finds herself amidst the conflicting, sometimes irreconcilable, identifications of others. What can she do? A lot of things, but nothing to secure the recognition she is yearning for. In this structure of power can the subject play only a minor role? Has ethics (as traditionally conceived) disappeared, because it is not clear which perspective, among the many which others supply, is correct? How can the subject but fail others since different things are demanded of her? These questions follow from the traditional ethical picture, but a different perspective on ethics seems to have emerged here. Indeed Lacan's psychoanalysis sets itself a different task. It does not prescribe who we should be or what we must do, but raises new questions about the place of desire in the search for wisdom and in the nature of obedience to the Law of Duty. It introduces a new kind of problem for ethical reflection, that is, that there is something in our desire that goes beyond what we think we want for ourselves. It raises the question of contingency in our lives in a new way, for it links this not to the good we can know, but to the inherent morbidity in our desire which takes us on paths we can neither design nor foresee. It holds that in our moral lives, in our moral destinies, there is no general wisdom. To live well is no longer to master one's life wisely, nor is it to submit to a master who teaches us how.

Desire condemns us to a kind of causality irreducible to either a social or a psychological determinism. The stumblings in our acts and tongues bear witness to the sense in which our libidinal bodies cause our symptoms, our dreams, our compulsions. Lacan introduces the question of causality into an ethical setting connected with the ancient problem of knowing how to respond to what happens to us. His psychoanalysis rediscovers the sense in which development is entirely animated by contingency, by *tuche*. He links the fragility of goodness to the morbidity of desire. The events that make up our libidinal destinies are events of a particular kind, forgotten in what we say and do, and in who we are and become. What happens to us is a matter of fortune (Aristotle's *tuche*) rather than choice (Aristotle's *proairesis*): things happen to us that we cannot regulate and so we forget them and repeat them in the disorder of our lives. This fortune is not a matter of determinism, rather it sets the unconscious working. Libidinal necessity means that our bodies never stop writing themselves in our destinies. Though our fortune as erotic beings can never be foretold, the way that fortune works itself out can be interpreted. The law of psychic causality is neither social nor psychological, but structural. This law structures the singular way desire works through our life.

Desire is so structured by repression that it appears to us an occasion for remorse or guilt. We are obligated or guilty sorts of beings before we even formulate just what our obligations or duties are, and the principles that would govern them. Lacan's question is therefore whether there can exist an ought or a must, a responsibility that is more than just another command of the super-ego. *Wo es war, soll ich werden*[4]: this *sollen* is something else than being guilty, and yet it is not a simple ought, something that causes or determines that one become. The *ich* to which the precept is addressed is not an ego, not a generic entity like Freud's or Kant's, the same in each of us; the precept is not in this sense an appeal to our humanity. The *ich* is an "I" that does not yet exist, that cannot yet know who it is and what it will become. The way "I" figures in our lives is through the improbable *tuche* (chance and fate) of our fortune. The particular ethical problem with which psychoanalysis confronts each of us is not knowing the law of our own erotic destinies. Previous ethical thought had sought to surmount this in the concept of a knowing subject that can transcend and master its own desire. Freud thought he had shown the existence of an eros that undermines this supposition. Lacanian psychoanalysis introduces the problem of a new kind of responsibility: the responsibility of our own desire.

The distance that separates us from classical ethics lies in the disharmony between the unconscious bodily inscription and what we say and think, an incompatibility between our eros and our ethos that according to Lacan is characteristic of our modern scientific civilization and its tragedies. No wisdom prior to myth or law, but a tragic universe, where the law in living is prior to the knowledge of the good and fundamentally incompatible with it; where one can transgress the law without knowing it, or only knowing it after the fact. Eros makes of us obligated sorts of beings prior to our observance or transgression of any particular obligation. Our eros, our desire, confronts us as an imperative or necessity we cannot locate in ourselves or in the world of our interests. The reason we cannot find it within or without, the reason for its sublime transcendence to us, is that it is structured by repression: the law is repressed desire. The value of sublimation is for Lacan the value of the capacity we have to represent to ourselves, this *réel* that would lie at the source of the idealizing ethical fictions secreted in the interval between Aristotle and Freud. Sublimation is the possibility civilization offers us for something else than the symptoms of our discontent. In it we satisfy just what we would otherwise satisfy in our symptoms, our imperious desire. We invest ourselves in sublimatory objects, which bring us the promise of a new kind of bond that would bring us together as subjects of the unconscious: the promise of a new erotics. The *réel* for Lacan is what we miss, what we come up against, the obstacle we stumble over—and miss: the inconceivable wonder that things are what they are and not some other way. This order does not permit a simple mirroring or coordination of the inner and outer world of the subject, because the elusive subject is also ordered, here as a feature of an original insufficiency. Rather than the cure of an ego-psychology, the care or concern of analysis for Lacan seeks to sustain this heart of insufficiency as desire.

THE LAW OF HUMAN BEINGS: THE LAW OF DESIRE

The law of human beings is the law of language, says Lacan. The human being ought to give up her narcissistic relationships with the other(s) and recognize the otherness of the Other according to the place a human being has in the order of being. This law regulates also the entry to reality. Lacan differentiates the object as mediated by language and the "pre-linguistical thing" or "Thing." By sublimation Lacan identifies that special relation in which an object becomes a Thing. Here too the task of the subject is to overcome her narcissistic relationships to objects: the completely satisfying object (*la Chose*) will bring with it the death of the subject of desire. The Law preserves the life of desire; the desire of a human being must adapt itself to the constraints of the symbolic system of language. The center of Lacan's thoughts on ethics is desire itself. The subject has to understand herself as a subject of desire. Because of the vital needs originating in the pre-linguistic being of the subject, which the subject cannot satisfy by herself, she has to direct herself to an other subject. The exteriority of the symbolic means that this also results in alienation. In its turn this causes the subject to will to reject her being as a subject of desire. As the subject has to remain a subject of desire (or alternatively die) and as the satisfaction that the subject aspires to goes beyond the level of needs and what is longed for, the subject of desire is referred to as an other subject: "Le désir est désir de désir, désir de l'Autre, soit avons-nous dit, soit soumis à la loi" (The desire is desire of desire, desire of the other, be it subjected to the Law) (Lacan, 1966, p. 852).

The ethical significance of desire is that human beings can relate to it in different ways. A human being has the choice of betraying her desire or living in accordance with it. It therefore offers itself as a criterion of guilt: of how true to it we are. Though through the symbolic order language protects a kind of possession that is narcissistic, ethically a human being has still the choice to respect the order of being or to dominate it. In this lies her responsibility. A human being is therefore guilty toward being, has to live the openness so that being can bring itself forward (Heidegger speaks of the *Entbergung von Seiendem*). Here what is envisaged is not only what is there, but also what is not there. The wall of language separates a human being from Being. Speaking justly (in German *das rechten Sprechens*) is the way Lacan conceptualizes the mission of her true relationship with being. Whatever the subject does she can never realize this aim fully. As no way of speaking can make the real exhaustively explicit, she can never live up to her responsibility. In the eyes of Lacan, only the mystic in her complete otherness is capable of this.

It is quite clear that ethics, at least in its traditional sense, has disappeared because the Lacanian subject does not know who she is. Nor can the inchoate subject identify a correct way of acting because of the possibility of multiple perspectives. Rather than constituting an autonomous subject, the law of language generates a subject who has to pay tribute to the chain of signifiers; in other words it is a subject of the unconscious. And though there is no need for a strong subject that is transparent to herself in the full-blown sense, one is confronted here with a subject that cannot find itself *in principle,* that would not recognize itself because "it" does not know how to look for "it"—the ever-shifting identifications, in ever-shifting metonymy of meaning. And incidentally, the process of metonymy is regarded as essential, for once through a process of metaphorization the subject is identified in a certain sense, it has to escape this metaphorization or forever be locked up in itself (possibly resulting in psychosis). For Lacan, there is only a minor place for the fact that to label someone is also to recognize her as a human being. And though this may be violent, it is (at least) at the same time a recognition.

The promise for education (as far as there is a message) may go back to something basic: the importance of being surrounded by people who care and indeed demand a lot of those whom they care for. Nothing is indeed more violent than being left out, not desired at all by the Other—at the extreme not being able to enter the symbolic order. Lacan's position hints at a new ideal of personhood, interpreting what one does and does not do to understand better how and why one desires what one particularly longs for. And maybe all that in order to be able to accept (at last, and each time anew) who one is, to find at least for a moment one's peace, and one's truth.

LACANIAN THEMES IN EDUCATIONAL PRACTICES

Above it was indicated how childrearing can be seen from a Lacanian perspective. Turning to the context of formal education one can see that the thoughts and actions of teachers and students are influenced by the imaginary, symbolic world of the school. Even if the student thinks and speaks to herself, the Other exists, choosing the words in language that can best be understood by her. The Other becomes a central concern, "it" controls the infant's first associations with her parents and forces her to attend to the world, teaching her to see it in terms of logic, rules and orderliness. Schools make an important contribution to society by reproducing the *status quo* both in its intellectual and cultural variants. Still, they have been able to maintain the fiction of neutrality and autonomy, providing significant ideological services to a capitalist society. Here the culture of the school is conceived as transmitted through pedagogic practices, validated by the political power of the state. These practices, in combination, provide students with a language that defines them and their place in the social system, definitions of "what is important for youth growing up in the inner city," for instance. In reality a litany of traditional values and beliefs are recited to them, which seek to define what is good and bad, who is intelligent and stupid, and what good manners ought to be in the classroom. Good taste and the norms of educational decorum are placed in front of children as a constant reproach: this is how you should act if you wish to be considered an intelligent and worthy person. Thus the socially correct attitudes and behaviors of classroom life are taught. Children are not to chew, fight, or throw things. They are not to leave their desks or talk without permission. The teacher has the right and duty to control their bodily movements and gestures, can force them to sit still and be silent, and can punish and humiliate them with a word. Rothstein (1993) argues that schools have always been tied to other agencies of capitalism, even as they denied such links. They have arisen from social and political customs and from the functional needs and beliefs of those who funded them. And in pursuing their own purposes, "they [have] developed a special history and practice, borrowing methods from mental hospitals, military and penal institutions, and the charity schools of the early nineteenth century" (Rothstein, 1993, p. 80). The organization of education systems seems to be opposed to change, insisting on a return to basics and a simpler past.

The insistent demands of Otherness are taught in the classroom, a world of words sustained by teachers where the primary Other is the teacher. It is the teacher who has the power to decide, who is the one pupils must attend to, who speaks where they listen. A collective voice of the Other is constructed, reflecting the background and levels of attainment of the children. Only internalization of the *mores*, moral understandings and language of the classroom permits students and teachers to speak and to be understood. It is, however, not something they consciously plan or execute. Early in their schooling, children become aware of the Otherness that teachers and other students represent. The Other in these instances is never an actual person, but always an unconscious construct in which the word is located and used by children and teachers alike. With their servile silence and submissive gestures, students seek to soften the coerciveness and authority of the all-powerful adult, summoning up and transferring behaviors and identifications from previous experiences with all-powerful parents. Mostly students seek recognition and acceptance as worthwhile and competent persons, and some measure of assurance and predictability in their relationship with the demanding teacher. "A very good answer" is not only an encouragement and praise but creates also the dangers of dependency and submissiveness. As long as the teacher ignores her role as a state-employed worker, as long as she is ignorant of the social functions of schooling in modern life, she cannot understand her true relationship to her students, Rothstein (1993) argues.

Here the unconscious is that part of an educational system's history that is marked by mythology, folklore and amnesia. It is the proscribed past that has forgotten its own roots and social functions. It can be uncovered in the words and phrases that teachers and students use when they speak to one another. It can be discerned in the traditions and folklore of schooling, and in the normative and ethical structures used to validate pedagogic practices. Every experience of failure and rejection in classrooms leaves personal scars. The humiliations of student experiences are often repressed and unavailable for conscious retrieval. But what has been forgotten still exists and affects the way students and teachers act. As the context of education reveals itself as serious and important, the child represses her social needs and desires. She accepts her subordinacy and regimentation because all of her own kith and kin have advised her to do so, and because of her own dependent status in her family and communal relations.

At another level, there is also an unconscious conflict between teachers and students as the child can never accept her institutional identity and the negation of her personal self. On some level she will struggle against the conscious and reasonable arguments of adults. In the symbolic order we may speak about unified efforts to achieve common goals, but the reality of the struggle for dominance in classrooms is a constant negation of such ideological pronouncements. A critical point may occur when children decide that they have nothing to gain by integrating themselves into the coercive educational environments of mass schools. Quite evidently, no education can occur without the consent of students. Teachers have decisional rights over students, but only so long as children are willing to concede these rights. During the day teachers take the place of the symbolic father. The teacher-student relationship can thus equally well be seen as an imaginary and a symbolic one. The unconscious elements in classroom discourses are denied, and consciousness and discipline are emphasized. The imaginary relationship between students and teacher is one of transferred affection and aggressiveness: two egos struggle to make sense of a socially produced situation, both trying to maintain their senses of self between narcissistic images of personal and institutional lives.

There are many educational examples where the Lacanian perspective might prove itself useful. When small children are doing well in mathematics, they might sometimes become fearful if confronted with more complicated problems. The child needs to be disturbed out of this kind of complacency and needs to be made to confront the mathematics problem. Instead of giving the correct answer, the teacher might try to help them to feel more secure, that they are up to this—thus not taking this task away from them. At the other extreme, in the writing of a PhD thesis, the adult student—while also working at a full time job—frequently struggles with the question of where it all leads to. Such a student will go through periods where the whole thing seems impossible, she thinks she is not able, she does not have the time to do the topic justice. But perhaps the struggle is internally related to the quality of the learning and to what is produced; a student's PhD work can come too easily. This may also more broadly be true of education. It points to the inappropriateness of separating what is learned and the learning involved from the person of the learner in a broad sense, though not of all learning of course, for example, learning to type. Here the supervisor should not try to answer but return the question and its difficulties to the student. Though she might try to rechannel the candidate's energy when she goes through a difficult time, it would be wrong for her to offer answers. Constantly available and maintaining that there are ways forward, she should refrain from giving one, instead creating the opportunities for the student to find one for herself. There is also the adult learner returning to study, perhaps someone who left school early having not done well. Typically such students are deeply anxious about coming into the alien institution and very worried that they will fail. They need more careful handling than their younger counterparts. Again there seems to be something about the sense of lack they feel which is internally related to the quality of their learning. Often such learners seek a kind of counselling from their tutors. But crucially they must learn to live with their lack and to confront it and to grow from it. Again it would be a betrayal to her real interests if the student were *not* frustrated, comforted but not confronted with real learning itself. Another case is the youth who fantasizes about a future career. There is an incredible range of choice in higher education and there is a tendency with the rapidly improving information and guidance on these matters to treat the decision in an excessively rational way. Again the student ought to become frustrated. The careers counsellor should acknowledge her desire and indicate alternatives, but she should stay away from indicating the answer. Her project ought to be a negative one, as again it is the student who has to find for herself what she wants to do. As for the pilgrim of earlier days, it is most important to travel. Here as elsewhere there is the message that you can't know what you really want unless you are confronted with something. In such a position the student of the British Open University may find herself not knowing what she wants to do, yet encouraged by her tutor's comment that she herself never knew what she wanted to do either. Teachers appear here as mentors who give advice but who are themselves as much learners as the learners. And as in sport, frustration and failure are sometimes desirable in teaching. This is at odds with finding *the* correct answer as suggested by the technological spirit in education; rather it points to the idea of self-realization in progressive education.

COULD IT BE OTHERWISE? LESSONS FOR THE FUTURE

Not only in the context of the family, but also in schools, children find themselves in a situation from which they cannot run away. What is generally the case for human relationships presses itself even more insistently in educational contexts. The alternative that Rothstein seems to have in mind (that we could indeed escape) is ruled out forever. Lacan teaches us that inasfar as we are not indifferent to others, inasfar as it matters to us that we mean something for them—and according to him it is, of course, not possible for a mental healthy human being to exist otherwise—we are part of a chain of expectations. Necessary and healthy as this might be, it also carries the risk of not finding one's truth among the contradictory discourses of others, or worse of being suffocated by their identifications (the imaginary level). It has been shown that this position generally stresses the importance of there being significant others, of caring and of keeping desire going, that is, making sure that there are enough channels open for one to find a pathway. Though not restricting one's movements as a parent or teacher through particular guidelines, this position does, however, prevent us going in extreme directions, in the search for limitless autonomy and authenticity, for absolute freedom. The worst sin educators might commit is therefore probably that of not reacting to their own children. In offering answers parents and educators make clear that there are answers (thus not abandoning them and leaving them completely on their own), that this is what they do, but that there are also other options open, exemplifying at the same time the groundlessness of human life. Due to the special relationship between parents and children, the child knows that she won't be left out if she chooses to act differently. She knows what it means to belong to them and learns to live with uncertainties within a particular range. And most of all she is characterized by the fact that she doesn't long for answers but for the recognition of herself by her parents. Thus she acts: "I don't want answers, I want you." And as for the educator, she should create space and time and make it clear that taking a position cannot be avoided, always bearing in mind the vulnerability of the child.

The Lacanian position thus challenges several pictures that are deficient and that held us captive, not the least that we know what we really want. In stressing the third person perspective and the way the infant is fixed into this order, Lacan finds a subtle balance. At the core of his stance is not how we have to justify what we do, not the offering of particular justificatory frameworks, but how justification itself is structured. How our discourses develop, and that they need not develop the way they do, that other options are possible, is made clear. Moreover it shows that every answer a person gives provokes new questions, bringing to the forefront other conflicts which can never really be sorted out, thus keeping alive the ineliminable life-long quest. It recalls Socrates' "know thyself" by indicating again how this it not really possible. This position also reminds us of the plasticity of human desire, of its multiple expressiveness, and helps us to resist a life, a politics, an ethics that are purely utilitarian, slave to instrumental rationality. For the subject herself, as for the Other, it must be kept in mind that things could be different and that we need to make sure that there is room for those alternatives. The Lacanian position reminds us over and over again that there are many rooms in the house of being and that transgressing this border by trying to delimit them is dangerous. An estrangement from herself will destroy the subject and put humanity itself at risk. The all-encompassing and revelatory nature of this perspective might well prove to be a sufficient answer to the question: Is this all we can sensibly say about education? It is indeed about learning to live with one's desire.

NOTES

1. Different authors figure in the *vom Kinde aus* movement, such as Montessori, Decroly, O'Neill, Steiner, Freinet and Dewey, on whose ideas different types of more radical educational institutions were based culminating in the *anti-autoritäre Pädagogik* in the late 1960s.

2. For a more elaborate general introduction to Lacan see Benvenuto and Kennedy, 1986.

3. Capitalized Law is used to refer to the Law-of-the-Father, of which the incest prohibition is the archetypical form.

4. The Freudian "es" refers to drives. The dictum "Wo es war, soll ich werden" refers to Freud's position that the structure of the ego is needed in order not to be overwhelmed by one's drives, nor by one's ideal-ego (cf. Freud's reality principle). Lacan will distance himself from Freud concerning this.

Chapter 9

Folly, Words, Wigs, Rags

The decision makers . . . allocate our lives for the growth of power. In matters of social justice and scientific truth alike, the legitimation of that power is based on its optimizing the system's performance - efficiency. The application of this criterion to all of our games necessarily entails a certain level of terror, whether soft or hard: be operational (that is, commensurable) or disappear.[1]

J.-F. Lyotard, *The Postmodern Condition* (1984, p. xxiv)

FOLLY

How are we to think of the *ends* of education? How are we to go about answering the question, What is education for? The question of the nature of education, of "who is the educated man," was a staple of philosophy of education as it developed, in the United Kingdom and to some extent in the wider English-speaking world, as a quasi-autonomous discipline in the 1960s and 1970s. The educated man (in much of the literature his gender was not in doubt) had liberated himself from the irksome contingencies of the present and the particular; or he had learned to structure his understanding of the world via such forms of knowledge as could be rationally distinguished. His education took the form of an initiation into "worthwhile activities." Whatever the variants, he was a recognisable and worthy heir of the Enlightenment tradition. Now if there is one thing that postmodern writers have persuaded us to distrust, it is these grand narratives of emancipation, rationality and progress. We take that point to need no elaboration here. What is less clear is how, in the wake of writers such as Lyotard, we are to go about questioning the nature and purpose of education in general, or indeed whether the question any longer makes sense. Perhaps, like the question What is Enlightenment?, it can only be looked at in historical terms, as who thought what and when, and under the determination of what historical influences. Perhaps even to ask the question has been revealed as folly.

One of the effects of the introduction of the National Curriculum of England and Wales in 1988 by the neo-liberal Conservative administration under Margaret Thatcher, was the stifling of debate on the question of the aims or ends of education. There were various reasons for this. A curriculum based almost wholly on familiar subjects such as mathematics, science and, geography, as the National Curriculum is, could be represented as intuitively obvious and in little need of overall justification. In line with this the National Curriculum quickly laid claim to a kind of middle ground which no one of common sense would dispute. Much was made of the idea of "entitlement" to its provisions, as if it was only a matter of restoring traditional and unquestionable benefits that had been taken away, presumably by progressives, socialists and other undesirables. And the pace of change[2] of the 'reform' of education naturally concentrated minds on questions of means, on implementation, to the detriment of serious thought about specifically educational desiderata or ends.

Certainly there are those who would have us believe that, like history, education—or at least arguments about what it is for—has come to a finish. A European White Paper on Teaching and Learning (1995), for example, declares that "Everyone is convinced of the need for change, the proof being the demise of the major ideological disputes on the objectives of education" (p. 9). A later section is entitled The End of Debate on Educational Principles; it tells us that "Heated debates concerning the organization of education and training systems—including debates on content and training methods—have taken place over the last few years. Most of these debates now appear to have come to an end" (p. 25). All philosophical questions are either solved, then, or declared redundant by bureaucratic *fiat*. All that remains is questions of *how*, of means: "The central question now is how to move towards greater flexibility in education and training systems" (p. 9). It is of course convenient for bureaucracies to specify aims and objectives and then call for an end to debate,[3] and the increasing tendency of governments to prescribe the detail of educational provision can seem to some to bring with it a welcome relief from awkward questions about ends:

in teaching generally, *the goals have already to some extent been set* . . . . Basic aspects of teaching and teaching competence may be contestable and teaching strategies are certainly argued about, but in school-based teacher education in the UK, for instance, we've already taken on a relatively specific set of purposes: our goal is to turn out people who are capable of teaching their subjects in British schools. Recently, in fact, the British government has attempted to spell out the nature of this capability in more detail than ever in the form of competence statements. (Tomlinson, 1996, pp. 62-63, emphasis in original)[4]

Here the conversational language ("we've": the full paragraph also contains an "isn't," an "it's" and a "we'll") and the relaxed "to some extent" and "relatively specific" operate to conceal the full prescriptivity of the system with which the writer appears prepared to collude. The reader will not be surprised to discover that Tomlinson's chapter is called The Effective Facilitator.

It is the notion of effectiveness, and its close relation efficiency, that have above all replaced proper consideration of ends. A culture in the grip of "effectiveness" and the technical/instrumental rationality of which it is an aspect takes ends as given, and is concerned chiefly with the means by which these given ends can be (efficiently) reached.[5] But surely whatever we want people to do we want them to do it effectively? The trouble is that talk of effectiveness is not so agnostic about ends as it pretends. It imports substantive ethical values of its own under the guise of ethical neutrality. Those values can be summarized in the phrase "measuring up:" do these people measure up? Are they meeting their targets, have they made the required *efficiency gains*? (If there is a phrase that encapsulates for our time the spirit of Orwell's Winston Smith, setting his features "into the expression of quiet optimism which it was advisable to wear when facing the telescreen,"[6] it is the phrase "efficiency gains.") It is Lyotard's great service that he helps us to see just what substantive values "effectiveness" introduces: compliancy with established systems and optimizing the system's performance. "The true goal of the system . . . is the optimization of the global relationship between input and output—in other words, performativity" (Lyotard, 1984, p. 11). In the world of education in the United Kingdom, the repeated emphasis that it is teachers' job to "deliver the curriculum" is a sign of the triumph of these values.

Writing two years after the publication of *The Postmodern Condition*, Alasdair MacIntyre (1981) observed that these are the values characteristic of a way of life where the bureaucratic manager has become a central figure. Acknowledging that we are unused to thinking of effectiveness as a distinctively ethical concept, MacIntyre wrote:

Managers themselves and most writers about management conceive of themselves as morally neutral characters whose skills enable them to devise the most efficient means of achieving whatever end is proposed. Whether a given manager is effective or not is on the dominant view a quite different question from that of the morality of the ends which his effectiveness serves or fails to serve. Nonetheless there are strong grounds for rejecting the claim that effectiveness is a morally neutral value. For the whole concept of effectiveness is . . . inseparable from a mode of human existence in which the contrivance of means is in central part the manipulation of human beings into compliant patterns of behaviour. (p. 71)

To be "effective," then, is to be good at finding means for predetermined ends. "Effectiveness" and its cognates become key terms in a culture where the devising of means has become a dominant activity, where consideration of values, of the ends to which means lead, no longer takes place to any significant extent: where we know where we stand, and make our arrangements and accommodations within the ends laid down for us.

WORDS

If the language of performativity, of effectiveness, has made it seem the mark of folly to ask what education is for, can we take one step back and examine language itself: can we ask what *language* is for? As we shall see, the technocrats who engineer the education system have anticipated us.

Of all the curriculum subjects English, as United Kingdom government ministers and advisers insisted on calling it (after a brief tussle in which "Language" was overthrown), seemed most likely to keep questions of educational ends alive. The purposes of English teaching, after all, had been a matter of vigorous controversy for over half a century, between, for example, proponents of utilitarian purposes such as filling in forms and understanding written instructions on the one hand and defenders of the great "literary heritage," or the refinement of sensibility, on the other. The government set up a Committee of Inquiry into the Teaching of English Language (thus generously making room for both contenders to the subject-title, but rendering literature invisible), which produced the Kingman Report in 1988. This was followed by two Cox Reports, *English for Ages 5 to 11* (1988; referred to below as *Cox*) and *English for Ages 5 to 16* (1989). What do these reports have to say about the ends or purposes of English teaching?

The absence of discussion of this question in Kingman prompted one of its members to publish a formal note of reservation: "what these educational aims should be, what English is on the curriculum for, is not really explored here with any rigour, but simply asserted" (1988, p. 77). *Cox* appears to be in no doubt that the issue must be addressed: "we needed first to be clear about the nature and purposes of English as a school subject" (1988, 2.1). Different views of the function of English teaching are listed in a succinct summary of the principal philosophies of the last thirty years or so. The tendency for views to be polarized is deplored.[7] We find the declaration that "the best practice reflects a consensus," not in the sense of a "timid compromise" but in that of "an attempt to show the relation between these different views within a larger framework." How odd to call this a consensus! It is tempting to see this, and the quest for a larger framework, as the continued yearning for some master narrative, so removed from the Lyotardian acceptance of incommensurability of language games and advocacy of irreducible difference, even unresolvable dissensus, the justice of the differend.

These reports are the Rosencrantz and Guildenstern of the National Curriculum.[8] Like those Shakespearian courtiers they were sent for by their political masters; and, similarly unclear about the possibilities of independence open to them, they exhibit the same mixture of confusion and disingenuity.

Hamlet:	You were sent for; and there is a kind of confession in your looks which your modesties have not craft enough to colour: we know the good king and queen have sent for you.
Rosencrantz:	To what end, my lord?
Hamlet:	That you must teach me . . .

The underlying performativity of these reports emerges in two features in particular. First, it emerges in the way that knowledge about language and skills with language figure so large in the attainment targets set for children of different ages. Where we lack a criterion by which to judge one kind of understanding more valuable than another, one attainment more sophisticated than its predecessor, it is natural to fall back on the notion of simple increase: more knowledge, more skills, are better than less. Thus "reading over a widening range of prose and verse" at one level and over "a still widening range of prose and verse" at the next and demarcating first "some sentences" and then "an increasing number of sentences" with capital letters, full stops and question marks (*Cox*, p. 42, 48). This is the language of industrial productivity and performance, in which the improving operative turns out more and more car exhausts which pass quality control.

Secondly, it is above all talk of effectiveness, efficiency and their cognates that stands in for proper consideration of the ethical in these reports and reveals their performative underpinnings. There are six examples of these terms in the first seven pages of Kingman, including two in the second paragraph. One sentence conveys the flavor well: "Information about language structure is most effectively made explicit at the moment when it is useful in real communication, so that the explicit statement consolidates the implicit awareness and effective learning occurs" (p. 14). Effectiveness is a function of what is made explicit (what else, after all, could be observed and measured?), and language is most nearly itself, it appears, in communication (and *real* communication, no doubt in the real world of business-like dealings) when language is ideally a neutral and transparent medium through which intention passes undistortedly. For Lyotard, by contrast, "'agreement,' 'consensus' and 'undistorted communication' disguise the basic conflictual nature of the language game" (Peters, 1995, pp. 33-34). *Cox* is similarly riddled with talk of effectiveness: children "need to be able to write clearly, appropriately and effectively" (3.22), "people need to be able to communicate effectively" (3.13) and so on.[9]

As with effectiveness, so with skills: *Cox* mentions language skills, interpersonal skills, listening skills, skills of concentration and assimilation, oral skills. Much could be said about the inappropriateness of calling concentration a skill, as if it was something we could choose to deploy just as we can choose to exercise our skills in riding a bicycle. The important point in the present context is that skills operate at the level of means, not of ends. The skilled carpenter, for example, has the know-how to make the dollhouse we order. As a carpenter he does not question our choice of ends and suggest a rockinghorse as less sexist. This is why reading is not a skill (though it may involve skills): does not becoming a reader (as opposed to being able merely to decode) involve among other things coming to value books, testing one's vision of the world against the vision they embody? Reading, that is, touches the ends and values of life. We see here how difficult it is to reconcile as complementary some of the aims of English teaching that *Cox* complains are too readily polarized, such as "reading for meaning and decoding" (3.5). When you think of reading as a skill you *are* siding with one polarity. Indiscriminate talk of skill, in short, is exactly what we would expect to find where there is no proper thought given to ends and values, where performativity reigns.

What conception of ends, then—the point and purpose of English as a curriculum subject, and the ends of education as a wider enterprise—are we left with in this scheme of things? The prevailing view of ends in the reports we have discussed is that they are simply *given*, in the shape of people's needs or what society requires. For example, the ends of English teaching are said to be given by the need to participate (effectively, of course) in a democracy, to cope with tax returns and manuals for the installation of washing machines (chap. 2). One passage is particularly revealing :

We live in times in which social and technological change is taking place at an unprecedented rate and we face an unknowable future. It may be difficult to suggest what bearing this predicament should have on the school curriculum, but to try to develop adaptability must be a sound strategy. Ability in language can contribute powerfully to adaptability. (p. 8)

In other words, when it has to be admitted that our ends-as-given-needs cannot be known or predicted satisfactorily, this very uncertainty is expressed as a need, the need for adaptability.[10] Here it does indeed seem that we are haunted, if not terrorized, by the inexorability of ends: when our ends are hard to determine ("an unknowable future") this very fact is expressed as a determinate end. At the same time however we find the very opposite idea here, that ends may be something we can select for ourselves at will. "Language expresses identity, enables co-operation, and confers freedom. . . . Language is the naming of experience, and what we name we have power over" (Kingman, p. 7).[11] How easily, it seems, language can be a transparent medium (see Chapter four) through which our purposes can pass to their objects!

The idea that language gives us the capacity to take what we want, whatever that happens to be, looks of course incompatible with the idea that our ends are given. But together these ideas make up a familiar picture of late twentieth-century man and woman, and in that sense they are complementary. In one part of their lives individuals are cogs working non-autonomously to ends set by others or by the supposed nature of things. In another part they exercise their will in acts of choice which are unconstrained by any other source of value. At one moment they are producers, part of a system controlled by others or by impersonal economic forces, and at another they are free-floating consumers able to take down any of the goods on the shelf as long as they have the money or the credit to pay for them. Many of these goods, moreover, are acquired for the sake of the fantasies they embody: they are not just what we contingently want but *have been sold to us*. They embody what we have been induced to want (the car has been sold to us on the strength of its image of conferring power, carefreeness, sexual attractiveness).

These reports, then, present us with a disturbing picture of education without ends, without any worked-out conception of what it is for. And this in turn leaves us with a model of the human being as learner that lacks something which we have come to think of as characteristically and importantly human: the possibility of deliberation (social as well as individual), of reflection about our goals and purposes, which is the process by which we arrive at our ends and values. For deliberation is redundant if ends and values are given, while if ends are the product of unconstrained choices, and values are subjective, deliberation can amount to little more than the scrutiny of one's wants to see which, as a matter of fact, is the most appealing.

Furthermore, in lacking an adequate conception of deliberation these reports seriously misrepresent the nature of language. For when we deliberate we struggle to work out our ends, uncertain sometimes even of the relative status of ends and means (as, for instance, when what we come to recognize that car ownership is not something we sought simply because it would make it easier for us to get from one place to another). Language is wholly bound up in this struggle. It is not an easy tool, something which when we have picked up the skill of working it we can safely use to achieve uncomplicated goals like persuading others to adopt our point of view or insinuating ourselves into different social groups.[12] Language has its necessary opacity, sets snares, can confuse or seduce, can point to itself rather than the supposed object of reference. The history of political slogans alone should warn us of the deviousness of language; advertising makes an industry of verbal as well as visual dazzle. While appearing to acknowledge this the reports we have examined exclude the possibility of the very deliberation necessary to understand the role of language in our lives. For we might train children to spot, say, sexual motifs in car advertisements successfully enough; but how, without wider deliberation about ends, are they to grasp that this may be thought manipulative and objectionable—that a woman's personhood is infringed when she is used as a marketing device, or a man's when he is expected to respond to it?

There is too, of course, a complete lack in these official government documents of any ironical awareness (to use Richard Rorty's phrase) that their own language games are incommensurable, that their own vocabularies are not final and immutable. No prescriptive, official government document can afford to emphasize the contingent, revisable nature of its own language game; and this, in the context of the relationship between language and human ends, means that it cannot but give us a misleading picture of how we stand.

In addition to this, literature is consistently marginalized by a view of English that foregrounds the skills of communication. And it is literature that characteristically problematizes the transparency of language and what we refer to elsewhere (Chapter four) as "the metaphysics of presence," often revealing too the part that *power* plays in obscuring our understanding of our ends and of language itself. This is the subject of the next section, whose title refers to the overt and unambiguous symbols of power still worn by counsel and judges in British courts of law.

WIGS

Joseph Conrad's novel *Heart of Darkness*[13] depicts a journey to the uttermost ends of the earth (the phrase is used more than once), located somewhere in Africa. The exploitative Europeans who finance the journey propose uncomplicated ends: "they were going to run an over-sea empire and make no end of coin by trade" (p. 14), but they devote no proper thought to what they are doing. The Eldorado Exploring Expedition, which epitomizes the greed and cruelty of the colonizing Europeans, is said to lack any "atom of foresight or of serious intention" (p. 44). At the heart of the jungle, and the object of the journey up the river which the narrator, Marlowe, leads, is Mr. Kurtz, fabulously successful in amassing ivory. But Kurtz has become a kind of god, his word has become law and his eloquence—his language skills, we might say—has become refined to the point where Marlowe actually thinks of him as a voice: "I had never imagined him as doing, you know, but as discussing" (p. 67). And that eloquence is used to establish power and possession by fiat: "'My intended, my ivory, my station, my river.' Everything belonged to him" (p. 70). Kurtz's relation to his ends is that of someone who believes he can determine at will what those ends shall be ("'By the simple exercise of our will we can exert a power for good practically unbounded,' etc. etc.," p. 72), and that they shall be his; and language is the medium through which he does so, as if language were wholly innocent and transparent. This makes language—contracts, letters and instructions—worthless and meaningless in *Heart of Darkness* when it proceeds from a will that, rather than simply exerting power, is corrupted by exploitative and power-based motives. Kurtz writes an eloquent report for the International Society for the Suppression of Savage customs,[14] yet at the same time he has "gone native" (in that revealingly Eurocentric phrase): he is himself taking part in "unspeakable rites." (Compare the words from Kingman quoted above: "Language expresses identity . . . language is the naming of experience, and what we name we have power over.") Kurtz redeems himself only when he is inarticulate, when his language fails him—when he acknowledges its opacity, we might say—and he whispers "the horror! the horror!" Only then does he come to some sense that his ends are not entirely his to shape. "Everything belonged to him, but that was a trifle. The thing was to know what he belonged to, how many powers of darkness claimed him for their own" (p. 70). Language has not proved a transparent medium to his ends. Kurtz's language, the language of the imperial European power that has sent him to Africa—the language of bureaucracy and capital—has (in Heidegger's way of putting it) spoken him. *Effective use of language gives us power*. Konrad's novel shows how language resists us.

In *Bleak House*[15] Charles Dickens shows us that the search for a kind of 'effectiveness' can lead us into narrow and inflexible conceptions of our ends, turning us into victims of the very (performative) system we thought our effective techniques would enable us to control. He draws a disturbing picture of what happens when language comes to be seen as given and intractable. Here capitalism, or more specifically its legal arm, has saturated language, in Lyotard's terms. The characters of the novel are with few exceptions trapped and baffled by language and signs, especially those emanating from the legal system and its ramifications. At the heart of the novel is the court of Chancery and the interminable case of *Jarndyce versus Jarndyce*, a web of legal jargon which has become an end in itself, and against which all other language games are required to be commensurable.[16] No sensible person can entertain hopes of the case being satisfactorily resolved, and finally the disputed estate is consumed in legal costs. Legal language has become self-referential, and preys on itself. Richard Carstone, one of the wards in *Jarndyce*, finds his life ruined by the case, not just in the sense that he loses what might have been his inheritance but in the sense that in such a world he cannot think properly about ends, about his purposes in life; and so, instead of deliberating, he plumps wildly for one career after another:

"I haven't the least idea," said Richard, musing, "what I had better be. Except that I am quite sure that I don't want to go into the Church, it's a toss-up." "You have no inclination in Mr Kenge's way?" suggested Mr Jarndyce. "I don't know that, sir!" replied Richard. "I am fond of boating. Articled clerks go a good deal on the water. It's a capital profession!" "Surgeon—" suggested Mr Jarndyce. "That's the thing, sir!" cried Richard. I doubt if he had ever once thought of it before.

Finally he becomes an articled clerk because he takes his end from the ineluctable nature of things: as an articled clerk he can come closer to the intricacies of *Jarndyce v. Jarndyce*. The performativity of the law claims him for its own.[17]

His education, notes Esther Summerson, the narrator at this point of the novel, had no power to counter the influence of Chancery:

He had been eight years in a public school, and had learnt, I understood, to make Latin verses of several sorts, in the most admirable manner. But I never heard that it had been anybody's business to find out what his natural bent was, or where his failings lay, or to adapt any kind of knowledge to him. He had been adapted to the verses. . . . I did doubt whether Richard would not have profited by some one studying him a little instead of his studying them quite so much. (p. 218)

His schooling, in short, had well prepared him for the idea that language is a natural fact, an authoritative given to which he must adapt himself. Reflecting on his inability to deliberate about his ends and goals and on the fact that "he was taken by the newest idea, and was glad to get rid of the trouble of consideration," Esther wonders "whether the Latin verses often ended in this, or whether Richard's was a solitary case" (p. 219).

If language really were like this for us, how should we live? We would indeed be terrorized, reduced to slavish, imitative representation, the abasement of our own distinct existence and identity before the true power and reality. Just so, the only name we have for the shadowy figure, yet on whom the plot of *Bleak House* turns, who makes the thinnest of livings by copying legal documents, is Nemo, no one. Or we might embrace the performativity of the system enthusiastically and unquestioningly, as the semi-illiterate Krook hoards old legal documents. Krook meets his end through spontaneous combustion, in a grim echo of the way *Jarndyce v. Jarndyce* is consumed by its own costs.[18] Like poor Miss Flite, unhinged by another suit in Chancery, we might try to keep alive our capacity for using language creatively, as if it were our instrument and not a natural fact. She keeps birds in cages. Their names are "Hope, Joy, Youth, Peace, Rest, Life, Dust, Ashes, Waste, Want, Ruin, Despair, Madness, Death, Cunning, Folly, Words, Wigs, Rags, Sheepskin, Plunder, Precedent, Jargon, Gammon, and Spinach" (p. 253). "Language is the naming of experience, and what we name we have power over" (above). Says Krook, "'It's one of her strange ways, that she'll never tell the names of these birds if she can help it, though she named 'em all.'"

But when the Lord Chancellor gives his judgment, Krook continues, Miss Flite will release her birds. That judgment simultaneously releases the characters of the novel from the legal language that has ruled their lives—they will then be free as birds, able to make their own choices and plump for whatever they like—and reasserts its power. Faced with such authority over human ends, the human capacity for naming is puny and brief.

"When my noble and learned brother gives his Judgment, they're to be let go free," said Krook, winking at us again. "And then," he added, whispering and grinning, "if that ever was to happen—which it won't—the birds that have never been caged would kill 'em."

They must be operational, or disappear.

Exasperated by our powerlessness in the face of such a system, we turn to experts for help. If our ends are fixed for us the experts are a kind of priestly caste who will intercede on our behalf, bureaucrats who can work the system; if we can plump for anything then they are experts in means, "effective facilitators," oiling for us the wheels of our choice. In *Bleak House* the lawyers, Kenge, Vholes and Tulkinghorn, are called on to mediate the mysteries of the law to their clients. In *Heart of Darkness* Marlowe is hired by the Brussels company as that most obvious symbol of instrumentality, the pilot of the boat that is to take them to their chosen destination. But Dickens' lawyers, so far from being mere acolytes or vicars of the mystery of language, are quite deliberately using it to further their own ends. Vholes, for instance, connives in the charade of Chancery because "Vholes and all the little Vholeses must eat," and Tulkinghorn's own dark purposes shape most of the novel's course. The law's victims might well reflect that "they allocate our lives for the growth of power." Conrad's Marlowe, so far from being a mere conveyor or instrument, is the narrator of virtually the whole of *Heart of Darkness* and as such it is he who gives us insight into the muddled understanding of language and of means and ends that runs through the novel.

RAGS

Lyotard has helped us to see that there is no master narrative, no authoritative language game, in which we can conduct our deliberations, whether about the ends of education or anything else. Philosophy in particular does not supply the master narrative for this purpose as it has traditionally been taken to do. Any language game, versions of philosophy included, will speak to us in ways that no other language game will, and say things that no other language game will say. Philosophy is left, as the deconstructionists say, to meditate on its destruction at the hands of literature (see below, Chapter twelve, p. 182): that is, to reflect on its own literariness, and its necessary failure to attain the status of a discourse that transcends the limitations of other discourses—a failure which is not regrettable, since it emancipates us from the fantasy of an ideal language and from foundationalism. Plato's dialogue *Phaedrus* is a text often referred to for this purpose. In it the philosopher Socrates seems to admit the claims of other discourses, notably that of myth. What is less often noticed is that the dialogue is also a rich source of understanding about ends and their relationship to language.

The dramatic context of the dialogue is that the young man Phaedrus wants to know how to live his life, with particular regard to the place in it of *eros*, usually translated as "love" but carrying associations of strong passions and loss of control. When the dialogue opens Phaedrus has been much impressed by the advice of the orator, or expert giver of advice, Lysias. (Phaedrus is very inclined to listen to experts. In the second sentence of the dialogue he tells us that he is walking in the countryside outside the city on the advice of his doctor.) Lysias has given Phaedrus thoroughly instrumental advice. Phaedrus wants to get on: then let him form a liaison with an older man who, without being "in love" with him with all the emotional turmoil and vicissitudes that might entail, will be in a position to promote his career.

The end is known in advance here. It is mutual advantage, and the search for it is to be prudential and rational to the point of cynicism. "You know how I am situated," begins the speech that Lysias has written as a model of how the older man should present his case: the speech that Phaedrus has written down and is carrying beneath his tunic, and which he relates enthusiastically to Socrates. "You know how I am situated" (Hackforth's 1972 translation), "You know the score." Lysias's prose is the language of efficiency, of business: clear but inelegant, colored principally by the kind of accountancy metaphors that lull us into believing that the only things that are real or valuable are those that can be quantified and costed, it is a triumph of performativity. (Hackforth calls it a "tedious piece of rhetoric," "flat, monotonous, repetitive.")

What the dialogue shows us is a different way of thinking about ends. It takes place on the banks of the river Ilissus, a place of sensual beauty where the wind Boreas was reputed to have snatched away the nymph Oreithyuia—a myth Socrates warns us is not to be rationalized. The learning about *eros* and its place in life that both Socrates and Phaedrus undergo involves receptivity, to each other and to the influence of the place. Socrates has left the city, the usual place of his philosophical activity, and is powerfully moved by Phaedrus's physical presence (234D). Phaedrus abandons the protection of a cold, prudential view of *eros* such as Lysias offers him and opens himself to Socrates (243E). Here each learns something about his ends and purposes by seeing them reflected, with subtle alterations, in another (cf. Martha Nussbaum's discussion of the *Phaedrus*: Nussbaum, 1986, esp. pp. 223 ff.). The mutual respect, verging on love, which each has for the other modifies, as they deliberate, their sense of what life is about and how to live it; and it modifies the kind of language that is admitted to be germane to their discussion. Love, awe, tenderness, and not just intellect or reason, are heard in the dialogue. We see that our capacity to think about our ends is shaped by the sense of what our ends might include, and shapes them in turn. To think prudentially about *eros*, whether to marry for love or advantage (to put it in modern terms) is to make one decision very much more likely than the other. The characteristic quality of my *eros* touches my intellect and the very language that I use. My thinking is colored by qualities it takes from the energy, intensity, honesty and truthfulness of my attachments. My sense of my ends changes as I apprehend them through the influence of the people and places by whom and which I allow myself to be surrounded.

In all this language is neither a ready instrument in our service, whatever our ends, nor is it an ineluctable given, an authoritative techno-science such as the Sophists cultivated (or so Plato tells us), susceptible to division into discrete techniques such as Exposition, Direct Evidence, Indirect Evidence, Probabilities, Proof, and Supplementary Proof (266E ff.). This is to make language into a rigid system of signs like the legal system in *Bleak House*, a recipe for the accumulative knowledge (*hypomnesis*) of experts in performativity rather than the flexible and sensitive use of words in the uncovering of human values and possibilities that Plato calls true memory.

This chapter has sought to show how Lyotard's repudiation of performativity, and its implications, illuminates some bewildering aspects of the world of education. It has sought to reveal the way in which the dominance of performativity, the language of efficiency and effectiveness, paralyzes our ability to think about our ends and purposes, as Phaedrus is paralyzed and seduced by the worldly realism of the Sophist Lysias. The way forward, if we are to learn to think again, is not of course to recover or build a competing grand narrative, a master discourse, in which to think about our ends, but to explore the manifold language games, many of which modernism has marginalized, and find how and where they are useful, how and where they can help us with what we want to understand. This is the spirit in which Socrates and Phaedrus move among different language games, including myth, dialectic, speculative anthropology as well as philosophy, their closeness to each other allowing them (Phaedrus especially) to make moves in languages which they would otherwise have feared and distrusted.[19] We need a keen eye for wigs, for the operations of power and the new (dis)guises which performativity wears, and we need to learn to move freely again among the rich plurality of rags, of language and forms of language. That very plurality fragments power, and diminishes its effectiveness.

NOTES

1. See also below (Chapter twelve, p. 175).

2. See Lyotard, 1984, p. 61: "Speed, in effect, is a power component of the system."

3. Compare *Education for Adult Life: The Spiritual and Moral Development of Young People*, a Discussion [*sic*] Paper produced by the United Kingdom's School Curriculum and Assessment Authority (1996), p. 10: there is "concern that prolonging the philosophical debate may already have hindered practical progress in schools."

4. See Lyotard, 1984, p. 48: "The transmission of knowledge is no longer designed to train an élite capable of guiding the nation towards its emancipation, but to supply the system with players capable of acceptably fulfilling their roles at the pragmatic posts required by institutions." The source of the example from Tomlinson (1996) is an unpublished paper on mentoring by Jean Howard.

5. As Lyotard (1984, p. 37) puts it, this is the result of "the blossoming of techniques and technologies since the Second World War, which has shifted emphasis from the ends

of action to its means."

6. George Orwell, *Nineteen Eighty-Four*, Part I, chap. 1.

7. "[P]eople set in opposition individual and social aims, or utilitarian and imaginative aims, or language and literature," Cox, 1988, 2.6.

8. See R. Smith, 1989.

9. *Key Stages 1 and 2 of the National Curriculum* (1995), the government's summary of the revised National Curriculum for 5 to 11 year olds, sets out the "General Requirements for English" for all Key Stages (i.e., up to the end of compulsory schooling). It lists what they should be taught to do, or what skills they should be taught to use, under the headings "To develop effective speaking and listening," "To develop as effective readers," "To develop as effective writers" (p. 2).

10. See Lyotard, 1984, p. 63: "The technocrats declare that they cannot trust what society designates as its needs; they 'know' that society cannot know its own needs since they are not variables independent of the new technologies. Such is the arrogance of the decision makers—and their blindness."

11. There are some interestingly similar remarks in the earlier (1975) Bullock Report, *A Language for Life*, most notably the vigorously foundationalist quotation from Gusdorf which prefixes chapter 4: "Man interposes a network of words between the world and himself, and thereby becomes the master of the world."

12. These two examples come from Kingman, p. 10.

13. All references are to the Penguin 1971 edition.

14. But there is "a kind of note at the foot of the last page, scrawled evidently much later, in an unsteady hand . . . 'Exterminate all the brutes!'" (p. 72).

15. All references to the Penguin 1973 edition.

16. This, we could say, dramatizes the way that meanings are internal to language, not external to it.

17. See Lyotard, 1984, p. 61: "The system . . . must induce the adaptation of individual aspirations to its own ends."

18. See Lyotard, 1984, p. 55: "A complete definition of the initial state of a system (or all the independent variables) would require an expenditure of energy at least equivalent to that consumed by the system to be defined." Lyotard illustrates the "impossibility of ever achieving a complete measure of any given state of a system" with a parable from Borges: "An emperor wishes to have a perfectly accurate map of the empire made. The project leads the country to ruin—the entire population devotes all its energy to cartography."

19. The *Symposium* works in the same way, adding autobiography to the language games.

Chapter 10

Learning by Heart

Knowing by heart is no knowledge; it is merely a retention of what has been given into the keeping of the memory. What we really know we can make use of without turning to the model, without turning our eyes to the book.

Montaigne, 1958, p. 57

How might someone be said to learn by heart? Classic cases are the memorization of historical dates, of multiplication tables, of songs, stories, poetry, and play scripts, and of telephone numbers. While the French also learn by heart (*par coeur*), the Dutch do it outside themselves (*van buiten*). Does anything turn on such difference? What, in any case, is a heart?

The now familiar distinction between surface and deep learning connects with aspects of method and content (see Entwistle, 1990, p. 135). Surface learning treats everything as not relatable or anchorable, concentrating on memorizing bits of information. Deep learning aims at understanding meaning by relating it to established ideas. There are facts and there are thinking skills. Facts become meaningful when thinking locates them in cognitive structures. What is to be learned may be anchorable in cognitive structures or it may consist in relatively isolated bits of information. But potentially anchorable facts are sometimes presented so that rote learning is encouraged, with meaningful connections overlooked. A curriculum might then be criticized for either the preponderance of subject matter that is not meaningful or its treatment of potentially meaningful content as if it were not.

Complaints to the effect that learning is not deep are familiar enough. We find them in Rousseau's concern that Emile should not have more words than ideas, in the satire of Mr. Gradgrind's teaching methods in *Hard Times*, and in countless books and government reports exposing the limits of purely didactic teaching. Good teaching has surely always recognized this. But must "the mere habituation, as knowledge got by repetition, from unintelligent memory" (*The Concise Oxford Dictionary*) of rote learning necessarily be condemned? Does the metaphor of surface and depth reflect an essentialism that is blind to the functioning of signs considered in Chapters one and three? And further, is not the broad sweep of the generalization about learning here at odds with the arguments of this book?

One objection to learning by heart is that the learner may know the words but not understand them; such learning, let us say, is ineffective. Gradgrind's rigid adherence to "facts" regardless of the context, or of anything remotely like cognitive perspective, seems amply to demonstrate this point. The child mimics the teacher with no more understanding than the parrot. The child sings along with the hymn woefully confusing the words. The student crams for exams memorizing key sections of textbooks. Such learning discourages understanding. A second objection is that, with advances in technology, learning by heart is a waste of time; such learning, let us say, is inefficient. The poets of ancient Greece demonstrated prodigious feats of memorization and recitation, as have storytellers through the ages. We can imagine a world where all the books have been burned, as in Ray Bradbury's *Fahrenheit 451*, where this might become necessary again. But we also know that technology, first of the printing press, then of archives and electronic databases, has made this extraordinary effort unnecessary. With the changes in access to knowledge, what we need are information technology skills rather than the burden of bodies of knowledge. With karaoke machines there is no need to remember songs. These are then formidable objections to learning by heart. Moreover, it may inhibit the growth of the ability to think for oneself. When Montaigne or Rousseau or Dewey rail against bookish learning, they see it as divorced from real experience and potentially incapacitating. What is learned in this way—unlike what is learned from experience—depends on a kind of faith: the learner must take things on trust. Suspicion of learning by heart raises questions of indoctrination and of authority.

But in some ways perhaps, and especially at the beginning, learning must be like this. This in turn involves a kind of sacrifice of the possibility of autonomy, in a submission that cannot as yet be explained. There have been indications of a reaction in favor of learning by heart, especially in primary education. Teaching methods in Taiwan apparently support the traditional view that learning tables by heart can be efficient and effective, equipping the child well for subsequent study. But are there ways in which learning by heart has educational value beyond the scales of these criteria, beyond efficiency and effectiveness?

If something is learned by heart, it becomes familiar. Familiarity, a kind of habituation, is evident in various aspects of learning. The student of a foreign language memorizes vocabulary. Words are then recalled actively in the student's speech and writing or encountered passively in the words of others. But this active-passive polarity scarcely does justice to the way words operate. The student's words meet her half-way. Sometimes she looks for a word; sometimes words come into her head unsolicited. The fact that the words have been learned makes these particular thoughts possible. Something seems to have been laid in store, something whose future use was unclear.

Following and repeating is all the more evident in first language learning, a matter of initiation rather than skills acquisition, indicative more broadly of cultural initiation. The child copies and the child remembers, much of this before understanding. That the child knows how to go on is the criterion for learning. In this initiation the child confronts the particular sounds and marks of our language, and words have astonishing resonance. "Tiger," perhaps, is a stripy word. Wednesday is fat, Wittgenstein is inclined to say, Tuesday is lean (Wittgenstein,

1953, p. 216e). Each child has her own idiolects; and sometimes these are handed down, actively fostered in the family scene. A different kind of familiarity is evident in the case of the actor who learns lines with progressive ease. The actor does not need to understand, but having the words opens new possibilities of thought: there is a store of texts that she can call to mind but which will also come into her thinking involuntarily.

What is learned by heart has a certain textual form—a nursery rhyme, some lines from a speech. One can know by heart not Elizabethan drama but specific speeches, not arithmetic but tables, not chemistry but the table of the elements. The specific formulation defies cashing out, reduction, or exchange and we cannot readily account for its value. Perhaps it exceeds rational command. Thus facility with language can be only badly described in terms of language skills. The know-how that is developed must be tied to a knowing-by-acquaintance where the happy familiarity with sounds and marks can extend into more complex forms:

Reflection upon language can help us to understand the edifying power and special status which Plato attributed to mathematics. Mathematical objects as non-empirical individuals may be compared with grammatical forms, the vision of which can joyfully excite the mind. A certain level of structure in any study may be accorded an analogous position, from which indeed we can see how any serious learning is a moral-spiritual activity. (Murdoch, 1992, p. 338)

Iris Murdoch's remarks, or Simone Weil's observations about the spiritual value of school studies (Weil, 1977, pp. 66-76), complicate the question of learning by heart by pointing beyond accustomed ways of thinking. There can be something inherently attractive in such forms and such particulars with far-reaching implications for our lives.

Something of this complication is evident in the expression itself. In the quotation from Montaigne at the start of this chapter a problem is already evident. While the first sentence condemns learning by heart, the subsequent commendation of "what we really know" states that this must not require turning to the book. Yet it is precisely when we know by heart that we do not need the book. Montaigne misses the oddity of the expression. Why knowing by heart? This is a puzzle that we will stay with. To intensify it let the etymology be recalled: in Latin to remember is *recordare*, to bring back to the heart.

Learning by heart will exceed the economy of teaching and learning. We must sound a note of the scandalous, in some sense defy the rationality of this economy. If what has been said so far in this chapter seems remote from moral education, we must now consider texts that—in a sense that we will come to—cause ethics to tremble. Jacques Derrida speaks of learning by heart as a storing up of riches, a "thesaurisation," as a learning beyond semantic comprehension. What is thus stored is not present and not in use; in the attic or the chest, sometimes arcane perhaps, these treasures exceed our calculable needs and any calculated use. Derrida quotes from the Gospel of Matthew, where the Latin (or the Greek) underscores the repetition:

Lay not up for yourselves treasures upon earth (*Nolite thesaurizare vobis thesauros in terra*), where moth and dust doth corrupt, and where thieves break through and steal. But lay up for yourselves treasures in heaven (*Thesaurizate autem vobis thesauros in caelo*), where neither moth nor rust doth corrupt, and where thieves do not break through and steal. For where treasure is, there will your heart be also (*Ubi est enim thesaurus tuus, ibi est cor tuum / hopou gar estin thesauros sou, ekei estai kai he kardia sou*). (Matthew 6: 19-21/Derrida, 1995a, p. 98)

The storing up of treasures is not instrumental for heaven is never to be made present. If one gives one's wealth to the poor, one commits oneself to an *an*economy of giving, a dissemination of value deeply linked with the infinite deferral that operates through language. There is renunciation here perhaps of the claim to have and of the claim to know, to make way for faith. This is a giving without reserve, a dissemination with no clear outcomes or calculable returns. We come to know such texts first through a repeating without knowing, as repetitions in the Sermon on the Mount tacitly show. Thesaurisation is a wording of the heart, revealing the heart's location, and releasing language to do its work.

We are suddenly in deep here. Do as you would be done by, an eye for an eye and a tooth for a tooth, the workings of rational self-interest, the social contract—these are economies of social morality that must be juxtaposed with the religious as this is dramatically explored in Kierkegaard's *Fear and Trembling*. Derrida's reading of this work leads through alms-giving, charity, revenge and the sacrifice even of what one loves most. The full scandal can be seen. Kierkegaard's text—written under the pseudonym of Johannes *de silentio* and with its "preamble from the Heart"—is a religious and ethical polemic on the horrifying story of Abraham's submission to God's will: that he make a sacrifice of his son, Isaac. Abraham's acceptance is unreserved; he neither offers nor seeks any explanation of what he must do. For this cannot be justified by any ethical principle; it is a violation of ethics. Abraham's action, the account insists, cannot ultimately be understood. It must be seen in terms of its singularity and of the Absolute, a sacrifice defying any satisfaction of a principle, hence any possibility of rational explanation. Abraham must remain silent. Yet the demands of the ethical must not disappear: (systematic) ethics must remain but as a temptation to Abraham. He is doing the right thing and he is doing the worst thing. The paradox and the scandal of this must be sustained.

There is an appalling fascination in this story. But for all its horror Derrida partially domesticates the scene. Sacrifice is critical for it points to the way our individual responsibility confronts us with particular circumstances where we cannot but do harm. Is sacrifice remote from our daily lives, confined, at most, to those terrible dilemmas that we sometimes face? Or, preferring to pursue conscientiously your job, to care for your family and friends, are you betraying those countless others—starving and homeless—to whom you have obligations? If we weigh up the goods and contribute our dues to charity (with a clear conscience that we are doing our bit), we are blinded in a kind of bourgeois complacency to what is at stake.[1] Recognizing responsibility, in contrast, must destabilize our accustomed ethical reasoning. Our dispassionate assessment of values, our confidence in ourselves as autonomous agents, our mastery—this kind of picture no longer holds steady once we confront the particular demands of our lives and their irresolvable conflicts.

It is not just that a utilitarian weighing of different values is shown to be wrong; *any* rule-governed ethics is unable fully to respond to the particular case. If the ethical viewpoint is destabilized or superseded, we are deprived of a public discourse and consigned to privacy. The circumstances of our choice are determined by that public world but in the unique moment of our decision we are alone. What is the structure of thought with which we must then confront our responsibilities? We need the structure of the conscience speaking silently to us and watching all we do, beyond the kinds of justification that ethical explanation might provide. Falling into that ethical language, we become hidden behind the social mask. At odds with the stability of oneself in one's roles there is the uncanniness of being a person. "What is this 'I,'" Derrida asks, "and what becomes of responsibility once the identity of the 'I,' trembles in secret?" (Derrida, 1995a, p. 92) Adopting the language of ethics involves seeing things in terms of the general and the universal; resisting this requires silence and secrecy, the work of a conscience that cannot be seen in public. The paradox of responsibility is that we must do both. Derrida adopts the ambiguous formula, *tout autre est tout autre*, where the tautology, "every other is every other," is in play with the incommensurability and intractability of "every other is every bit other."

This interiority, neither innate nor a naked confrontation with the world through experience, is not given but accomplished. It is not the interiority of the solipsist, nor yet the realm of Sartre's radical freedom and the *acte gratuit*. We reach this interiority by way of our initiation into language and culture, first by repetition and observance. From language and culture we arrive at the moment of decision, but then we are alone. Ultimately, like Abraham, we cannot account for ourselves—hence scandal and paradox. And we know that others have this same interiority. This recognition of others is not a matter of Hobbesian prudence nor yet of Christian altruism: a mature moral perspective must acknowledge the other's uniqueness and her strangeness to herself.

The paradox embraces the conflict between the singularity and secrecy of the absolute demands of a particular moment and the publicity of culture and language. How can the absolute demands of the particular avoid being dissolved in the language of the general? How can responsibility be retained? Speaking, says Kierkegaard, relieves us for it translates into the general. In Derrida's words, "Once I speak I am never and no longer myself, alone and unique" (Derrida, 1995a, p. 60). Singularity dissolves in the medium of the concept. In contrast, an infinite responsibility is bound to silence and secrecy; this, one might say, is the silence of action. Responsibility *in general* involves answering for oneself, committing oneself to language (and hence substitution) and to certain roles (and hence substitution): presenting oneself before one's fellows. Kierkegaard says that ethical exigency is regulated by generality. As Derrida puts it: "The ethical involves me in substitution, as does speaking. Whence the insolence of the paradox: for Abraham, Kierkegaard declares, the ethical is a temptation. He must therefore resist it" (Derrida, 1995a, p. 61). Responsibility *in the absolute*, a counterweight to accountability, involves silence, non-repetition, secrecy, non-substitution: presenting oneself before God (otherwise before one's conscience).

It would be easy to get stuck here, to urge that if Abraham's actions can be approved this must be on the basis of reasons—for what else can approval mean? What is required is not an avoidance of the temptation of ethics but a reappraisal of the values incorporating them into the system. It is important to resist this, however, again to maintain the paradox. This may be elusive but, as paradox, how else could it be? Abraham might say: it is God's will. This is less a reason than beyond reason.

In "Sauf le Nom," Derrida writes of negative theology with its canons of aphoristic texts and its tradition of repetitions.[2] The aphorism is taken on trust, accepted without full comprehension: "These works repeat traditions; they present themselves as iterable, influential or influenceable, objects of transfer, of credit and of discipline" (Derrida, 1995b, p. 51). The aphorism does not speak dogmatically to us but enigmatically and recurrently. This body of theology is imprinted on the tongue of the speaker in "a language that does not cease testing the very limits of language, and exemplarily those of propositional, theoretical, or constative language" (p. 54). Thinking on such words leads beyond habitual paths of reasoning. Any naturalistic ethics and tidy subject-object relation are dissolved. The body itself comes to be seen as inseparable from thought and from the word, in a way that extends deep into the religious tradition.

Asking what the heart is generates a kind of alternative physiology. The heart is not a pump, not even a receptacle, but a construction from the laying down of treasures, a treasure chest of words. The ear hears the silent voice of the conscience: what you hear in your head compellingly all the time is not sounds but words. The tongue bears the imprint of the body of theology, informing your words and the response you can make. The eye, unlike the public eye or the eye of surveillance, lights up your inner life. The repeated phrase "thy father which seeth in secret" (Matthew 6) indicates a structure of subjectivity that secretly witnesses all that you do:

Once such a structure of conscience exists, of being-with-oneself, of speaking, that is, of producing invisible sense, once I have within me, thanks to the invisible word as such, a witness that others cannot see, and who is therefore at the same time other than me and more intimate with me than myself, once I can have a secret relationship with myself and not tell everything, once there is secrecy, and secret witnessing within me, (there is) what I call God in me. (Derrida, 1995a, pp. 108-109)

The heart constitutes a thesaurization of your response to the world, made possible by the words that you are given, and making possible the invisible answering of your inner life. Reflect on these words and this idiom. The force of the language here reminds us how much the kind of language we use determines what we can think. This is to displace the transmissional and the constative with evocation and invocation—the prayer, the apostrophe, the encomium, the address *to you*, a calling to that answering of your inner life.

How important the language must be that frames education. Premodern and religious contexts revive for us an idiom in which a different conception can be expressed. In place of the transmission of content, teacher and learner can perhaps be seen as in service of a subject, at least of something beyond themselves. The aim of complete mastery starts to look like a kind of blasphemy excluding mystery and the ineffable. Naturalistic ethics is exposed in its shallowness by the revival of the concept of evil, something that is beyond the reach of technical solution. (Too secular a language prevents the expression of this.) The semiological medieval world, in Charles Taylor's phrase, implies less an indoctrination than an imprinting with texts, texts that function through dissemination. It is significant that Derrida has spoken of dissemination in terms of the loss of the father. Let us retrace elements in that family scene.

In our initiation into the mother-tongue we find a kind of home that is both familiar and uncanny. We are closer to ourselves than we can see yet our words remain other and deferred. Sometimes we look for words, as if searching in a darkened attic; our words come like ghosts to meet us halfway. In the poem *North*, Seamus Heaney tells himself to "Lie down in the word-hoard," invoking his ancestral Northern past, and the rich laying down of words and sounds in the Anglo-Irish dialect. The hoard of treasure is a thesaurus of words impressed on the heart. These words and thoughts can come (and sometimes must come) involuntarily. These are well-springs of thought. In a more recent poem, remembering childhood again and revisiting home, Heaney answers to his father's teasing words in this recollected scene:

> "Oh you go now! Run, son, like the devil
> And tell your mother to try
> To find me a bubble for the spirit level
> And a new knot for this tie."
>
> But still he was glad, I know, when I stood my ground,
> Putting it up to him
> With a smile that trumped his smile and his fool's
>   errand,
> Waiting for the next move in the game.[3]

The wit here foregrounds the word, and this predictable idiosyncratic little joke of the father (now dead) is disseminated here in this repetition. In the interstices of language there are surprising connections and reinforcements to be articulated, dark spaces maintaining their silence. Consider the play of "spirit level" here, its wandering iteration in this poem called "The Errand," where the errant Heaney remembers the home he has left, in this collection called *The Spirit Level*. There is the spirit of the father revived here, inspirational to the writer, and spirit as the provisional settlement in the familial, and in the political, "game." The words yield these possibilities. But consider also other resonances: how responsibility requires response. Heaney responds to his father by accepting the responsibility of standing up to him, of levelling with him. As a young man Heaney leaves the family farm: he stands his ground by leaving his ground.

The sources and springs that these words provide are anarchic forces against rigidity and indoctrination. W. B. Yeats speaks of "the foul rag and bone shop of the heart," a disorderly and unpromising source that yet offers unexpected gifts (Yeats, "The Circus Animals' Desertion," 1965, pp. 201-202). Sherlock Holmes berates Dr. Watson concerning what he calls the lumber room of the mind. Against the sharp clarity, the economy, of Holmes' mind can we accept and welcome the contingency and jumbliness, the rags, the sheer thereness, of what is known in this way? Against Holmes, it may be that those particulars of the heart, in their textual specificity and familiarity, draw from us a kind of love, as for the recollections of a song or a religious text, or for the remembered words of a lost father. Children go back again and again to the same story, wanting the repetition of words they know by heart. This may be a retreat into nostalgia, a sentimental longing for home. But it may nurture a sense of the words as familiar yet still to be received, like those of the aphoristic religious text, where mastery is not an option but humility is required. Then knowing by heart may not be so far removed from that perfectionist longing in education, evoked in Plato's *Symposium* by Eros. It may also incline us to think along lines suggested by Meister Eckhart and Dionysius the Areopagite: "love is of such a nature that it changes man into the things he loves" (Heidegger, 1975, p. 176).

Learning by heart cannot be avoided. In fact, people take pleasure in it, strutting their stuff as quiz show experts or flaunting their fluency in their favored jargon. In Steiner schools small children learn poetry in languages foreign to them. British Muslim children chant the Koran uncomprehendingly. Yet they are not untouched by these words: the words are charged with sound and context and play a role in their lives. While for many the liturgy of the church no longer figures prominently, we are confronted with the mass media as never before. Advertising jingles, pop songs, catch phrases from television series, football chants, strings of swear words that trip off the tongue, and media clichés are, as it were, absorbed into the system. Some find satisfaction in specialized jargon, perhaps degenerating into an arid technicism. For others, it is the loop of a neurosis where a personal story obsessively repeats itself. Violence on television may or may not have its harmful effects; the implications of what is learned by heart in this way, however, are more general and more pervasive, greater also perhaps than the effects of any lesson in moral education.

We have to talk and how we talk and see our situation is a product of the kinds of language we have. How we see our situation is already a moral matter: the moral life is not separable from the language we have for seeing the world. When you have something awful to face do phrases from Shakespeare or the Bible or from the *Readers' Digest* or *Hello* magazine come to mind? In which terms do you see things? The language of efficiency and effectiveness inculcates a kind of moral Esperanto, where skills acquisition displaces attentive appreciation, where the dogma of technicism are surreptitiously passed on, and where words are reduced to instruments of communication. Like the language of no place, the moral landscape that is implied lacks a topography and names of places, positions being determined by spacial coordinates. Preoccupation with the acquisition of skills, with credit accumulation and transfer, with tariffs of punishments and rewards, says something about the kinds of return, the acquisitiveness perhaps, to be expected from learners. For, although something might be made of skills in relation to memory, the inadequacy of skill-talk for the way language is learned and for our mature linguistic competence is evident when it is acknowledged what, and how much, must (continue to) be received. Complacent presumptions in favor of instrumentalism and acquisitiveness can then give way to receptivity and responsiveness.

Knowing things by heart has a deep attraction and this defies the economy of teaching and learning. It exposes limitations in that economy and the need to think beyond its criteria of success. These matters are surely a part of moral education; they help to show why education is always a moral matter.

Teaching and learning can stimulate the heart to beat faster. Stimulants carry a risk. The learner puts herself on the line, anxious about making mistakes, about failing, about being shown up, about . . . seeming . . . daft. The teacher faces the class in circumstances that can go well or awry. There is a critical edge in the challenge of speaking and, of course, risk of disorder. The body itself is exposed to potential ridicule, even to danger. Policy and practice have generally suppressed this risk, seeing only its unruly side. Where learning outcomes are safely predetermined a circle of calculation can be sustained. It is no accident that, in this same book on Abraham and Isaac, Kierkegaard rails against preoccupation with outcomes. "Lecturers," cut off from the convulsions of existence, have lost sight altogether of the fact that

ever since the Creation it has been accepted practice for the outcome to come last, and that if one is really to learn something from the great it is precisely the beginning one must attend to. If anyone on the verge of action should judge himself according to the outcome, he would never begin. Even though the result may gladden the whole world, that cannot help the hero; for he knows the result only when the whole thing is over, and that is not how he becomes a hero, but by virtue of the fact that he began. . . . [I]t is the outcome that arouses our curiosity, as with the conclusion of a book, one wants nothing of the fear, the distress, the paradox. One flirts with the outcome aesthetically; it comes as unexpectedly and yet as effortlessly as a prize in the lottery and having heard the outcome one is improved. (Kierkegaard, 1985, pp. 91-92)

Sardonic wit exposes the shallowness of this safe curiosity where responsibility is diminished. The gift of the lesson, learning by heart, the risk of teaching represent a different economy, an aneconomy which engages more deeply otherness and responsibility. This different economy makes way for different ideas of *oikos* (home) and of language:

There is an economy but it is an economy that integrates the renunciation of a calculable remuneration, renunciation of merchandise or bargaining [*marchandage*], of economy in the sense of a retribution that can be measured or made symmetrical. In the space opened by this economy of what is without reserve there emerges a new teaching concerning giving or alms that relates the latter to giving back or paying back, a yield [*rendement*] if you wish, a profitability [*rentabilité*] also, of course, but one that creatures cannot calculate and must leave to the appreciation of the father as he who sees in secret. (Derrida, 1995a, p. 107)

One must act justly without seeking recognition for it. One must give alms without seeking reward. One must teach and learn without wanting "results" (and without intending to build a personal portfolio or record of achievement, or to acquire skills), in renunciation sometimes of the claim to know. Reward is then of an incalculable kind and not to be seen. Dissemination works through these practices, just as it works through the growth of understanding and the growth of the person, and its effects are deferred.

The following list (and the ragged supplement of phrases it gives way to) revisit the words we have dwelt on:

Economy	*Aneconomy*
Efficient and effective learning	Learning by heart
Transmission or facilitation	Giving
Resources (standing-reserve)	Sources
General or universal	Particular
Rule-governed ethics	The absolute
Commensurability	Incommensurability
Replaceability	Irreplaceability
Others as commensurable	*Tout autre est tout autre*
Ascribed identity	Unique identity
Role	Person
Natural being	Spirit
Hard eyes	Lidded eyes
Eye, receiver of light (focused to inspect)	Eye lighting internal field (of conscience)
Ear as receiver of sound	Ear as response to silent call
Heart as pump	Heart as place of treasures
Wigs.	Rags
Language as communication	Uncanny (re)source in language
Home (the familiar) as ordinary	Home (the familiar) as uncanny
Delivery	Gift (dose—that which is given)

The list gathers contrasts that are drawn in this book. Efficiency and effectiveness are not enough: the ragged supplement must unravel them. Such disparity will generate endless difficulties for education but it is this supplement that is the more important.

The lack that motivates the learner becomes an erotic longing, a kind of perfectionism without perfectibility: wholeness to be prayed for, not to be attained. A world apart from the perfectibility of the smoothly functioning cycle of economy, this is a resistance also against other totalizing claims—explicit and substantive ideals of the good life. It recognizes something of the necessary secret of the sign, of its iterability; hence of the secrets of our thought and our lives. It sees human being as non-natural and spiritual, where the thesaurization of the heart is at the heart of education. Awareness of the workings of dissemination in teaching provides a sense of home, and hence of the familiar, as a place with a diaspora within. It opens the possibility of a teaching without reserve.

NOTES

1. This is, of course, poles apart from the kind of argument advanced by Peter Singer, who questions the extent of the moral difference between shooting a few peasants and failing to give money to Oxfam. For a discussion of this in relation to remorse, see Raimond Gaita's *Good and Evil* (Gaita, 1991, pp. 43-65).

2. The key text here is "Sauf le Nom" (Derrida, 1995b), though the preoccupation with negative theology is more general. An indication of what negative theology is about, drawn from this text, is provided by the following lines from Angelus Silesius (in Derrida, 1995b, p. 52):

> *Der unerkandte GOtt*
> Was GOtt ist weiss man nicht: Er ist nicht Licht, nicht Geist,
> Nicht Wonnigkeit, nicht Eins [Derrida's Version: Nicht Wahrheit, Einheit, Eins],
> nicht was man Gottheit heist:
> Nicht Weissheit, nicht Verstand, nicht Liebe, Wille, Gütte:
> Kein Ding, kein Unding auch, kein Wesen, kein Gemütte:
> Er ist was ich, und du, und keine Creatur,
> Eh wir geworden sind was Er ist, nie erfuhr.

3. "The Errand" from *The Spirit Level* by Seamus Heaney. Copyright © 1996 by Seamus Heaney. Reprinted by permission of Farrar, Straus & Giroux, Inc. and Faber and Faber Ltd.

Chapter 11

The Learning Pharmacy

What does the development of open learning tell us about teaching and learning? What does concern about this development show?

I

"Open learning" has become a slogan for change. Developed especially in further education and community colleges and extending to universities, it claims a key role in the learning society. A technologized conception of teaching and learning, shaped significantly by psychology and information technology (IT), it is promoted sometimes as a kind of educational panacea. It would be pointless to try to pin down a term that has come to be used in a loose and opportunistic way. Let us instead assemble a sort of Ideal Type of what we will call "the technology of open learning" and juxtapose this against standard criticisms.

Open learning involves the use of prepared learning packages *to which the student makes a largely written response and where the role of direct contact with the tutor and with fellow students is minimal.* Distance-learning *courses and drop-in* learning centers *extend access to make education available at a time and place to suit the student.* Diagnostic systems *determine the student's learning needs and provide accreditation of prior experience and learning.* Standardized qualifications, *within a* unitized modular curriculum, *provide clear and flexible learning paths enabling the tailoring of a* learner-centered *curriculum to suit the individual. The uniform (binary) language of* competence *provides accreditation with maximum clarity. Learning is an instrument for the achievement of competence.*

A second glance at the above may cause one to ponder ways in which these aspects of practice coalesce with more conventional teaching and learning. Slavish adherence to a textbook may be similar to reliance on the learning package. The large-scale lecture may minimize interaction between the teacher and the learner. Conversely, communication between tutor and student in correspondence courses may incorporate refinement and sensitivity. But the jargon phrases in our caricature purport to reconceive practice in a language more precise than ordinary usage. What do they imply? Maximum availability, diagnosis, norms of functioning—not so much a cafeteria curriculum as that of an all-night pharmacy perhaps.

There are various sources of resistance to such developments. First, such practices involve a reductivism. Content becomes information, readily manipulable in the economy of course materials, students' responses and assessment. Skills are isolated from context. Behaviorism, extensively criticized in education, here emerges in new forms. Second, although open learning claims to offer learner-centeredness, this is conceived in consumerist terms with individually tailored learning opportunities clearly taken off the peg. The prepared text subordinates student to materials: teaching is less student-centered than resource-driven. The rhetoric of student-centeredness has been used to win over teachers of a progressive bent, but it serves the demands of efficient management. Beyond such objections, however, there is a deep-seated resistance to the displacement of classroom contact. Live and immediate classroom exchange has an authenticity that open learning methods can only palely imitate. The teacher is the source of a master discourse, the traditionalist might say, an authoritative voice whose presence leads the learner toward a contemplation of truth. Crucial to education is classroom interaction, the progressivist will emphasize, the goal of which is personal growth and self-mastery. The Open University is a good thing, it is said, but it is a substitute, suitable for people who are unable to attend mainstream university courses. More radical forms of open learning debilitate the very idea of education: that they become common features of that mainstream is preposterous.

How might the force of these positions be more precisely identified? One needs to know what one is discussing; otherwise, as we shall hear, one is bound entirely to miss the mark. Traditionalists, liberal educators and progressivists criticize open learning. The present approach seeks to disturb presuppositions, to probe these differences in order to lead beyond them. The force of these conflicting positions is to be exploited. If the aim of this chapter is to establish a clear account, this will come to be repeatedly transgressed. The argument, like the practice, will exceed its bounds, opening deep questions about teaching and learning.

The live classroom lesson is opposed to the learning package, as speech to writing. The uncanny parallel between these oppositions raises the ancient question. It stylizes the issue to see how far the tensions between the arguments point beyond them.

II

At a late stage in Plato's *Phaedrus*, in the context of the continuing enquiry into the relationship between philosophy and rhetoric, at a point when the main argument seems well concluded, Socrates is concerned to emphasize the primacy of speech and the dangerous nature of writing.

The dialogue, as we saw in Chapter nine, poses the question of whether the advances of someone who is madly impassioned with love are to be preferred to those of someone who is not. For the purposes of the present chapter it is not necessary to dwell on the substance of the major part of the dialogue but its presentation is worth recalling. The first position that is examined is expressed in the form of the written speech of Lysias, which Phaedrus reads aloud. Socrates condemns Lysias' speech not only for the content of his argument but for its style. Phaedrus urges him to provide an alternative speech, and swears by the nearest plane tree that he will not let him leave until he does so, here in the presence of this same tree. Socrates delivers his speech and it seems that he has the argument sewn up. But when he is about to leave, his divine sign—a demon which has often held him back when he is about to go astray—intervenes. He realizes the inadequate nature of the speech he has presented and is compelled to attempt another. The dialogue becomes deeper, Socrates' second speech being formed around the grand allegory of the soul as a winged chariot with two horses, one obedient to command, the other wayward. Then in the middle, as if by a hinge, the dialogue swings to a reconsideration of the art of rhetoric and its relation to philosophy. The argument comes to rest in a modified conception of rhetoric and of the non-rational—less condemnatory than that found in some earlier dialogues. The passage on the relation between speech and writing seems like an unnecessary digression, a passage that might have been edited out. It is partly because of this untidy structure that the dialogue has in the past been thought to be unsatisfactory.

For present purposes it will be appropriate to pass by the range of issues raised in the main body of the dialogue to focus on writing and speaking. The myth that Socrates recounts in this respect is worth going over in some detail. The Egyptian demigod Theuth presents to King Ammon his various inventions and invites Ammon's comments. When it comes to the invention of writing, Theuth says, "Here is an accomplishment, my lord the king, which will improve both the wisdom and the memory of the Egyptians. I have discovered a sure receipt for memory and wisdom." But the king replies:

Theuth, my paragon of inventors, the discoverer of an art is not the best judge of the good or harm which will accrue to those who practise it. So it is in this case; you, who are the father of writing, have out of fondness for your offspring attributed to it quite the opposite of its real function. Those who acquire it will cease to exercise their memory and become forgetful; they will rely on writing to bring things to their remembrance by external signs instead of on their own internal resources. What you have discovered is a receipt for recollection, not for memory. And as for wisdom, your pupils will have the reputation for it without the reality: they will receive a quantity of information without proper instruction, and in consequence be thought very knowledgeable when they are for the most part quite ignorant. And because they are filled with the conceit of wisdom instead of real wisdom they will be a burden to society. (Plato, 1973, pp. 96-97)

Writing is not the first of Theuth's inventions: he is responsible for number and calculation, geometry, astronomy and various kinds of draughts and dice. Let's credit him with some further achievements. As accessories to writing Theuth has invented the printing press and the photocopier, the microchip and hence information technology, and beyond this hardware the technology of open learning.

The advantages of each of the god's inventions have apparently been considered at some length but when it comes to writing Theuth is allowed only a brief comment: writing is "a sure receipt for memory and wisdom." What is being claimed here? Wisdom is promised because of the access to information that writing provides. Without writing one is confined to hearsay. The modern library might stand as testimony to the truth of this claim. Memory is enhanced—made more reliable and more extensive—by the availability of writing, which reminds us of what we have forgotten. For memory and wisdom, writing is "a sure receipt." It is the best guarantor of wisdom in that, in contrast to memory, it is unlikely to fade or fail: it is the means by which we can check when our memory is not clear. The elaborated account also emphasizes the vast archives and databases that writing and the related IT make available. Notwithstanding the possibilities of distortion, good reliable information is at our fingertips in an unprecedented way.

Given the terms of this expanded picture let us recapitulate the critique staked out by the King and Socrates. Theuth has fundamentally misunderstood and misrepresented the effects of his invention. Writing has an allure that has taken him in. Those who acquire it will become forgetful, relying on external reminders rather than their own inner resources. It is a recipe for reminding, not memory. As for wisdom, it may yield the reputation of this, not the reality: the amassing of quantities of information without instruction will induce a superficial knowledgeability which is really ignorance. In their "conceit of wisdom" such people will become a burden on society.

The claims and the criticism can be seen to fall under the twin headings of memory and wisdom. Behind the criticisms there is the assumption of two hierarchies: the priority of speech and the immediacy of present experience. If some uneasiness is felt about extending an argument about writing *per se* to a technical development *within* writing, that is, the technology of open learning, it is worth noting Michel Foucault's observation that the position taken by Socrates itself evidences an anxiety of a topical kind. This concerns the *hypomnemata*, the personal notebooks that had at the time become popular. (Consider modern anxieties over the ambivalent role of video cameras.) Foucault rightly locates the importance of the discussion of speech and writing within the larger question in the dialogue of whether or not a particular type of discourse gives access to truth. In phrasing that harbors a haunting indictment of certain aspects of education, Foucault suggests that the nature of the *hypomnemata* is "not to pursue the indescribable, not to reveal the hidden, not to say the non-said, but, on the contrary, to collect the already-said, to reassemble that which one could hear or read, and this to an end which is nothing less than the constitution of oneself" (Rabinow, 1991, p. 365). This is to be seen in contrast to the bringing to light of the *arcana conscientiae* of confessional literature. Other contrasts will be made later.

The first hierarchy, the priority of speech, is captured succinctly in Aristotle (*De Interpretatione*) and nicely accords with common sense. Thoughts are transmitted through spoken words, and speech can be converted into writing. Thoughts exist independently of their formulation in words, speech independently of writing, but there can be no writing independent of a background of speech and no speech without a background of thought. The hierarchy can be extended upwards toward an ideal of thought in logic, the secure point that holds the structure in place. Thought exists potentially at least independently of the contingencies of language; the nature of writing, which Socrates calls a "kind of shadow" of living and animate speech, is at a further remove. The thinker in earnest will not, as Socrates scathingly comments, sow his seed in the "black fluid called ink" (Plato, 1973, p. 98).

In the *Seventh Letter* Plato acknowledges the parts played by name, definition and representation in the development of knowledge but regrets that these factors, though they may tell us what anything is like, are inadequate to reveal its essential being. Thus, "no intelligent man will ever dare to commit his thoughts to words, still less to words that cannot be changed, as is the case with what is expressed in written characters" (p. 138). The inadequacy of language is explained in terms of the arbitrary nature of signs and their instability when combined in definitions. More subtly, language lulls us into a willingness to neglect the search for truth—an awareness of the essence of a thing—in favor of a manipulating of the instruments of name, definition, representation and knowledge (in its more limited forms).

The second hierarchy concerns the authenticity and importance of present experience. Thus direct apprehension is presumed to be superior to what is remembered. What is remembered is superior to what we are reminded of, or about which we are told by another. In remembering, the original experience is brought to our awareness in an immediate way. The mediation of a speaker who reminds us dilutes the authenticity and distorts the content of the experience. Being informed by what is written extends the mediation to debilitate the experience still further. This weakening is all the more evident in view of the lowly place of writing in the first hierarchy.

Immediacy of awareness in Plato is to be understood in terms of the intelligence or vision of ultimate truth, and such awareness has a certain kind of content. Without this specific content, however, the idea of immediacy can be seen still to have a potency that has been widely influential—for example, in empiricism and in a certain Romantic tradition that has shaped progressive education. Direct awareness of this kind appears to be secure and thus to offer a foundation for other judgments; it is as if we take it for granted as our ultimate reference point—the ocular proof that so obsesses Othello. Free from mediation, it is not compromised by the opinion and unreliability of others.

This second hierarchy links with the first: in relation to one's thoughts language is taken to be a medium of expression. Hence the self-presence of thoughts put into words is no longer immediate. Given this, the conversion of the thoughts into writing, which is subject to severance from its author, extends the mediation. It is a further objection of Socrates that the audience of the written word cannot be satisfactorily determined: writing "cannot distinguish between suitable and unsuitable readers" and is "quite incapable of defending itself" (p. 97). What has seemed the purity of thought is thereby subject to contamination.

Running through both hierarchies is a dichotomy between the inner and the outer in which the former—the possibility of a pure inside, uncontaminated, unpenetrated—is favored. Writing and being reminded are outside the inner sanctum of direct intelligence of truth. Existing in external signs rather than within our own resources, they are the field of play in which falsehood and mere appearance deceive us. The second hierarchy overlaps with the first. Memory gained from an original intelligence of truth is not vulnerable: "there is no danger of a man forgetting the truth, once he has grasped it, since it lies within a very small compass" (p. 141). The lack of exercise of the memory, however, may lead to forgetfulness. Thus, a pernicious effect of writing is the facilitation of being reminded (and of its content of opinion [*doxa*] and illusion), not of memory (and of its content of intelligence). At a deeper level the combination of the hierarchies crystallizes an opposition in conceptions of thought, between the potentially clear ideas that are the hallmark of philosophy and the shifting and unreliable signs that are the stuff of language and literature.

It would be gratifying in some ways if the matter could be left there with Socrates' critique, with the apt indictment of "the conceit of wisdom" and with the implication that the shallow behaviorist conception of understanding that open learning theories and packages sometimes enshrine makes them a potential burden on education. But the hierarchies on which the condemnation is based are not unproblematic.

The first hierarchy is vulnerable to criticism along the lines of Wittgenstein's position in the so-called Private Language Argument. A public practice of language is necessary for the ability to think. Essential to thought is rule-following. The idea of a rule is conceptually bound to the making of mistakes and so there must be a society to register mistakes, for the notion of a private mistake is incoherent. It is also necessary that there are public signs, marks perceived through the senses. Only out of such public signs in everyday practice can logic—or any ideal of language—develop.

That signs can be severed from context was one of the roots of the anxiety about writing. This is not to say that they do not need a context to make sense but that they are repeatable or quotable and available to new contexts. Iterability and citationality are necessary to their being signs at all. Following Wittgenstein, we need to eradicate the idea that meaning is a process that accompanies a word (1953, p. 218e). Following Derrida, we should eradicate the idea that a sign is full or saturated with meaning. Signs come to us bearing the imprints of their earlier uses. As they leave us they are available to interpretation and relocation, their meaning never fully determined. Meaning exists, as does our thinking, in and through this openness of the sign to further uses. Severance is the condition for there being signs (or thought) at all. And as we have seen, a sign functions not through a direct matching with concept or thing but through systems of difference. Ideas of a pure realm of thought or a direct representation are dispelled; translation becomes transformation.

What this brings to light is the way that the obvious detachability of the written sign—its severance from its author—is not something that differentiates it radically from speech. Rather, writing manifests openly the detachability that is essential to utterances also. Thus the objection concerning severance that Socrates raises against writing must apply to speech also. The presence of the speaker is not the safeguard against the misunderstanding of the sign that Socrates seems to imply.

The clarity and assurance that characterize Plato's concept of memory point toward an ideal in which what is truly known (essentially timeless) is present as a vision, written on the soul; what has happened to provide intelligence of this casts its light vividly into present noumenal awareness. Yet, if the preceding Wittgensteinian arguments are sound, memory must be constituted out of those public practices of speaking about the past, of reminding and of correcting.

The idea of immediacy of awareness in Plato, however, is more subtle. Coming to know something requires something more than seeing it truly once. It needs to be made secure in the mind by the repeated demonstration or vision of its truth. The picture is not one of instruction but of the learner coming to see for himself with the aid of the prompting and helpful questioning of a sympathetic teacher. The doctrine of *anamnesis*, so liable to arouse incredulity in the contemporary reader preoccupied with the *doxa* of information, is impressive in the quality of attention and awareness it depicts. Even though the matter may be explained for him, the learner must see the matter for himself. What is known requires a certain response; without this it is not really known. The modern inclination, supported by the acceptance of a fact-value dichotomy, is to see the quality of awareness as a contingent matter, independent of whether or not something is known.

"A concept forces itself on one," remarks Wittgenstein (1953, p. 204e). Mathematical proof is compelling in the way that the isolated empirical fact—say, the date of a battle—is not: one cannot entertain the possibility that the former is incorrect once one has seen it in the way that one can with the latter. If the knowledge Plato is concerned with can be seen in terms of the compulsion of certain pictures, with conditions that frame other enquiry, the pervasive significance of such a quality of awareness becomes more evident. In these terms the position of Plato is obviously far more subtle and complex than that voiced here by Ammon and Socrates.

Along these stylized lines the present argument finds fault both with the technology of open learning and with the crude terms of the position from which the critique is made. Let us pause to stabilize the discussion by recalling the key features in the original positions. Open learning was characterized in terms of the availability of prepared learning packages requiring minimal direct contact with a teacher, its systematic articulation of different courses, its accreditation of competence and its tailoring to individual need. It was opposed by a faith in the immediacy of classroom contact as the authentic source of learning, usually with the teacher as authoritative voice. Both involve a claim to mastery and a securing of the conditions of learning—the former in the control of rational systems and the technical accomplishment implied by competence, the latter in the master discourse of the teacher or the authentic experience of the group.

What follows is an attempt to find the pulse of anxiety in these two positions and to feel for a way of reconceiving practice. As this chapter's title signals, as some of the preceding arguments have indicated, this involves turning in the direction of Jacques Derrida's reading of the intricate and subtle play of the dialogue's language in his "Plato's Pharmacy" (Derrida, 1981a, pp. 61-171).

The fleeting reference to Pharmaceia, nymph of the medicinal spring where the dialogue is set, both heralds and hides what is to come. In the legend Oreithyia is playing in this spot with Pharmaceia when Boreas, the north wind, abducts her. The pattern is there: Oreithyia's virginal purity, the play of Pharmaceia, rape and death. Asked if he believes the legend, Socrates says that he might emulate the intellectual professionals and rationalize it by saying that Oreithyia was blown from the rocks and fell to her death. Rather than speculate about legends, however, he prefers to accept the common story and thereby give his attention to the quest for self-knowledge. Socrates' desire for clarity of thought is not to be assuaged by the analytical techniques of the demythologizers. Yet it seems to be compromised by the seductiveness of this place on the river bank, its charms sensuously evoked by Socrates' appreciative words : the trees are "splendidly tall and shady" and with "the finest possible fragrance," the water "beautifully cool," the air "delicate and sweet" and "throbbing in response to the shrill chorus of the cicadas," the grass slopes providing "perfect comfort" for the head (Plato, 1973, pp. 25-26). In the detailed topography of this enchanted place Socrates does not seem to be a native, disinclined as he is to venture beyond the walls of the town, the center of learning; indeed he is *atopos*. But this adjective speaks also of his oddness in another sense, an oddness he might have avoided had he joined company with the professionals. If he is out of place, he is not unready and no professional regime holds him back from the life of philosophy, his leisure, his *schole*: without shoes as usual, he is ready to get his feet wet as they step into the river. He responds spontaneously to philosophical discussion as to the environment.

An etymological echo of Pharmaceia's name runs through the dialogue, a minor term to unsettle the body of the text. It is the charm by which Phaedrus lures Socrates out of the city, the place of learning and self-possession; it is the written text of Lysias which Phaedrus hides under his cloak; it is books; at the end of the dialogue it is no less than writing. The recipe for memory that writing provides is a *pharmakon*. Just as Pharmaceia plays, it will echo like this:

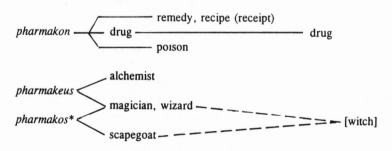

* a word absent like Lysias, meaning seeded like Lysias' text

Derrida shows the change that is undergone, the ambiguity that is suppressed, when this term is translated. The *pharmakon* can be both the healing medicine and the intoxicating drug, perhaps also the quick fix. The ambiguity attaching to the word is similar to that found in "drug," but this is lost in *remède* or "remedy:"

It cancels out the resource of ambiguity and makes more difficult, if not impossible, an understanding of the context. As opposed to "drug" or even "medicine," *remedy* says the transparent rationality of science, technique, and therapeutic causality, thus excluding from the text any leaning toward the magic virtues of a force whose effects are hard to master, a dynamics that constantly surprises the one who tries to manipulate it as master and as subject. (Derrida, 1981a, p. 97)

The *recovered* ambiguity may serve to show through writing the tensions traced above—between logic and language, between philosophy and literature, between the atemporal and the dynamic. The *suppressed* ambiguity is necessary to sustain those oppositions, those origins of mastery and security, through which Western thought inaugurates itself: "It is precisely this ambiguity," Derrida suggests, "that Plato, through the mouth of the King, attempts to master, to dominate by inserting its definition into simple clear-cut oppositions: good and evil, inside and outside, true and false, essence and appearance" (p. 103). The *pharmakon* in its ambivalence "constitutes the medium through which oppositions are opposed, the movement and the play that links them among themselves, reverses them or makes one side cross over into the other (soul/body, good/evil, inside/outside, memory/forgetfulness, speech/writing, etc.)" (p.127).

Theuth's promotional introduction of his product, "with a humility as unsettling as a dare" (p. 94), may be naive or disingenuous. It fails to acknowledge the product's other side and, in its almost transparent one-sidedness, dramatizes the partiality of meaning. The ambiguity that Pharmaceia introduces into the dialogue works in favor of the claims of unreliability but also makes evident something of the richness of the sign.

If ambivalence about the condemnation of writing is hinted at here, it is perhaps played out in the structure of the text as dialogue and the absence of any framing narration. Of course, Socrates' is the dominant voice but, as was pointed out earlier, his own position is called into doubt and then, under supernatural influence, recast. Phaedrus, who seems to sense that Socrates is overstating his case, wins some concessions from him in the closing lines, where Socrates begins to seem slightly ruffled perhaps. Beyond this there is the continuing question of the relation between Socrates and Plato—the nature and function of the artifice Plato employs, the space that opens between the "real" Plato and the fictionalized Socrates. The untidy composition of the dialogue has been a cause for dissatisfaction. This composition leaves something hanging in the air, a demonstration of the sort of uncertainty that may indeed attach to writing, a partial unruliness prefigured in the image of the chariot with two horses. And it should be remembered that Plato's central thesis in the dialogue has been established through myth, which, of course, seems to be on the "wrong" side of the list of oppositions in Socrates' account of writing and speech. These features of style do not show anything conclusively. But then it is of a piece with the suggestion that Plato is presenting an equivocal position that they should not.

It is worth considering also the extended metaphor of growth and procreation with its implicit hierarchies of dominance and authority. Theuth is father to his invention and so, it is alleged, not its best judge ("you, who are the father of writing, have out of fondness for your offspring attributed to it quite the opposite of its real function" [p. 96]). As father to the thoughts expressed in words, the speaker will not cast them abroad indiscriminately but will tend them carefully. Writing may yield quick results, but the growth of ideas in the reader is forced to maturity too soon with the result that the roots are not properly embedded. The living and animate speech of a man with knowledge, on the other hand, will be implanted in the listener in such a way that it will grow to maturity over a longer period but with a vigor and endurance which is otherwise lost.

This imagery incorporates a dynamism, however, that works toward the subversion of the centers of stability and that undoes Socrates' apparent intentions. It is a feature of growth, of plants and of children, that neither the gardener nor the parent is fully in control. The whole enterprise is subject to contingency: things are fragile and may not go according to plan. If this were not the case, the concepts of parenthood and gardening would not be what they are. This imagery may be a gesture of recognition toward the openness of words. But if this gesture is made, it is not clear in the dialogue where it directs us.

Socrates' position shows some signs of weakening in response to Phaedrus' comments. When Socrates suggests that ideas committed to writing are subjected to a forced growth, as in a hot house, the division in the imagery, which has elsewhere confined writing to inertia, is transgressed. Phaedrus picks this up and compliments Socrates on the distinction with the result that Socrates acknowledges the difference between seriousness and what is legitimately undertaken in a different spirit. Thus "gardens of literature" (p. 99) may be the result of writing, serving both as agreeable pastimes and as aids to memory when the forgetfulness of old age sets in. Moreover, such pastimes are held to be far superior to drinking parties and kindred pleasures. The condescension of this resembles the modern philistine reduction of the aesthetic to the decorative and the peripheral. In any case there is a hollowness to Socrates' stance given his recourse earlier in the dialogue to literary tropes.

The two hierarchies were dismantled by showing the role of the non-present in both speech (or thought) and present experience. The very functioning of metaphor is central to the issue here. Metaphor works through the non-present and as such, and in the dialogue's own terms, it is at one with writing itself.

The *pharmakon* and its translation show how metaphoricity is possible. The possibility of the term precedes and exceeds the opposition remedy/poison. Writing precedes and exceeds logic and the literary trope. It opens the space in which the literal and the non-literal become possible; it opens the violent space of the transference of a non-philosopheme into a philosopheme, the "very passage into philosophy" (Derrida, 1981a, p. 72). It shows how the attempt to settle ambiguity, to resist dynamic change, to achieve a purity in structural oppositions, to legislate, is repeatedly compromised and contaminated. In the excess there is a displacement of simple opposition. In Derrida's words:

All translations into languages that are the heirs and depositories of Western metaphysics thus produce on the *pharmakon* an *effect of analysis* that violently destroys it, reduces it to one of its simple elements by interpreting it, paradoxically enough, in the light of the ulterior developments it itself has made possible. Such an interpretative translation is itself as violent as it is impotent: it destroys the *pharmakon* but at the same time forbids itself access to it, leaving it untouched in its reserve. (p. 99)

So also the reduction of myth to questions of historical fact may close off the avenues of access that a less sophisticated reading might provide. The translation instances, and at the same time suppresses the very idea of, the unreliability of writing, hostile as this would naturally be to the metaphysics of the modern Western world. Modernity's idea of the natural is constituted through oppositions that writing exceeds. As Derrida points out, the operation of the *pharmakon* for good or ill is always from a certain point of view. If writing involves a corruption of the nature of speech or thought or logic, medicine involves an interference with the body's natural functioning including the natural functioning of its disease. Behind this is a conception of the natural which is characteristic of modern metaphysics. With this there is an idea of the real, and of definition in terms of essential characteristics, that has driven analysis. The critique of the hierarchies above points to the ways in which that picture of the natural and of the real is disturbed.

Socrates, cast in the *Gorgias* and the *Hippias* as the *pharmakeus* or alchemist, exceeds his own arguments. In the *Symposium* his voice is linked with that of Eros, exerting a magnetic attraction on his listeners. In Iris Murdoch's words, "He [Eros] lacks goodness and beauty, he is a lover who is forever seeking these, he desires wisdom which is supremely beautiful, he is a creative spirit, he is tension, exertion, zeal (206b). He is, in the strong and eloquent words of Diotima, a terrible magician, an alchemist (*pharmakeus*), a sophist" (1992, p. 343). It is energy that these words connote, the desire for pure vision exemplified in this needy and intermediate creativity. Socrates' dialectic is given the stamp of rhetoric; it becomes literature.

Dialogue itself, lacking the tidiness of a treatise, makes possible a sort of friction. In the *Seventh Letter*, Plato remarks: "It is only when all these things, names and definitions, visual and other sensations, are rubbed together and subjected to tests in which questions and answers are exchanged in good faith and without malice that finally, when human capacity is stretched to its limit, a spark of understanding flashes out and illuminates the subject at issue" (Plato, 1973, p. 140). The tone here and the metaphor of heat suggest an understanding of dialogue that is at odds, for example, with modern revivals of "Socratic method," in tension perhaps with "Platonism." Warmth generated by the exchange of ideas is the source of the spark of understanding. The further denigration of writing that immediately follows this remark is odd if not disingenuous. It implies that writing rules out the possibility of precisely that exchange of ideas that Plato's writing of the dialogue both demonstrates and makes possible for the reader. The sense of the unreliability of the sign is fostered in such a way as to lead beyond the overt position that Socrates articulates, and beyond this denigration. The text unravels to undo its apparent intent.

III

What can be salvaged from the dismantling of these rival ideals of purity with their claims to mastery—of the technology of open learning, and of authentic immediate classroom experience?

Translation and transformation, openness and closure, writing and technique, speech, paternity—we want to pull together the threads of these arguments with the notion of perfectibility. This can be found, on the one hand, in the aspiration toward control, in the matching of learning and accreditation, in maximal availability, and in a refined articulation of course materials with students' needs; on the other, in the authenticity and authority of the immediate experience of the classroom. It is toward a breaching of these ideals that the present text must lead.

Let us try a detour that will take us away from the supplement on writing and speech and back into the earlier sections of the dialogue. The ideal of rational control, it was said, provides a link between the technology of open learning and the authentic immediacy of the classroom. What is the fate of rationality and rational self-possession (*sophrosune*) in the *Phaedrus*?

The compromising of the argument of the dialogue with the literary is of a piece with the pull of the wayward horse, the intervention of Socrates' demon, the wild riverbank, and the drone of the cicadas. In "'This story isn't true': madness, reason, and recantation in the *Phaedrus*," Martha Nussbaum identifies a sleight of hand: Phaedrus was in fact in exile at the time the reported events were supposed to be taking place. She charts the developing acknowledgment of madness (*mania*) in the dialogue. In earlier dialogues the intellect must remain in control. Now, sober sense is merely human whereas madness comes from God (Plato, 1973, p. 47). In an argument that will carry conviction with the wise though not with the merely clever, madness is contrasted with technical accomplishment. As Nussbaum puts it: "Poetry inspired by 'madness' is defended as a gift of the gods and a valuable educational resource; non-mad styles are condemned as retentive, lacking in insight" (1986, p. 210). In contrast with the measuring, counting and reckoning activity of the rational intellect, madness will be closer to passivity and receptivity. Socrates' first speech is sober and controlled: "In every discussion . . . there is one and only one way of beginning if one is to come to a sound conclusion; that is to know what one is discussing; otherwise one is bound entirely to miss the mark" (Plato, 1973, p. 36). But this sobriety contrasts with, is upstaged by, the humor in the parenthetic remarks; for example: "Tell me, my dear Phaedrus, do you think, as I do, that I am inspired?" (p. 37).

Eventually it is the mad impassioned lover who is favored. As Socrates warns, "intimacy with one who is not in love, mingled as it is with worldly calculation and dispensing worldly advantages with a grudging hand, will breed in your soul the ignoble qualities which the multitude extols as virtues" (pp. 65-66). There is a growing recognition of the philistine emptiness of rational calculation, of a merely technical expertise, and of that concern with fact that veils the deeper insights that a legend might reveal. The advances of the non-lover are not to be preferred; the demythologizing of the professional intellectuals is not to be emulated. There is a new recognition of that needy creativity occasioned by incompleteness: the experience of madness has led to a more sceptical view of the good of self-sufficiency (Nussbaum, 1986, p. 230). The *Phaedrus* opens a way from mastery.

The emotional intensity of Nussbaum's account is achieved partly through its progressive demonstration of the way in which the argument converges with the relationship between the characters: the physical proximity of Socrates and Phaedrus; the sensuous qualities of the scene. If dialectical argument relates to abstract contemplation, the personal story here involves an attention to particulars. And yet this presence incorporates what is not present, in the sense of the personal history of the individuals, in their exposure to circumstance, in the way they are changed through the dialogue; and in the lure of the absent Lysias' speech that has drawn Socrates out of the city. Attachment to another person leads beyond itself. Presence in the *Phaedrus* then is impure and complicated. The mastery that other forms of teaching and learning might incorporate is jeopardized as both teacher and learner are changed and destabilized in the process. In the disequilibrium of *erastes* and *eromenos* both are seduced by the reflection in the other of something "beyond beingness or presence" (Derrida, 1981a, p. 167), something necessarily deferred. With this there is a sense of motion and receptivity, as of finding a way through the woods, and this is energizing.

The energy that shines through Nussbaum's reading rests on casting Phaedrus in a certain light: his name and various etymological connections in the text suggest that there is something radiant about him; Socrates is struck by his beaming face as he reads; learning is connected with images of light and bedazzlement. Yet the light in Phaedrus is also to be complicated. Ferrari finds in Phaedrus' radiance something closer to flashiness: he sees a very different and rather superficial character, a literary agent and dilettante, who tends toward trivialization and who makes from the written text an antiquarian fetish of original performance and the truth of events (Ferrari, 1990).

But this difference over the character of Phaedrus does not prevent a drawing together of the accounts in terms of a theme of reading that might be exemplary for learning. Nussbaum's elaboration of this elsewhere is revealing. In "Flawed Crystals: James's *The Golden Bowl* and Literature as Moral Philosophy" she explores the ways in which the aspiration to perfection has a stultifying effect on moral development (1990, pp. 125-147). The safety of not harming is coupled with an aestheticisation of persons and of morality and an unwillingness to "burst out of the tight circle of harmony" (p. 129), a modern denial of original sin.

Nussbaum suggests that there is in the effort of reading a text of this sort an indication of the sort of attention that the moral life requires. The receptive-responsive attitude that is required of teacher and learner in the *Phaedrus* has its counterpart in this process of reading—of Henry James and of the *Phaedrus* itself. There can be no simple collection of information: there is in the text a resistance to reading that requires a patient attention, and a tracing and retracing of its patterns. If this admits a developing, faltering insight, this involves also a creativity in the face of the text's gaps.

Insight and creativity are suppressed by faith in a pure presence, in the immediacy of classroom experience and in the atemporal contemplation of the rational intellect, but also in the emphasis on context-independent performance. In contrast, reading points not to a universality beyond the present and the particular but rather toward the ways in which the present is mediated, textual, traced by the non-present.

The character of Lysias is an emblem of the reading the *Phaedrus* especially might require. Lysias is an alien, not entitled to vote or to own land, or to be present in person in a lawsuit. Speechwriter and word wizard, he is the outsider, perhaps also the convenient scapegoat (*pharmakos*) for this scene. Lysias is not present. Plato seeds his text, as Ferrari puts it, with the speech of Lysias (1990, p. 210). Is this genuinely written by the real Lysias or is it Plato's pastiche? The undecidability of this requires of the reader a response that draws attention to the nature of writing and of reading. Speech provides no magic formula for settling the question, for evading the problems associated with writing. The undecidability creates a sort of vertigo, a sense of the impossibility of foundations.

The rich romanticized reading of Nussbaum may sometimes intimate a latent essentialism, a danger of which would be a kind of aestheticization of imperfect-ion, of the lost center and the *Unheimliche*. But words are breached, persons are breached, necessarily and originally. Original sin without the Fall: sin architraced. Preoccupation with perfection and with imperfection then may hold back iterability's releasement into creativity and nomadic joy. Wholeness in Plato's text comes to seem equivocal: neither lost nor to be attained, but to be prayed for, epitomized by the dialogue's inconclusive closure with Socrates' praying in quiet benevolent humility.

Imperfection, flawed crystal . . . cracked pot, hinge, break: breach, *la brisure*. Can we make this bridge from Nussbaum's reading to Derrida's pharmacy? In reiterating the ways in which perfection might suppress education this bridge will be crossed and re-crossed.

Translation, naively imagined, maintains a constant portable signified attached to a changing signifier. In the passage from ordinary language to a purified technical (or philosophical) language also the signified is secure. The conversion of learning into the uniform language of competencies is similarly imagined: ideas are encoded in the learning package to be acquired by the learner and recoded for accreditation. There is a perfect matching, as between a text, its translation, and the ideas contained. The smooth-running systems of open learning offer convenience and unlimited availability, economies of scale, and the perfect articulation of method with product: only teach what can be tested. They have perhaps their *hypomnemata* in endless memoranda, reports, and lists within organizational structures that this language in part determines. Skills are portable and exchangeable. Behavioral objectives and commensurability assist in the monitoring of staff performance and the creation of an arena of surveyability, in the name of efficiency and effectiveness. These contemporary translations contribute to a certain unbreached formation of the self. Cosmetically packaged Records of Achievement and other techniques of profiling represent the self so as to suggest the possibility of synoptic description and transparency. Assessment provides a complete examination of the learning that has been undertaken. The student's learning "hits" objectives in a progressive management of the self, sometimes inflated as autonomy; this is the complement of the management of the institution that this curriculum makes possible.

Writing itself runs the risk of absorption: a possibility contained in the *pharmakon* is its possible translation. The point where writing comes to be seen as a means, an instrument, for the conveying of words coincides with the emergence of a certain conception of the technical. This is the order of the well-kept "Chinese" pharmacy where standardized formulaic classification covers over difference.[1] Technicism's ideals of stability and commensurability offer purity of a kind. In the illusion of completeness possibilities of teaching and learning are foreclosed. Technicized writing, however, is not what it seems. The simple conversion of performance for credits without remainder is also exceeded, and becomes theatrical. Not just competence but the aura of competence and rational control supervenes, an advertisement for itself. The text hides the rules of its game. Beyond translation there is transformation.

It is transformation of a sort that practice undergoes in and through this technicized language, the increasingly dominant discourse of education. Derrida refers to Plato's anagrammatical writing where different meanings are at play in the use of a single signifier. The translation effects "a neutralization of the citational play, of the 'anagram,' and, in the end, quite simply of the very textuality of the translated text" (Derrida, 1981a, p. 98). The neutralization of educational discourse leads to a kind of sterility, commandeering practice in such a way as to exclude alternative possibilities that were previously animated by it; practices are either normalized or made to seem perverse. Undecidability and open-endedness are excluded in the translation of *pharmakon*; unreliability and uncertainty are suppressed by the technology of open learning in the name of a purportedly innocent objectivity. Everything is revealed within a horizon of calculability. Everything is made safe.

"You look like the sort of person who wouldn't go to a party."[2] This cutting classroom remark to a teacher exposes a site of ridicule, humiliation, adoration, inspiration . . . indifference; site also of the bee, gadfly, snake and sting ray (*narke*), anaesthetizing and vivifying. The remark requires the confrontation with the body, not virtual presence at the flick of a switch. This dynamic cutting space is the critical edge of the *pharmakon*, a force whose effects are hard to master, a force for good or ill. The learner necessarily goes beyond fixed meaning, beyond curriculum objectives and beyond aims; beyond, therefore, any stable authority of the teacher, whose language is never saturated but forever to be breached. Far from being a threat to meaning this is its condition.

Plato's text and Derrida's trafficking with it conjure multiple messages about teaching and learning: against planning and control with a lack of spontaneity; against intellectual expertise as skills to be used; against pedagogy as the encyclopaedic knowledge of the manipulation of behavior; against the compartmentalization of one's life. What is learned is not to be separated from the way it is learned, how to live not a preparatory question but a part of the good life. Illusions of mastery and perfectibility are dispelled.

"Platonism," Derrida will imply, is shored up against the entry of the Stranger. For the Stranger threatens

the domestic, dialectical mastery of the pharmacy, the proper order and healthy movement of goods, the lawful prescription of its controlled, classed, measured, labelled products, rigorously divided into medicines and poisons, seeds of life and seeds of death, good and bad traces, the unity of metaphysics, of technology, of well computed binarism. The philosophical, dialectical mastery of the *pharmaka* that should be handed down from legitimate father to well-born son is constantly put in question by a family scene that constitutes and undermines at once the passage between the pharmacy and the house. "Platonism" is both the general rehearsal of this family scene and the most powerful effort to master it, to prevent anyone's ever hearing of it, to conceal it by drawing the curtains over the dawning of the West. (Derrida, 1981a, p. 167)

The incursion from the outside threatens parricide. But Derrida disperses Plato's centers of authority, of good/sun/father/capital, disturbing the home and this family tree, contaminating philosophy with literature. The light becomes mysterious and lunar: this supplementary logic is the realm of Theuth.[3]

As the centers of authority withdraw or disappear, where are the teacher and the learner in the family scene of the classroom or the ideal home of open learning? Deep in education is a patriarchal handing down. Socrates has figured as the original voice in this line. Now his demon and the cicadas speak through him. What is said is written by Plato. Does Plato preserve the voice of Socrates or commit it to the dead letter in an ironic parricide?[4] The authoritative authorial voice is absent, direct apprehension of the truth an "impossible *noesis*" (Derrida, p. 167). *Logos* already a representation (of *eidos*), representation involves repetition, hence the possible play of the supplement. Far from being a threat to meaning, this is a condition for education. Myth, Socrates says, is repeating without knowing; in the same way learning begins. Without authoritative mastery, Socrates still leads, but now humbly, and in prayer. The teacher directs the erotic attention to no theological source—"for if at the limit an undeferred logos were possible, it would not seduce anyone" (p. 71)—but through the inconclusive open text of the lesson. This teacher is impassioned but knows nothing, veritable scapegoat for today's smart profession.

In the deep diffusion of learning in our lives, in its extended illegitimate family of practices, there is no uniform recipe. Obvious irony: that teaching and learning without these tidy suppressions avoids the closure of open learning. Obvious prayer: that the advances of the humble *mad* teacher be preferred.[5]

NOTES

1. In "Outwork" Derrida appears, according to Barbara Johnson, to allude to Mao Tse Tung's criticism of his comrades who classify things according to their external features instead of their internal relations, as in the complex systems of the Chinese pharmacy (Derrida, 1981a, pp. 23-24n).

2. David Bastow described this genuine case.

3. In the Egyptian myth Theuth is charged by the sun-god with the responsibility of taking over from him in his absence. So the moon is born.

4. As Walter Brogan has it: "Can Plato write in such a way as to defer and postpone the loss of Socrates' daimonic power to elicit the effects of the father's presence? Or is his writing a mere mimicry, a violent patricidal repetition that both re-enacts and renounces Socratic discourse?" (in Silverman, 1989, p. 22).

5. The substance of this chapter appeared in a different version, authored by Paul Standish, in *Imprimatur, 1*(2/3), 1996. We thank the editors for permission to reprint.

Chapter 12

Reading Education

Her Majesty's Chief Inspector of Schools in England, Chris Woodhead, devoted part of his 1997 annual lecture to criticism of educational theory and research: "So much that is written about education is quite simply second rate. . . . I believe much current thinking about education to be woolly, simplistic or otherwise corrupt" (1997). We have some sympathy with the criticism, although we do not share Woodhead's apparent desire to solve the problem by sweeping much research and writing about education into oblivion. This is too reminiscent of what Lyotard calls "terrorist behaviour:" "The decision makers' arrogance . . . consists in the exercise of terror. It says: 'Adapt your aspirations to our ends—or else'" (1984, p. 64) (see also Chapter nine). We return to Mr. Woodhead in the last section of this chapter, throughout which we ask: What are the significant features of writing about education today? How is educational theory different now from how it was in the past? How are we to 'read' education? We examine a number of extracts, which seem to us characteristic of our postmodern time.

LISTS

It is immediately striking that a large proportion of material currently being published on education consists less of continuous prose than of lists, bullet-points and decimally-numbered paragraphs. The National Curriculum, in England and Wales, bears some responsibility for this, together with the advice on how to implement it that it has spawned. Further responsibility lies with the computing software that enables such lists to be created at the touch of a few keys: it is a fine example of how the new technology is not merely a splendidly efficient means toward existing ends but begins to change the shape of writing and of thinking. Lists may appear eminently clear (on clarity, see below); they take us directly to the practical, setting out the advantages and disadvantages of various courses of action, telling us what to do and how to do it. They seem to be one form in which writing strains to deny its own textuality, attempting to be as close as possible to action and practice (as if action consisted essentially of discrete, atomic pieces of behavior: thus word-bites mirror action-bites, one might say).

A striking example comes from regulations governing the training of Secondary school teachers (Department for Education Circular No. 9/92, Annex A):

Newly qualified teachers should have acquired in initial training the necessary foundations to develop:

2.6.4.   an awareness of individual differences, including social, psychological, developmental and cultural dimensions;

2.6.5.   an ability to recognise diversity of talent including that of gifted pupils;

2.6.6.   the ability to identify special educational needs or learning difficulties.

There are twenty-seven "competences," expressed as the outcomes of the training intended to produce them. They refer of course to what young teachers should be able to *do*, not to what they should *know*. Here there seems to be a total confidence that language maps unproblematically onto reality, that beneath the talk of competences we will find entities called abilities; and that beyond them there are other entities called, e.g., "learning difficulties," the transparency guaranteed by the fact that the teacher will "recognize" or "identify" them. Since these regulations concern the accreditation of training courses we must imagine a world in which the inspector's scrutiny passes through trainer, trainee and pupil to the giftedness or special need (see also Chapter four).

RHETORIC

It is not only in its fondness for lists that much current writing on education reveals this tendency, although this is a particularly vivid way in which it does so. The literature on school effectiveness is another rich field. Here, for example, is Michael Barber (1995):

Awareness of the characteristics of effective schools is widespread; effective leadership, involvement of all staff in decision-making, consistency in policy implementation, parental involvement, intellectually challenging teaching . . . the litany [*sic*] is familiar (see left) [at left there is of course a list]. Now attention at school level is shifting from these characteristics of school effectiveness to the strategies required to achieve effectiveness; in other words, to school improvement. [Punctuation as original]

There are many ways in which this passage could be analyzed. We might, for example, note that effectiveness seems to require effectiveness, and that the key to all this is, remarkably, school improvement; or we might complain at the statements of the obvious—fancy intellectually challenging teaching making for better schools! What we want to draw attention to, in the light of the ideas discussed in this chapter, is that the language of school effectiveness manifestly constitutes a *rhetoric*, a language that revels in its own apparent hard-headedness, realism, moral superiority and talk of outcomes. Key words in the list to the left of Michael Barber's article include professional, firm, purposeful, responsibility, positive, high demands, and of course effective (three times). This rhetoric attempts to conceal its own rhetorical nature by seizing the language of action and, as if only too aware of its flimsy textuality, of the action that will lead to real action ("to the strategies required to achieve effectiveness") and action done better ("to school improvement"). It is the language of action, but no more than language nevertheless. In Derrida's vivid image, we are being asked to read by the light of the word "day." Compare the words with which Lysias's speech in the *Phaedrus* begins (see Chapter nine): "You know how I am situated," "You know the score." We are men of the world, men of action. We are interested in effectiveness.

One further illustration is particularly interesting since it comes from a Government White Paper (*Choice and Diversity*, 1992) where, as the precursor of legislation, language might lay claim to especial unambiguousness. As an incipient "performative" in this context the "presence" of language might seem to be given both by its origins in the speaker's intentions and its effect in the world of political action.

1.22   There is little point in having good, regularly inspected
        schools, first rate teachers and the National Curriculum
        well taught and assessed, if all of our children do not
        attend school, remain there, and learn throughout the
        whole of the school day.

This seems incontrovertible. There is no point in my giving you paper to write on if you fold it up into paper planes. Clearly not. But the sentence is complex, and includes devices which were given names when rhetoric was studied. The understatement of "little point" (clearly there is no point, not little point) was called *meiosis*; "attend school, remain there, and learn throughout the whole of the school day" is an ascending tricolon (compare "friends, Romans, countrymen"). There is a more complex tricolon in "good schools," "first rate teachers" and "the National Curriculum well taught and assessed," for here the first leg is expanded to include "regularly inspected." The effect is to emphasize that since we have or are about to have all the elements of the first tricolon we must have the elements of the second too. And since two of the elements of the first are subject to legislation (first rate teachers being impossible to guarantee by law), the need for further legislation to cover two elements of the second (learning too frustrates the legislator) is accordingly established. The fact that the first two cola are irregular and do not ascend smoothly prevents an excessive neatness which might sound glib. The rhetoric of course enhances, rather than detracts from, the impression of simplicity (the passage begins with two monosyllables, and almost with four since "little" here means "no," and ends with six). The feeling is conveyed that very basic but very profound (this is the effect of the rhetorical devices) truths, questionable only by imbeciles, are here being conveyed in the voice of sonorous common sense.

Rhetorical and textual, then; but the sentence further denies its textuality by sounding a very distinctive *voice*: testily asserting the obvious in the tones of an authority confident in the value of regularity, standards and examinations, the voice is unmistakably reminiscent of a certain sort of schoolmaster commenting on the futility of the best bread rolls being purchased if they are then thrown around the dining hall. (One feels that some literary critics would also make much of the fear that underlies the sentence: that the children - the signifieds whose presence is essential for the whole thing to work - might undo the whole structure by absenting themselves.)

EDUCATIONAL THEORY

None of the examples above comes from what could be called educational theory. But such theory has been no quicker to acknowledge its own textuality. Culler writes that "the idea of a discipline is the idea of an investigation in which writing might be brought to an end" (1987, p. 90); if that does not seem quite right for the educational disciplines it would nevertheless be true to say, perhaps, that they hoped to proceed as if their writing, their textuality, might seem wholly unproblematic. Philosophy of education was philosophy, and so aimed at truth and rationality, and literature was something else: this was less case of the "ancient quarrel between the artists and the philosophers" than a sublime indifference to the former on the part of the latter.

[T]o understand philosophy you need to appreciate the distinction between concepts, as defined, and words. It should be obvious, now that it is clear what a concept is, that they are distinct, but they are obviously also closely related. . . . *Philosophical analysis* must include conceptual analysis in addition to preliminary verbal analysis. What constitutes conceptual analysis is a thorough, precise, and detailed unpacking of a concept. (Barrow, 1981, pp. 7-9)

This is the Enlightenment Project in full blossom: the aspiration to bring light and clarity ("obvious . . . clear . . . obviously") where before there was darkness and ignorance. And who, it might be asked, can be against clarity? The very objection seems to invite a "transcendental" response, of the sort popular in the heyday of analytic philosophy of education, to the effect that clarity is a virtue that the very questioning of it seems to presuppose. It is not our intention here, of course, to elevate unclarity to the status of a general good. But Barrow's "clarity" is not entirely unproblematic either. His conception of philosophy is rooted in a firm distinction between philosophy and literature, between the literal and the metaphorical: a distinction that writers such as de Man have shown cannot be systematically sustained, for the enterprise of controlling metaphor cannot extricate itself from metaphor. "The literal is the opposite of the figurative, but a literal expression is also a metaphor whose figurality has been forgotten. The philosophical is condemned to be literary in its dependence on figure even when it defines itself by its opposition to figure" (Culler, 1987, p. 148).

Barrow's own text richly displays this figurality. After the repeated (and rhetorical) insistence on the need to lay things out in full view ("distinction" and "defined" as well as variations on "obvious(ly)"), he uses two metaphors. The first is that of the reiterated "analysis." It brings with it the authority of the laboratory, where scientists clinically (and thoroughly: the effect of the reiteration) break complex matter down (the meaning of "analyse") into its constituent parts, using powerful microscopes to examine the results of their operations. The second is that of "unpacking," which suggests that concepts are rather like tea-chests: you take out the contents to see what you've got. As with the rhetoric of clarification, the root idea is that of *seeing what is really there*, things of indubitable reality that nevertheless present themselves as a blurred and confused jumble to those who lack the appropriate techniques or capacity.

Some recent writings about educational theory have gone one step further, not merely repressing the textuality of theory but asserting that practice is theory, and constitutes the best form of it. The author of *Teaching as Learning: An Action Research Approach* (1993), Jean McNiff, claims confidently that "Education is not a field of study so much as a field of practice" (p. 5). In his foreword to the book Jack Whitehead writes:

The majority of work on educational theory is presented in terms of conceptual structures rather than a form of enquiry. . . . An alternative view to this . . . is that you and I should take the lead in generating a living educational theory by producing descriptions and explanations for our own educational development in our professional work in education. Rather than conceive theory in terms of a set of conceptual relations, this text offers a view of theory in terms of embodied explanations for the way of life of individuals . . . embodied in the sense that they are part of the individual's practical responses to questions of the form, "How do I improve my practice?" (p. xii-xiii)

Here, it seems, there is no text (despite the use of the word "text") to scrutinise, since theory can only be embodied in practice. Now practice too can be regarded as part of the system of signs, the "text" which Derrida tells us we cannot stand beyond; yet Whitehead regards McNiff's practice as validated outside of any such "text" by her personal commitment, expressing the hope that readers will "respond with a sensitivity and quality of criticism which does not violate her integrity" (p. x). The denial of textuality is accompanied, and of course in a sense caused, by the aspiration to seek validity and meaning not in the system of differences constituted by the text but by what the text reflects—not, on this occasion, hard facts but the commitment of the author. Appropriately enough McNiff includes some poems as an appendix: their publication "is the realisation of the values I am expressing. It is an important part of the book, not only in the sense that it communicates my inner thoughts" (p. 109). Here we have that "self-presence of the cogito, consciousness, subjectivity," which Derrida has criticized as the "metaphysics of presence" (1974, p. 12).

We have noted elsewhere (see Chapter four, p. 50) that what Derrida calls logocentrism always assumes the priority of the first of a pair of terms (literal/metaphorical, etc.). Theory/practice is one more pair of such terms, and if the priority once was *theory*, which was held to be translated into the inferior *practice*, then the reversal of the priority demonstrates logocentrism no less.

MISSING CHILDREN

15. We also have to be aware of the negative impact that the theorising of the academics can have on the teacher. I remember sitting some years ago listening to a professor lecture on primary education. What he said struck me as opaque, impossibly abstract, remarkable mainly for the ostentation of his academic references. Talking afterwards, however, to teachers who had been in the audience I found that they had not responded in this way at all. They were deeply impressed by the wealth of learning . . . more than one said to me that it had just reminded him once again how little he knew about the business of teaching children. In terms of bringing a lecture alive, teaching a child to read they, in all probability, knew much more than their lecturer.

16. The longer I do this job, the more important I think it is to question the way in which academics and researchers mystify the business of teaching (and, indeed, children's learning). Good teachers know and care about what they are teaching; they have high expectations of their children; they use a range of teaching methods skilfully and appropriately. I am not for one moment wanting to suggest what they do is straightforward. Far from it: they perform, with enormous skill, an immensely complex practical task. I do not, however, think that much that is written about the demands they face connects with the day to day reality of their experience. [punctuation as original]

In this annual lecture (Woodhead, 1997), referred to at the beginning of this chapter, academics are condemned for their posturing, theorizing and obfuscations. How does the text achieve its effects? First, it presents the Chief Inspector whose voice we hear as a plain man. He is, we note, not Christopher but Chris. He does not report simply that there was a lecture given by a professor (a *professor* lecture on *primary* education: the obvious absurdity of the juxtaposition warns us what to expect): he tells us that he was *sitting*, as it were found himself doing that in the midst of his busy life, as you and I might remember we were standing at the bar that evening. "Talking afterwards, however, to teachers"—we can picture him, in some kind of foyer or public area, cup of tea in hand, in relaxed conversation, as befits a plain man. But between these two bluff vignettes of ordinary life there intervened something so odd that the listener was struck. As he sat innocently and listening in his plain man way, it must have been odd if it struck him (the plain man is not given to over-sensitivity; in fact earlier in his lecture he recommended to schools the virtue of fortitude), and indeed did so at the time and not on reflection afterwards (this is the force of the past tense of the verb). What struck him? Something that was "opaque, impossibly abstract, remarkable mainly for the ostentation." The ascending tricolon suggests the lecturing professor is too clever by half. Within this ascending tricolon lies another, ascending more slowly, consisting of the nouns central to the first (the professor is too clever by more than half): opaque, abstract, ostentation. The vowels with which these words begin slow the reader. "Talking afterwards, however, to teachers" restores the easy conversational flow, beginning with "I remember sitting some years ago," which the professor had the ill manners to interrupt.

This plain man is at one with his teachers, who are also plain people: "More than one said to me . . . " is a sentence of numerous plain monosyllables. He is also, no doubt by contrast with the professor, a man of (attractively rueful) *experience* ("The longer I do this job") who, far from being a highly-paid civil servant whose relationship with government is complex and contentious, merely does a *job*, like other ordinary folk do. There is something of the blunt John Bull in him, challenging the academics and researchers in the name of what was plain before they mystified it, like the heroic reporter of the television consumer program who challenges the seller of fake insurance. With his foot in the door, and the professor's rottweiler thundering down the hall, Mr. Woodhead gives defiant voice to some plain truth:

Good teachers know and care about what they—
They have high expectations of their—
They use a range of teaching—
Once more unto the breach, dear friends, once more

In his hour of truth and defiance the Chief Inspector speaks in iambic rhythms—the iambic pentameters of Shakespeare:

Look, in this place ran Cassius' dagger through
See what a rent the envious Casca made . . .

Now look again at his own Shakespearean lines:

Good teachers know and care about what they—
They have high expectations of their—
They use a range of teaching—

They are not so finished, so perfect, as to be glib or over-lyrical; or is it that he is interrupted? Of course: the professor has intervened again, in his unwelcome way: are you suggesting that teaching is a simple matter? No indeed, replies Mr. Woodhead, forced now to abandon the pentameter for the same lowly prose as his questioner. What teachers do is not straightforward, not if it raises them alongside Antony, Henry V, King Lear. And then we are back in full swell with the bard:

Far from it, they perform with enormous skill
And Brutus was an honourable man.

Thus the text achieves its effects. With academic, associate opaque, abstract, ostentatious (and, in the end, what is *written*, despite the early promise of a lecture, "what he said"); with Mr. Woodhead and the classroom teacher associate by contrast transparency, day-to-day reality, and plain directness—the directness of a *voice* of one who sits, talks afterwards, drinks tea, does a job—yet undeniably a text nevertheless. Teachers, we note, bring lessons alive in vivid immediacy: texts are for others, the children whom they teach to read.

Here at least the children are permitted to figure briefly (to be strictly accurate there is only one child, "a child," being taught to read in the text). In the previous sentence the children appeared only to be negated: the plain teacher (who was in any case wrong, and misled by the professorial villain of the piece) claimed to know little about teaching them, and the sentence could finish after "teaching" with no loss of meaning. Children, it would seem, add nothing meaningful to education. Again:

They have high expectations of their—

The pentameter requires a monosyllable to close: it is not quite right, not smooth, if it finishes with "children" (though Shakespeare is happy with greater irregularities). Children do get in the way, their presence as irregular variables in school threatening to disrupt the orderly system of monitoring standards over which the Chief Inspector presides. They, and their learning, are best tucked away in parentheses (para. 2), where they can be mystified by academics and researchers without too much risk of the infection spreading. Little danger of child-centeredness, the heresy which the Chief Inspector has a mission to extirpate, when the children are so effectively removed from the center of the picture.

Still, a strange contradiction (an *aporia*, Derrida might call it) lies at the heart here. Is teaching simple or complex? The academics have mystified it, so it is presumably simple, yet Mr. Woodhead calls it "immensely complex." If there is a paradox here perhaps it is resolved partly by describing the complexity as "practical," and partly by blaming the academics and researchers for it. It seems to be because the professor had induced him into false consciousness of some sort that the plain teacher thought he knew little about teaching children and was persuaded to believe it was complicated. So perhaps teaching really is a simple business, then? Goodness, how complicated it all is. Perhaps it really would be better if teachers did not try to think about it at all.

DECONSTRUCTING EDUCATION

[Deconstruction denies] "that philosophy has access to truths which literature can only obscure and pervert by its dissimulating play with language and fiction. . . . Philosophers like Locke and his latter-day positivist descendants devote a great deal of their thought to establishing a discourse of dependably logical and referential meaning, such that philosophy can carry on its work undisturbed by the beguilements of rhetoric." (Norris, 1983, p. 3)

Metaphor, whose expulsion deconstructionists see as fundamental to the philosophical project, constantly returns to haunt the philosopher. Figurative language cannot be kept at bay, and thus, in de Man's words, philosophy becomes "an endless reflection on its own destruction at the hands of literature" (quoted in Norris, 1983, p. 3). That is to say, in perhaps the most famous of Derrida's formulations, there is "nothing outside the text:" there is no escape from the textuality of things, from figurative language. We deceive ourselves if we think there is, our attempts to find something which can "place a reassuring end to the reference from sign to sign" (Derrida, 1974, p. 49) bound to be undone by the "hidden articulations and fragmentations within assumedly monadic totalities" (de Man, 1979, p. 69) in the way that the deconstructionist critic likes to show.

Deconstruction shows the ordinary and everyday in a new light, revealing its extraordinariness. In this it operates at the leading edge of the eclectic theory which is now often regarded as the successor to philosophy as traditionally conceived. To quote Culler again:

The works we allude to as "theory" are those that have had the power to make strange the familiar and to make readers conceive of their own thinking, behaviour, and institutions in new ways. Though they may rely on familiar techniques of demonstration and argument their force comes—and this is what places them in the genre I am identifying—not from the accepted procedures of a particular discipline but from the persuasive novelty of their redescriptions. (1987, p. 9)

The task of redescribing, of making the world seem stranger than we thought, is not a new one to philosophy. It can be argued that this is precisely what the pre-Socratics were doing, having the courage of their own metaphors, as Nietzsche perceived, and declaring our familiar world to be really all fire, or water, or air. One way of reading Plato is as showing us that knowledge, justice or virtue are immensely more odd and complicated than we supposed, requiring the attention not just of analysis but of myth, simile and analogy if we are not to settle into our characteristic human habit of over-simplification. How remote this is from the common perception of theory as a structure of generalizations under which individual phenomena can be subsumed. Theory that jolts us into seeing the world with fresh eyes shows us its singularity, the "difference" of one thing or person from another. Thus Lacan, for example, sees the task of revitalizing psychoanalysis as being "to disengage from concepts that are being deadened by routine use the meaning that they regain both from a re-examination of their history and from a reflexion on their subjective foundations" (quoted in Kermode, 1990, p. vii).

This conception of theory, and the activity of offering deconstructive readings, is unlikely to be popular. The hostility which "French theory" has roused needs little illustration (see, for example, Palmer, 1992, p. 3); Derrida's ideas are often taken to lead to the consequence that any text or interpretation is as good as any other, and deconstructionists are supposed to believe that there is no such thing as reality, only text, in the same rather tiresome way as previous generations of philosophers sometimes pretended to believe that the tables and chairs around them did not really exist. As for the power of making strange, Roger Scruton, for instance, argues against the kind of theoretical thinking that "refers things with which we are intellectually at ease, to a hypothesis . . . which implies that we do not really understand them" (1983, p. 61). The same writer would have us believe that "figures of speech are open to their meaning. They are vivid, immediate, unambiguous" (1981, p. 47). Those who would have us live by their text must first be careful to persuade us that texts are innocent, transparent guides to the state of the world.

Paul de Man shows us why Derridean ideas are bound to be opposed with such hostility. He writes that "the linguistics of literariness"—that is, the revealing of irreducible textuality—"is a powerful and indispensable tool in the unmasking of ideological aberrations. . . . The resistance to theory is resistance to the use of language about language. . . . The resistance to theory is resistance to the rhetorical or tropological dimension of language" (1982, pp. 363-368). Always and inevitably we are situated in relationships where power operates, including our own power. We must *read* education if we are to understand where power lies and how it effaces or masks itself. If education is a practice, then education is a text.

Prospect

So you think that relativism is a spectre, that language is a rich plurality of rags, that we are not masters of ourselves, and that Socrates, the founder of Western philosophy, is irrational, even mad?

Yes. We think that there are forms of relativism that are plainly wrong and that these are pernicious for education, but that relativism has also been constructed as a spectre to bedevil any attempts to move beyond universalistic and ethnocentric presumptions in thinking about education. We think that language is not a seamless cloth but patchy and diverse. We think that assumptions concerning self-mastery fly in the face of the evidence that careful study of language and of social relationships provides. We think that Socrates' faith in rationality is less complete, and that Plato's writing of Socrates is more complex, than is sometimes assumed.

What are we to make of this? Why don't you write more clearly? If something can be said, it should be said clearly. If it can't be said clearly, it is better to say nothing at all.

We need to be allusive and sometimes perhaps elusive—not to obscure but to try to probe matters that cannot be brought simply and unequivocally into the light. We mean to resist the many prevalent interpretations of postmodern thinkers that seem to us to miss the point. We have resisted also the idea that anything goes and that everything is a matter of interpretation. There is room for a distinction between the kind of reading that reacts creatively and does something with the material at hand and an ill-informed reading that gets it all wrong.

Why don't you provide a clear and systematic exposition of what postmodernists say?

Sometimes we don't and sometimes we do. Sometimes the very idea of systematicity is put in question by the postmodernist writers we consider. We have varied our approach according to different topics, themes and thinkers, and according to what we have felt motivated to do by the different practical problems in education that we have each encountered.

But the ideas you refer to and the way you develop them yourselves are not simple. Why does everything have to be so complicated?

The difficulty is inherent in the practical problems. Less rigorous thinking offers easier "solutions." We feel obliged to try to make sense of these difficult ideas because they offer ways forward in educational theory and practice. Not to do this would lull us into confusion and complacency; easier solutions would make more opaque those practical problems that should be our concern.

Why do you speak of "education after postmodernism?" Isn't this all rather modish and just a little politically correct? It's not clear that any new theory of education is evident in this book.

There is a vague sense that we live in conditions of postmodernity and in educational theory there has for some time been much talk of postmodernism. Sometimes this is little more than lip-service to a term that has become, it is true, somewhat modish; sometimes, however, this taps deeper streams of thought. Given that this has happened, that postmodernism now has come to figure prominently in educational research, we wanted to ask how education looks different. How do we make sense of these different strands of ideas that have threaded their way into the thinking? Postmodernism is no longer new, but we are not satisfied with the way it has been received in education. In another sense, however, we want also to advance ideas *after the style of* postmodernism as well as to see how education looks after we have worked through some of the writings of certain postmodernist thinkers.

You are postmodernists then?

We don't think this is a helpful question, and we might say that we don't much care. We find some things written by some writers whom people commonly style postmodernists to be valuable. We draw on those texts and try to do something with them to exploit their relevance to education. By doing this we acknowledge the nature of textuality, of the threads of these ideas that weave together and tie up with others, and of their availability to a reworking of the kind we are engaged in. Speaking of *ideas* lulls us into those logocentric assumptions that postmodern thinking puts into question. This book reminds us that words *count* by interweaving its themes in different styles of discourse.

Doesn't this have the effect of preventing you from sustaining a coherent argument?

We do not believe that "a coherent argument," a univocal programmatic argument, is possible here, or, for that matter, even desirable. We see the presumption in favor of a unified argument as a problem for education because of its tendency to obliterate other insights. Of course, we are not against coherent arguments: we believe we have provided these. But they tend to be local rather than all-encompassing. Moreover, we do not think that unified coherent arguments are best attacked by unified refutations, which themselves remain within the same ambit: our strategy is rather to subvert and destabilize, to become ironic, and sometimes to change the subject.

Why do you disregard established traditions of progressive or radical educational theory?

Little is said about these traditions in this book partly because we do not see these as dominant forces in the present educational scene. There are attractive elements in such movements but they also are often limited by the false assumptions they tend to espouse—especially concerning the idea of the human subject and the conception of knowledge itself. We have some sympathy with claims that progressivism tends to hold a sentimentalized or romanticized view of the learner. More importantly, we think it fails fully to acknowledge the social character of knowledge and understanding. Where this is recognized, it tends to be interpreted in terms of a social constructivism that fails to acknowledge our inheritance of public forms of thought, and fails to acknowledge their relation to truth. The thinkers we are concerned with write in response to the texts of the past, not to recover hallowed truths but to rework those texts, as any repetition must inevitably do.

In your chapters on ethics and desire you seem to be saying that the idea of the human subject has changed. But whose idea of the subject are we speaking of here?
One would need to look in detail at the development of the self through a series of philosophers—at least, since Descartes—to trace this, something beyond the scope of this book. In another sense, however, the more central concern for education is the dominance in everyday thinking of a certain conception of the autonomous individual. Such thinking, we contend, is there in modern curriculum policy with its conception of the free agent whose education consists in the acquisition of a range of competences but also in the far more rounded and rich idea of a liberal education, with its robust philosophical underpinning. The individualism that these ideas support does not stand up to the kind of scrutiny to which communitarian arguments can expose them nor to the more rigorous consideration of language that poststructuralism provides. These ideas about language have profound effects, altering assumptions about the working of desire in ways that are deeply disruptive for conceptions of autonomy and for our understanding of personal relationships. Foucault, Lyotard and Derrida, as we have said, shift the idea of the self in such a way as to shatter the unified conception of the autonomous subject that has been taken for granted in educational theory and practice.

Much contemporary debate concerning morality puts into question changes in family relationships. You have touched on this in various ways, it seems.
Think what has happened. Wide coverage of cases of child abuse and increasing child labor have perhaps inevitably cast the family in a different light. No longer are we inclined to assume that the family provides happiness and fulfillment for all its members. The context of trust has been undermined in a way that all the current reaffirmations of family values cannot repair. In education we hear again the language of (children's) rights. Parents' right to choose freely their way of life no longer entails a right to direct their children's lives to their own ends. Interaction between parents and children has moved into the arena of public scrutiny, beyond the walls of the family home. And where the language of rights predominates the recognition of difference can be eroded, especially when ethics and religion are involved. In the wake of child-centeredness, parents encourage children to make choices for themselves. But for some parents this licences a

withdrawal from responsibility. With pressures of money and time, with too much to do, parents are increasingly absent from family life, their role partially given up to the professionalized functions of the daycare center and child-minder. Parents face conflicts between the demands of their work and the needs of the child: entrusting children to strangers often brings guilt. Time away from work is busy with housekeeping and with the need to relax; little is left to spend with the children. A compensating earnestness about acquiring "parenting skills" and spending "quality time" with the children takes on the style of professionalized childcare, while with self-conscious promotion of "values in education" schools take over some of the functions of the home. A professional and political agenda sets the new "family" values. In the absence of consensus in society at large the realm of values is progressively conceded to the expert and the technician. Everything becomes governed by performativity.

When we look at the way educational provision might change in the future, isn't your refusal to take a systematic approach to education going to stand in the way of progress?
It depends on the context and it depends on the system. Generally it is the obsession with system that stands in the way of progress.

You have talked repeatedly about the problems of performativity. This seems to amount to an anxiety you have about measurement and testing. Don't you think that testing is necessary in education? It is difficult to imagine how we might go about raising standards if there were no testing: we simply wouldn't know whether we were making progress or not. Furthermore, education is a very expensive business. Surely teachers should be accountable for what they do and it is not unreasonable to expect value for money.
We see performativity as a danger but it would be a mistake to interpret our concern as a hostility to measurement. Educational measurement is by no means simply an educational matter and the public understanding of such measurement is itself a problematic and deeply political issue. Beware of thinking: only teach what you can test. With this there is the preoccupation with the application of the criterion of efficiency to everything we do in education: be operational or disappear. We want to stop in her tracks the new manager who thinks she has the masterplan that will sweep away what has gone before and systematically resolve all our problems.

How far is the book prescriptive? What are the implications for practice?
If by implications you mean clear-cut prescriptions—do this, don't do that—then there probably are not many. Part of what we are concerned to emphasize is precisely that teachers should not be following tidy prescriptions. If they are, this erodes education by undercutting what teaching and learning should be about. It sells short those they will educate.

It's often thought that postmodernism wants to subvert the canon but you keep going back to Plato.
Yes, Plato, Shakespeare, Dickens. We do not think that postmodernism wants to subvert the canon so much as to engage with it in a new way, to give it vibrancy, perhaps to make it tremble, for only with some movement can it live. Postmodern writing characteristically and self-consciously responds to other texts. Hence there is no place in postmodernism for that kind of thinking that imagines that we can simply start from scratch, in education or anywhere else. We do not advocate throwing out the Great Books but rather reading them in a creative and responsive way. For this you need also to be introduced to what is outside the dominant paradigm.

Are there no authorities? Are there no experts?
There are experts and there are authorities. There is a shift, however, in the way that mastery must be considered. In the first place, the aspiration to masterful control comes to seem illusory, a source of problems in our thinking. There is space instead for a kind of humility where the expert is characterized in part by her ability to see how little she knows. This is not a matter of scepticism—you can't really know anything—but rather a kind of responsive openness: the teacher is in thrall to what she studies and teaches. And this responsiveness is a dimension of responsibility. The more we are confident that our thinking can lead to mastery the more this sense is suppressed.

So what should schools be like then?
We have no blueprint—the very idea of a blueprint is at odds with the arguments of this book. But we are prepared to make some suggestions, obvious ones, we hope, in the light of the previous chapters. Educational institutions need to be released from the performativity, the jealous scrutiny, one might say, that has come to dominate them. This not only fixes an administrative net over what they can do; more perniciously it alters the very idea of what education is about in the minds of teachers, learners and the public at large. Crucial factors in this performativity are managerialism and information technology. Of course, institutions have to be managed and, of course, information technology is immensely valuable. But these become degenerate when they are allowed to dominate the institution because their instrumental value is blown up into instrumentalism and this has deeply distorting effects on conceptions of the good that shape education. Part of what is implied here involves giving responsibility back to teachers. With this shift there is a reduction of control on what is going on and hence increased risk. But we see the anxiety about risk as itself anti-educational. In place of large-scale control we need more human scale. Acknowledgement of the diversity of language and of what we do with language should lead to a broader understanding of what education is and can be.

So that brings this simulacrum of a dialogue to a close? You seem to have all the answers. And you do have some recommendations.

Ours are, it is true, the controlling voices in this all too brief dialogue, and it is one in which we cannot but have the last word. But we do not think this last word resolves things; rather that it opens them in a new way. In the text of this book we have tried to write neither a potted guide to postmodernism nor a tidy prescription for the education that should come after it. Rather, we have tried to respond to the kind of bewilderment that is increasingly felt by thoughtful educators by drawing from, and reacting to, some of the writings commonly bracketed as postmodernism. We want people to read what is going on in education in an active, critical way, a way that does not simply absorb the dominant paradigm and that does not accept that teaching and learning involve just the transmission of a fixed content—be this information, skills or received opinion. And we see this as the only fit way to honor the past and to prepare for the future.

References

Ahlberg, J., & Ahlberg, A. (1986). *The jolly postman, or other people's letters*. London: Heinemann.

Annas, J. (1993). *The morality of happiness*. Oxford: Oxford University Press.

Baier, A. C. (1994). *Moral prejudices*. Cambridge: Harvard University Press.

Barber, M. (1995, October 6th). From characteristics to strategy. *Times Educational Supplement* (School Effectiveness Section), p. 2.

Barrow, R. (1981). *The philosophy of schooling*. Brighton, Engl.: Wheatsheaf.

Baudrillard, J. (1983). *Simulations* (A. Bass, Trans.). New York: Semiotext(e).

Bauman, Z. (1990). *Thinking sociologically*. Cambridge, MA: Blackwell.

Bauman, Z. (1994). Morality without ethics. *Theory, Culture & Society, 11*, 1-34.

Benhabib, S. (1994). Democracy and difference: Reflections on the metapolitics of Lyotard and Derrida. *The Journal of Political Philosophy, 2*, 1-23.

Benvenuto, B., & Kennedy, R. (1986). *The works of Jacques Lacan. An introduction*. London: Free Association Books.

Bernstein, R. (1987). Serious play: The ethical-political horizon of Jacques Derrida. *The Journal of Speculative Philosophy, 1*, 93-117.

Burningham, J. (1977). *Come away from the water, Shirley*. London: Jonathan Cape.

Calhoun, C. (1995). Standing for something. *The Journal of Philosophy, 92*, 235-260.

Caputo, J. D. (1988). Beyond aestheticism: Derrida's responsible anarchy. *Research in Phenomenology, 18*, 59-73.

Carr, W. (1995). Education and democracy: Confronting the postmodernist challenge. *Journal of Philosophy of Education, 29*, 75-92.

Cavell, S. (1979). *The claim of reason: Wittgenstein, skepticism, morality and tragedy*. London: Oxford University Press.

Child, M., Williams, D. D., Birch A. J., & Boody, R. M. (1995). Autonomy or heteronomy? Levinas's challenge to modernism and postmodernism. *Educational Theory, 45*, 167-189.

Choice and diversity: A new framework for schools. Presented to Parliament by the Secretaries of State for Education and Wales by command of Her Majesty (1992). London: HMSO.

Cooper, D. (1983). *Authenticity and learning. Nietzsche's educational philosophy*. London: Routledge & Kegan Paul.

Cox. (1988). *English for ages 5 to 11: Proposals of the Secretary of State for Education and Science and the Secretary of State for Wales*. London: HMSO.

Cox. (1989). *English for ages 5 to 16: Proposals of the Secretary of State for Education and Science and the Secretary of State for Wales*. London: HMSO.

Crisp, R., & Cowton, C. (1994). Hypocrisy and moral seriousness. *American Philosophical Quarterly, 31*, 343-349.

Culler, J. (1987). *On deconstruction*. London: Routledge & Kegan Paul.

Davion, V. (1993). Autonomy, integrity, and care. *Social Theory and Practice, 19,* 161-182.

Deleuze, G., & Guattari, F. (1992). *A thousand plateaus: Capitalism and schizophrenia* (B. Massumi, Trans.). London: The Athlone Press.

De Man, P. (1979). *Allegories of reading*. New Haven: Yale University Press.

De Man, P. (1982). The resistance to theory. In D. Lodge (Ed.), *Modern criticism and theory* (pp. 355-371). London: Longman.

Department for Education. (1995). *Key Stages 1 and 2 of the National Curriculum*. London: Department for Education.

Derrida, J. (1974). *Of grammatology* (Gayatri Chakravorty Spivak, Trans.). Baltimore: Johns Hopkins University Press.

Derrida, J. (1978). *Writing and difference* (A. Bass, Trans.). London: Routledge & Kegan Paul.

Derrida, J. (1981a). *Dissemination* (B. Johnson, Trans.). London: The Athlone Press.

Derrida, J. (1981b). *Positions* (P. Foss, P. Patton & P. Bleitchman, Trans.). Chicago: University of Chicago Press.

Derrida, J. (1983). The principle of reason: The university in the eyes of its pupils (C. Porter & Edward P. Morris, Trans.). *Diacritics* (Fall), 3-20.

Derrida, J. (1987a). *Of spirit: Heidegger and the question* (G. Bennington & R. Bowlby, Trans.). Chicago: University of Chicago Press.

Derrida. J. (1987b). Le facteur de la vérité. In *The post card: From Socrates to Freud and beyond* (A. Bass, Trans.). Chicago: University of Chicago Press.

Derrida. J. (1988). *Limited Inc*. Evanston, IL: Northwestern University Press.

Derrida, J. (1991). *The Other heading* (P.-A. Brault & M. B. Naas, Trans.). Bloomington: Indiana University Press.

Derrida, J. (1992a). Mochlos. In R. Rand (Ed.), *Logomachia: The conflict of the faculties* (pp.1-34). Lincoln: University of Nebraska Press.

Derrida, J. (1992b). *Acts of literature* (Edited by D. Attridge). London: Routledge.

Derrida, J. (1992c). *Given time: 1. Counterfeit money* (P. Kamuf, Trans.). Chicago: University of Chicago Press.

Derrida, J. (1994). *Specters of Marx: The state of the debt, the work of mourning, and the new international* (P. Kamuf, Trans.). New York: Routledge.

Derrida, J. (1995a). *The gift of death* (D. Wills, Trans.). Chicago: University of Chicago Press.

Derrida, J. (1995b). *On the name* (Edited by T. Dutoit; D. Wood, Trans. "Passions"; J.P. Leavey Jr., Trans. "Sauf le nom"; I. McLeod, Trans. "Khora"). Stanford, CA: Stanford University Press.

Derrida, J., & Ewald, F. (1995). A certain "madness" must watch over thinking. *Educational Theory, 45,* 273-291.

De Wachter, F. (1994). Post-modern challenges to ethics. *Ethical Perspectives, 1*(2), 77-88.

Dewey, J. (1966). *Democracy and education*. New York: The Free Press, Macmillan.

Dreyfus, H. (1980). Holism and hermeneutics. Symposium with Richard Rorty and Charles Taylor. *Review of Metaphysics, 34,* 3-23.

Egéa-Kuehne, D. (1995). Deconstruction revisited and Derrida's call for academic responsibility. *Educational Theory, 45,* 293-309.

Eliot, T. S. (1968). *Four quartets*. London: Faber & Faber.

Entwistle, N. (1990). *Styles of learning and teaching: An integrated outline of educational psychology for students, teachers and lecturers.* London: David Fulton.

European Commission (1995). *Teaching and learning: Towards the learning society.* Brussels: Author.

Ferrara, A. (1994). Authenticity and the project of modernity. *European Journal of Philosophy, 2,* 241-273.

Ferrari, G. R. F. (1990). *Listening to the cicadas: A study of Plato's Phaedrus.* Cambridge: Cambridge University Press.

Foucault, M. (1974). *The order of things.* London: Routledge.

Foucault, M. (1984). Politics and ethics: An interview. In P. Rabinow (Ed.), *Foucault reader* (C. Porter, Trans.). New York: Pantheon.

Foucault, M. (1988). The ethic of care for the self as a practice of freedom. In J. Bernauer & D. Rasmussen (Eds.), *The final Foucault* (pp. 3-20). Cambridge, MA: MIT Press.

Gaita, R. (1991). *Good and evil.* London: Macmillan.

Giroux, H. (1993). Literacy and the politics of difference. In C. Lankshear & P. McLaren (Eds.), *Critical literacy: Politics, praxis and the postmodern* (pp. 367-377). Albany, NY: State University of New York Press.

Gordon, T. (1975). *Parent effectiveness training: The tested new way to raise responsible children.* New York: Wyden.

Greenberg, C. (1961). Modernist painting. *Arts Yearbook, 4,* 101-108.

Hackforth, R. (1972). *Plato's Phaedrus, translated with introduction and commentary.* Cambridge: Cambridge University Press.

Harré, A., & Kransz, M. (1996). *Varieties of relativism.* Oxford: Blackwell.

Heaney, S. (1975). *North.* London: Faber & Faber.

Heaney, S. (1996). *The spirit level.* London: Faber & Faber.

Heidegger, M. (1962). *Being and time* (J. Macquarrie & E. Robinson, Trans.). Oxford: Blackwell.

Heidegger, M. (1966). *Discourse on thinking* (J.M. Anderson & E.H. Freund, Trans.). New York: Harper & Row.

Heidegger, M. (1971). *On the way to language* (P. Hertz, Trans. "Words"; J. Stambaugh, Trans.). New York: Harper & Row.

Heidegger, M. (1974). *Identity and difference* (J. Stambaugh, Trans.). New York: Harper & Row.

Heidegger, M. (1975). *Poetry, language, thought* (A. Hofstadter, Trans.). New York: Harper & Row, Harper Colophon.

Hertzberg, L. (1988). On the attitude of trust. *Inquiry, 31,* 307-322.

Hughes, T. (1982). *Selected poems. 1957-1981.* London: Faber & Faber.

Johnson, B. (1980). *The critical difference.* London: Johns Hopkins University Press.

Kamuf, P. (Ed.). (1991). *A Derrida reader: Between the blinds.* New York: Columbia University Press.

Kant, I. (1979). *The conflict of the faculties* (Mary J. Gregor, Trans.). New York: Abaris Books.

Kearney, R. (1993). Derrida's ethical re-turn. In G.B. Madison (Ed.), *Working through Derrida* (pp. 28-59). Evanston: Northwestern University Press.

Kermode, F. (1990). *Poetry, narrative, history.* Oxford: Blackwell.

Kierkegaard, S. (1985). *Fear and trembling* (A. Hannay, Trans.). London: Penguin.

Kierkegaard, S. (1996). *Papers and journals: A selection* (A. Hannay, Trans.). London: Penguin.

Kingman (1988). *Report for the committee of inquiry into the teaching of English language.* London: HMSO.

Kiziltan, M., Bain, W., & Canizares, A. (1990). Postmodern conditions: Rethinking public education. *Education Theory, 40,* 351-369.

Krajewski, B. (1992). *Traveling with Hermes.* Amherst: University of Massachusetts Press.

Lacan, J. (1966). *Ecrits.* Paris: Editions du Seuil.

Lacan, J. (1973). Seminar on "The Purloined Letter" (J. Mehlman, Trans.). *Yale French Studies, 48,* 38-72.

Lindsay, C. (1992). Corporality, ethics, experimentation. Lyotard in the eighties. *Philosophy Today, 36,* 389-401.

Lynch, E. (1996). *Reading: The dismal scheme of things.* Unpublished B.A. dissertation. University of Durham, United Kingdom.

Lyotard, J.-F. (1984). *The postmodern condition: A report on knowledge* (G. Bennington & B. Massumi, Trans.). Manchester: Manchester University Press.

Lyotard, J.-F. (1986). *Le postmoderne expliqué aux enfants.* Paris: Galilée.

MacIntyre, A. (1981). *After virtue.* London: Duckworth.

Martindale, C. (1993). *Redeeming the text.* Cambridge: Cambridge University Press.

McCarthy, T. (1978). *The critical theory of Jürgen Habermas.* Cambridge, MA: MIT Press.

McKinney, R. H. (1992). Towards a postmodern ethics: Sir Isaiah Berlin and John Caputo. *The Journal of Value Inquiry, 26,* 395-407.

McLaren, P. (1994). Critical political agency, and the pragmatics of justice. The case of Lyotard. *Educational Theory, 44,* 319-340.

McNiff, J. (1993). *Teaching as learning: An action research approach.* London: Routledge.

Meek, M. (1992). Children Reading—Now. In M. Styles (Ed.), *After Alice* (pp. 172-187). London: Cassell.

Miller, A. (1980). *Am Anfang war Erziehung.* Frankfurt am Main: Suhrkamp.

Montaigne, M. de. (1958). *Essays* (J.M. Cohen, Trans.). London: Penguin.

Murdoch, I. (1992). *Metaphysics as a guide to morals.* London: Chatto & Windus.

Myerson, G. (1994). *Rhetoric, reason and society.* London: Sage.

Norris, C. (1983). *The deconstructive turn.* London: Routledge.

Nussbaum, M. (1986). *The fragility of goodness.* Cambridge: Cambridge University Press.

Nussbaum, M. (1990). *Love's knowledge: Essays on philosophy and literature.* Oxford: Oxford University Press.

Palmer, F. (1992). *Literature and moral understanding.* Oxford: Clarendon Press

Peters, M. (Ed.). (1995). *Education and the postmodern condition.* Westport, CT: Bergin & Garvey.

Peters, M. (1996). *Poststructuralism, politics and education.* Westport, CT: Bergin & Garvey.

Plato. (1973). *Phaedrus and letters VII and VIII* (W. Hamilton, Trans.). London: Penguin.

Rabinow, P. (1991). *The Foucault reader.* London: Penguin.

Rand, R. (Ed.). (1992). *Logomachia: The conflict of the faculties.* Lincoln: University of Nebraska Press.

Rorty, R. (1989). *Contingency, irony, and solidarity.* Cambridge: Cambridge University Press.

Rothstein, S. W. (1993). *The voice of the other. Language as illusion in the formation of the self.* Westport, CT: Praeger.

Scruton, R. (1981). *The politics of culture.* Manchester: Carcanet.

Scruton, R. (1983). *The aesthetic understanding.* London: Methuen.

Silverman, H. J. (Ed.). (1989). *Continental philosophy II: Derrida and deconstruction.*

London: Routledge.

Smeyers, P. (1995). Education and the educational project I: The atmosphere of postmodernism. *Journal of Philosophy of Education, 29*, 109-119.

Smith. F. (1973). *Psycholinguistics and reading*. New York: Holt, Rinehart & Winston.

Smith, R. (1989). English to what end? In F. Coffield & A. Edwards (Eds.), *Working within the act* (pp. 8-11). Ouston, Co. Durham: Educational Publishing Services.

Staten, H. (1985). *Wittgenstein and Derrida*. Oxford: Blackwell.

Tomlinson, P. (1996). *Understanding mentoring*. Buckingham: Open University Press.

Veyne, P. (1993). The final Foucault and his ethics. *Critical Inquiry, 20*, 1-9.

Weil, S. (1977). *Waiting on God* (E. Craufurd, Trans.). London: Collins.

White, J. (1973). *Towards a compulsory curriculum*. London: Routledge & Kegan Paul.

White, S. (1991). *Political theory and postmodernism*. Cambridge: Cambridge University Press.

Wittgenstein, L. (1953). *Philosophical investigations/Philosophische Untersuchungen* (G. E. M. Anscombe, Trans.). Oxford: Blackwell.

Wittgenstein, L. (1969). *On certainty/Über Gewissheit* (Edited by G. E. M. Anscombe & G. H. von Wright; D. Paul & G. E. M. Anscombe, Trans.). Oxford: Blackwell.

Wittgenstein, L. (1980). *Culture and value* (P. Winch, Trans.). Oxford: Blackwell.

Wittgenstein, L. (1993). *Ludwig Wittgenstein. Philosophical occasions 1912-1951* (Edited by J. C. Klagge & A. Nordmann). Indianapolis: Hackett Publishing Company.

Woodhead. C. (1997). *Do we have the schools we deserve?* London: Office for Standards in Education.

Yeats, W. B. (1965). *Selected poetry*. London: Macmillan.

Author Index

Subject Index

About the Authors

NIGEL BLAKE is Lecturer in Educational Technology at The Open University, England.

PAUL SMEYERS is Professor, Department of Educational Sciences, University of Leuven, Belgium.

RICHARD SMITH is Senior Lecturer, School of Education, University of Durham, England, and is editor of the *Journal of Philosophy of Education.*

PAUL STANDISH is Lecturer in Education at the University of Dundee, Scotland.

Critical Studies in Education and Culture Series

Beyond Comfort Zones in Multiculturalism: Confronting the
Politics of Privilege
Sandra Jackson and José Solís, editors

Culture and Difference: Critical Perspectives on the Bicultural Experience in
the United States
Antonia Darder

Poststructuralism, Politics and Education
Michael Peters

Weaving a Tapestry of Resistance: The Places, Power, and Poetry of a Sustainable Society
Sharon Sutton

Counselor Education for the Twenty-First Century
Susan J. Brotherton

Positioning Subjects: Psychoanalysis and Critical Educational Studies
Stephen Appel

Adult Students "At-Risk": Culture Bias in Higher Education
Timothy William Quinnan

Education and the Postmodern Condition
Michael Peters, editor

Restructuring for Integrative Education: Multiple Perspectives, Multiple Contexts
Todd E. Jennings, editor

Postmodern Philosophical Critique and the Pursuit of Knowledge in Higher Education
Roger P. Mourad, Jr.

Naming the Multiple: Poststructuralism and Education
Michael Peters, editor

Literacy in the Library: Negotiating the Spaces Between Order and Desire
Mark Dressman

ISBN 0-89789-511-8

90000>

HARDCOVER BAR CODE